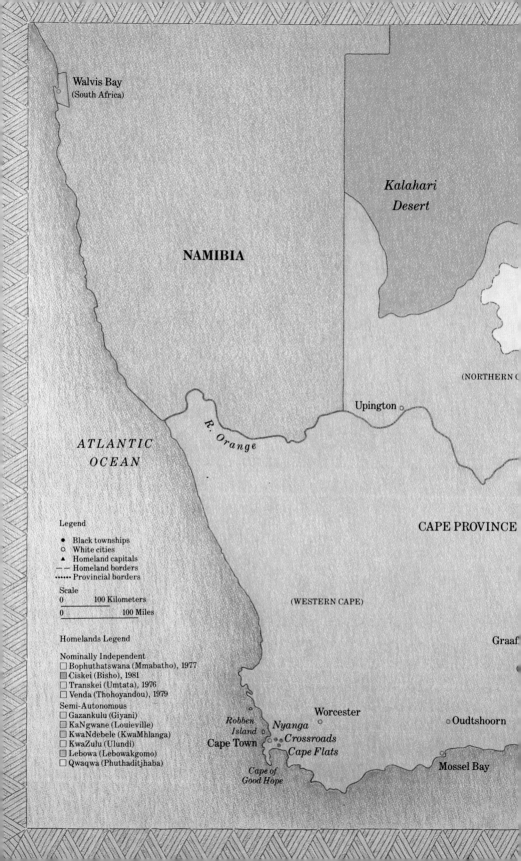

Walvis Bay
(South Africa)

*Kalahari
Desert*

NAMIBIA

(NORTHERN C

Upington ○

*ATLANTIC
OCEAN*

R. Orange

CAPE PROVINCE

Legend
● Black townships
○ White cities
▲ Homeland capitals
– – Homeland borders
••••• Provincial borders

Scale
0   100 Kilometers
0   100 Miles

(WESTERN CAPE)

Graaf

Homelands Legend

Nominally Independent
▢ Bophuthatswana (Mmabatho), 1977
▢ Ciskei (Bisho), 1981
▢ Transkei (Umtata), 1976
▢ Venda (Thohoyandou), 1979
Semi-Autonomous
▢ Gazankulu (Giyani)
▢ KaNgwane (Louieville)
▢ KwaNdebele (KwaMhlanga)
▢ KwaZulu (Ulundi)
▢ Lebowa (Lebowakgomo)
▢ Qwaqwa (Phuthaditjhaba)

Worcester

*Robben
Island*   *Nyanga*   ○ Oudtshoorn
Cape Town   *Crossroads*
            Cape Flats

*Cape of
Good Hope*   **Mossel Bay**

Minerals Legend
Au Gold
Co Cobalt
Cr Chromium
Cu Copper
Fe Iron
Mn Manganese
Ni Nickel
Pl Platinum
Ti Titanium
U Uranium
V Vanadium
C Coal
D Diamonds
O Oil

**SOUTHERN
AFRICA**

Legend
••• Major Roads
••• Major Roads/Railroads
+ Major Railroads
— Pipelines
1 Cahora Bassa Dam
2 Kariba Dam

Scale
0   200 Kilometers
0   200 Miles

THE LAST YEARS OF APARTHEID: CIVIL LIBERTIES IN SOUTH AFRICA

THE LAST YEARS OF APARTHEID: CIVIL LIBERTIES IN SOUTH AFRICA

**JOHN DUGARD
NICHOLAS HAYSOM
GILBERT MARCUS**

EDITED BY **JOHN DUGARD**

South Africa **UPDATE** Series
FORD FOUNDATION—FOREIGN POLICY ASSOCIATION

Copublished by the Ford Foundation and the Foreign Policy Association

© Copyright 1992 by the Ford Foundation

Printed in the United States of America
Library of Congress Catalogue Card Number: 92-070233
ISBN: 0-87124-145-5

Editorial assistance provided by Alicia Anthony, Sonia Kane, Margaret Nichols, and Alice Tufel

Book design by Samuel N. Antupit
Map design and illustration by Lea Cyr
Composed by The Sarabande Press
Printed on acid-free paper by Science Press

CONTENTS

Preface   ix

Foreword   xi

Chapter I: THE LAW OF APARTHEID
John Dugard   3
Constitutional Control   4
Racial Classification   9
Political, Territorial, and Social Segregation   10
Political Repression   21
The Courts and the Law of Apartheid   27
Conclusion   31

**Chapter II: CIVIL LIBERTIES UNDER
EMERGENCY RULE**
Gilbert Marcus   32
The Origin of Emergency Powers   32
The Genesis of Security Legislation   35
The Emergency: Powers of the Security Forces   39
The Emergency: Role of the Judiciary   49

Chapter III: THE TOTAL STRATEGY: THE SOUTH AFRICAN SECURITY FORCES AND THE SUPPRESSION OF CIVIL LIBERTIES

Nicholas Haysom	55
The Total Strategy	56
The Security Forces	59
The Government's Response to Revolt	73
The De Klerk Era and the Demise of the Securocrats	89
Conclusion	93

Chapter IV: BLACKS AND THE ADMINISTRATION OF JUSTICE

John Dugard	95
Black Participation in the Administration of Justice	95
Black Attitudes Toward the Law and Its Institutions	102

Chapter V: LOOKING AHEAD

John Dugard	112
Constitutional Options and Issues	115
Nature of the State	116
Constitutional Checks and Balances	120
A Bill of Rights	123
The Future of the South African Legal Order	134

Appendices

A. Address by State President F. W. de Klerk, February 2, 1990	139
B. Public Safety Act, 1953, Security Emergency Regulations	155
C. Freedom Charter, June 26, 1955	162
D. ANC Constitutional Guidelines for a Democratic South Africa, 1988	167
E. Summary of State President F. W. de Klerk's Address, February 1, 1991	172
F. ANC Constitutional Proposals, April 1991	176
G. Constitutional Rule in a Participatory Democracy, September 4, 1991	189

Notes

Chapter I: The Law of Apartheid   201

Chapter II: Civil Liberties Under Emergency Rule   205

Chapter III: The Total Strategy: The South African
              Security Forces and the Suppression of Civil
              Liberties   209

Chapter IV: Blacks and the Administration of Justice   217

Chapter V: Looking Ahead   220

Selected Bibliography: Civil Liberties in
South Africa   224

Selected Annotated Bibliography: South Africa   226

Key Events in South African History   232

Index   247

PREFACE

In 1981 the Study Commission on U.S. Policy Toward Southern Africa, funded by the Rockefeller Foundation and chaired by Franklin A. Thomas, published a report on the results of a two-year study. The report, entitled *South Africa: Time Running Out (SATRO),* contained an extensive review of South Africa's history, people, economy, and social and political systems; a survey of South Africa's relations with its neighbors and the rest of the world; and interviews with South Africans across racial, religious, and economic lines. The book concluded with an analysis of U.S. interests in South Africa and laid out a framework for U.S. policy in southern Africa, with specific objectives and actions for U.S. public and private groups. *SATRO* has been reprinted and has become a seminal teaching and reference resource. It is probably still the most comprehensive treatment of South Africa and U.S. policy available.

Since 1981 events have moved swiftly in southern Africa. South Africa's political landscape has been transformed by a combination of internal and external pressures, the most important being a black rebellion of unprecedented scope, intensity, and duration. South Africa's neighbors in the region paid a high price in human suffering and economic dislocation as the result of Pretoria's destabilization policy and their own internal conflicts. But they also had the satisfaction of seeing both the achievement of independence by Namibia, Africa's last colony, and the initiation of a genuine dialogue between blacks and whites in South Africa itself. The international climate changed significantly, with the superpowers cooperating on regional issues, thus effectively ending the cold war in southern Africa. In the United States, southern Africa's increased importance was reflected in the controversy it aroused as a domestic issue and in its new prominence on the foreign policy agenda.

Many parts of *SATRO* have become dated, although others, particularly the policy section, remain relevant. It was therefore decided to update the work with a series of publications covering the 1980s. The intention of the series is to produce a comprehensive journal of record and an analytical resource suitable for teachers, students, and policy makers as well as for a broader audience. Each book deals with a single topic related to South Africa and is written by one or more specialists. In addition to the text, useful supplementary materials such as bibliographies and chronologies, copies of original documents, and maps are included. Together, the books provide a thorough assessment of a pivotal decade in the history of southern Africa.

The South Africa UPDATE Series is produced under the aegis of the Ford Foundation's Southern Africa Study Group and the guidance of an editorial board consisting of academics, former U.S. government and UN officials, journalists, and business, labor, and foundation executives. The opinions expressed in the books, however, are those of the authors.

John de St. Jorre
Editor
South Africa UPDATE Series

Note: This book uses the term "black" to embrace collectively Africans, people of mixed descent known as "Coloureds," and Indians. The individual terms are used when referring to each group separately. Also, money figures in the text are given in South African rand without a U.S. dollar equivalent because of the fluctuating value of the rand during the 1980s. When the decade opened, R1.00 was worth U.S. $1.25; at the decade's close, the rand's value had dropped to U.S. 40 cents.

FOREWORD

In the 1990s South Africa is poised to enter a new era in which the black majority will have the determining voice in government and people's basic rights will no longer depend on the color of their skin. At the beginning of the decade, the National Party government, which ruled South Africa with an iron fist for more than forty years, denounced its own racist ideology of apartheid and started a process leading toward negotiation with its most bitter opponent, the African National Congress (ANC). South Africa at last has the potential to become a just society, in which the law is used to advance—rather than suppress—human rights.

During the 1980s many apartheid laws providing for social segregation were repealed or relaxed, and South Africa became a more racially integrated society. For example, the "pass laws" requiring blacks to account for their presence in the cities by the presentation of an identity document—a symbol of both the pettiness and the brutality of apartheid—were repealed, and blacks were permitted to take their place more fully in the social and, particularly, the economic life of the country. But the decade ended with the edifice of apartheid still intact. People remained classified along racial lines, schools were still segregated, residential racial zoning continued, 87 percent of the land was reserved for exclusive white ownership, and above all, the franchise continued to be denied to Africans, who comprise over 70 percent of the population.

In February 1990 a political revolution occurred in South Africa when President Frederik W. de Klerk announced the end of apartheid, withdrew the ban on popular black political organizations, and initiated a process of negotiation aimed at the establishment of a just political order in South Africa. Since then all but one of the discriminatory laws constituting the policy of apartheid have been repealed. The sole survivor is the Constitution itself, which excludes Africans from the franchise. This discriminatory law will remain in force until a new, nonracial constitution is agreed upon by the representatives of all the people of South Africa. Until then it is premature to speak of the total downfall of the apartheid state, despite the country's dramatic move in that direction.

This book examines the final years of apartheid in South Africa, including the methods that were employed to suppress opposition to apartheid and the ways in which it remained in force. Chapter I describes the law of apartheid and its demise over the past ten years. Chapter II examines the security legislation that was employed to suppress opposition to apartheid and focuses on the state of civil liberties under the successive states of emergency that governed the country—or parts of it—from July 1985 to October 1990. Chapter III analyzes the role of the security forces in the suppression of human rights and the violence that has characterized South African society during the past decade. Chapter IV describes the role of blacks in the administration of justice in South Africa and examines the alienation of the black community from the "white man's" law of apartheid. It also considers how this alienation may affect the future of South African law. The final chapter is devoted to constitutional options for the future. Proposals for a new constitution are discussed in the context of prevailing political attitudes, and the prospect for a bill of rights enshrining racial equality, personal liberty, affirmative action, and the redistribution of land and wealth is examined.

While this book focuses on the 1980s, the decade is not viewed in isolation. The previous thirty-three years of apartheid are taken into account and prospects for the future are assessed. The hopes engendered by the release of Nelson Mandela and other political prisoners, the unbanning of popular political parties, and the start of political negotiations form a recurring theme. But apartheid, with its racist and repressive legal order, is a historical reality that cannot be forgotten as South Africa enters a new era.

During the 1980s the three contributors to this volume were staff members at the Center for Applied Legal Studies (CALS), a sociolegal research unit of the University of the Witwatersrand that monitors the South African legal system and works for the dismantling of the apartheid legal order through the media of research, public education, and public interest litigation. Several other members of CALS helped in the preparation of this study: Laurel Angus assisted in research and editing; Lydia Levin, our research librarian, helped to retrieve and collate data; and Colleen Renew patiently typed and collated the manuscript. I am most grateful to them for their help in a CALS team effort.

John Dugard

THE LAST YEARS OF APARTHEID:
CIVIL LIBERTIES IN SOUTH AFRICA

Chapter I
The Law of Apartheid
John Dugard

In 1948 the National Party came to power in South Africa on the political platform of apartheid (racial separateness). During the 1950s, using the instrument of the law, the new government proceeded to construct a political order in which rights, powers, and privileges were allocated on the basis of skin color and a system of rigid racial separation and white domination was secured. Opposition to these measures was brutally suppressed by an arsenal of repressive security laws. Apartheid brought notoriety to South Africa, which gradually found itself relegated to the status of a pariah state in a world committed to the principles of racial equality, decolonization, and majority rule. For three decades, the apartheid state remained in place, although challenged by internal opposition and increasing international pressure.

During the 1980s apartheid began to crumble as opposition, both internal and external, gained momentum. Key racist laws were repealed or relaxed, political rights were extended to persons other than whites, and the term apartheid was denounced by its inventors. In 1989 President Pieter W. Botha, who had become prime minister in 1978 and president in 1984, was forced into retirement and was succeeded by Frederik W. de Klerk. This heralded a liberalization in government policy, culminating in President De Klerk's address to Parliament on February 2, 1990 (see Appendix A). In this speech, De Klerk announced the lifting of legal restrictions on political opposition groups and called for negotiations between all political and racial groups in order to establish "a totally new and just constitutional dispensation in which every inhabitant will enjoy equal rights, treatment and opportunity in every sphere of endeavour—constitutional, social and economic."[1]

In 1991 the race classifications laws, the racial zoning laws, and the Land Acts, which reserved some 87 percent of the land for exclusive white ownership, were repealed. The Internal Security Act, which provided the legal apparatus for the brutal suppression of opposition to apartheid, was radically amended. This left the 1983 Constitution, which is premised on racial separateness and excludes Africans completely from the franchise and participation in the central legislative process, as the sole survivor of the apartheid legal order. It will remain a constant reminder of apartheid until a new, nonracial constitution is approved. Although apartheid as a legal system is virtually dead, South Africa remains a society in which race is still a determining factor in the allocation of political, economic, and social rights. Forty years of legislated racism have left an indelible mark on South African society that cannot be erased overnight.

This chapter describes the workings of apartheid during the 1980s by examining its three principal features: constitutional control; political, territorial, and social segregation; and political repression. In the 1990s a reformed National Party government is committed to a nonracial constitution, the abandonment of segregation, and the adoption of a bill of rights to secure greater protection for individual liberty. But the legacy of apartheid remains, and it is important to examine it in order to illuminate the harm that has been done, the progress that has been made, and the obstacles that must still be overcome before South Africa becomes a nonracial, democratic society.

Constitutional Control

South Africa is currently governed by its third Constitution, which was adopted in 1983. The first was enacted by the British parliament in 1910 to create a union of the four British colonies of the Cape of Good Hope, Natal, Transvaal, and the Orange River Colony. Proposals for a U.S.–style federal constitution with a bill of rights were rejected by the founding fathers. Instead, they chose a constitution closely modeled on that of Britain. Although a federation was rejected in favor of a unitary state, the separate identities of the four colonies were retained by recognizing them as provinces with limited legislative and executive powers. They became the Cape Province, Natal, Transvaal, and Orange Free State. The franchise was limited to whites in the Transvaal, Orange Free State, and Natal. The small number of Coloured and African voters in the Cape Province was removed over the years by a succession of devious constitutional maneuvers. By 1956 Africans had lost all their voting rights, and Coloureds in the Cape Province were voting on a separate voters' roll to elect four members to represent them in the all-white parliament.

The paramount principle of the British, or Westminster, system upon which the first constitution was based is that of parliamentary supremacy. This principle, which frees parliament from any legal curbs on its lawmaking powers, is justified in Britain on the grounds that parliament, elected by means of universal franchise, represents the will of all the people in a relatively homogeneous society. In South Africa, the principle had no justification because the Parliament made no claim to represent all the people. Nevertheless, the principle was used as a device for justifying the exercise of uncontrolled white legislative power over the black majority. The National Party, claiming that it acted in accordance with British parliamentary rules, was thus able to enact its policy of apartheid into law without serious obstruction from the courts.[2]

The second constitution, enacted by the Parliament of the Union of South Africa in 1961, created a republic, with a state president replacing the British queen as nominal head of state.[3] But the Westminster parliamentary form was retained. Executive power was vested in a prime minister and cabinet that enjoyed the confidence of the majority party—the National Party—in the legislature. The Parliament remained a whites-only body, elected by white voters. The principle of parliamentary supremacy was reaffirmed by a provision in the constitution describing the Parliament as the "sovereign legislative authority" and denying to the courts the competence "to pronounce upon the validity of any Act passed by Parliament."[4] The provincial system was retained, but the powers of the provinces were eroded over the years.

In the late 1970s, notably after P. W. Botha became prime minister, the National Party government devised a new constitution that would co-opt the Coloureds and Indians into the parliamentary system while enabling the whites to maintain political control. The result was the Republic of South Africa Constitution Act of 1983, which enfranchised Coloureds and Indians—but not Africans—and established a tricameral Parliament consisting of separate legislative chambers for whites, Coloureds, and Indians.[5] Although the new constitution departed from the Westminster model and was heralded by the government as an exercise in consociational democracy, it succeeded in maintaining white control of the political system.

Parliament under the 1983 Constitution consists of three chambers:

- House of Assembly, with 178 white members elected by whites to represent some five million whites;
- House of Representatives, with 85 Coloured members elected by Coloureds to represent three million Coloureds; and
- House of Delegates, with 45 Indian members elected by Indians to represent nine hundred thousand Indians.

The constitutional machinery for the operation of this tricameral Parliament is highly complicated. Although provision is made for joint sessions of the three houses, when it comes to the adoption of legislation, each chamber deliberates separately. In the event of disagreement, the will of the majority in the white House of Assembly—that is, the ruling National Party—prevails. This is achieved through the instrument of the state president.

Although he has far-reaching executive and legislative powers, the state president is not popularly elected. Instead, he is chosen by an electoral college of eighty-eight people, which includes fifty members designated by the House of Assembly, twenty-five members of the House of Representatives, and thirteen members of the House of Delegates. In practice, this means that the majority party in the House of Assembly sends a built-in majority of delegates to the electoral college, ensuring that its candidate is elected.

The Constitution gives the state president the power to control the tricameral Parliament like a puppet master. He decides which matters are to be disposed of by each house on its own and which matters are to be voted on by all three houses sitting separately or, if necessary, by a special procedure to resolve deadlocks. If the state president decides that a matter concerns the interests of only one of the three racial groups, he will categorize it as an "own affair" for that group and refer it to the house of that group for final legislative determination. The Constitution lists a number of matters that belong to the category of own affairs, such as social welfare, education, art, culture, recreation, health, housing, agriculture, and local government. But this list is not intended to be exhaustive, and ultimately, it is for the state president to decide whether a particular matter is the own affair of one population group, in the sense that it affects "the maintenance of its identity and upholding and furtherance of its way of life, culture, traditions and customs."6 Should the state president decide that a matter is not the own affair of a particular house, it becomes a "general affair" to be decided by all three houses. This crucial determination by the state president is final, and no court of law may question its correctness.

A bill designated as a general affair, passed by all three houses sitting separately, becomes law when it has been agreed to by the state president. Should any disagreement among the three houses arise, however, the state president will refer the matter to the President's Council, whose decision is deemed to be the decision of Parliament.

The President's Council is not an independent arbiter but rather the alter ego of the state president and the majority party in the House of Assembly. Its sixty members consist of twenty chosen by the House of Assembly, ten by the House of Representatives, five by the House of Delegates, and twenty-five appointed by the state president—fifteen of his own choice and ten nominated by the opposition parties in the three houses. Thus, the state president and the majority party in the House of Assembly together control thirty-five members of the council, a built-in majority.

This elaborate constitutional scheme ensures that, in practice, the majority party in the House of Assembly controls the legislative process in a number of ways. First, its appointed state president ensures that any matter principally affecting white interests will be decided by the House of Assembly as an own affair.

Second, if a bill concerning the South African public at large, including blacks, and consequently designated as a general affair, is rejected by either the House of Representatives or the House of Delegates, it may be passed by the alter ego of the House of Assembly—the President's Council. In this way, for example, a controversial amendment to the Internal Security Act, extending arbitrary police powers of detention, was passed in 1986 by the President's Council after being rejected by both the House of Representatives and the House of Delegates.7

Third, in the event of a boycott of Parliament by either the Coloured or Indian chamber or both, the will of the House of Assembly will prevail, since the constitution empowers the remaining house, or houses, to perform the function of Parliament in such a case.

Executive government is vested in the state president, who

normally holds office for a five-year term, with no restriction on reelection. In the exercise of executive powers, the president acts on own affairs on the advice of three separate ministers councils chosen by the majority parties in the white, Coloured, and Indian chambers, and on general affairs on the advice of a Cabinet drawn almost exclusively from the majority party in the white chamber.

The third branch of government—the judiciary—hardly features in the 1983 Constitution. The courts are expressly excluded from questioning the validity of the state president's decisions and acts of Parliament.[8] Proposals for a bill of rights and judicial review in the Constitution were rejected.

Both the 1910 and 1961 constitutions achieved a limited decentralization of power by means of the provincial government system. The 1983 Constitution makes no provision for provincial government, and in 1986, this system, which had been introduced in 1910 as a concession to the federalists, was finally repealed.[9] Elected provincial councils were abolished and multiracial provincial executive committees, whose members are appointed by the state president, were established to administer the affairs of the four provinces.

The architects of the 1983 Constitution proudly portrayed it as an exercise in consensus politics. In reality, it is nothing of the kind. It is a skillfully constructed arrangement that, behind the facade of multiracial cooperation, retains the twin cardinal principles of earlier constitutions: white domination and legislative supremacy. Like its predecessors, it provides the dominant group within the white community, the Afrikaners—about three million out of a total of five million whites—with a constitutional instrument to determine both their own destiny and that of the rest of the population, numbering over twenty-six million.[10] A coercive police and military apparatus, given legal form and funding by this Constitution, ensures that the Afrikaners retain their ability to impose their will on South Africa.

The 1983 Constitution was not popularly acclaimed. In November 1983 it was approved by a 66 percent majority in a referendum held for whites only. The government refused to allow the holding of similar referenda for Coloureds and Indians, so that the elections to the House of Representatives and the House of Delegates in August 1984 became a test for the acceptability of the Constitution by those communities. In the Coloured elections, only 57 percent of the eligible voters registered, and of this number, 30 percent voted, which means that only 17.1 percent of the eligible Coloured voters cast their votes. Although 79.2 percent of the eligible Indian voters registered, only 20.3 percent actually voted, reflecting an overall percentage poll of 16.08 percent.

In 1984 South Africa was plunged into a state of turmoil. Many factors contributed to this situation, but there can be no doubt that the 1983 Constitution, with its sham democratic forms for Coloureds and Indians and its exclusion of Africans, was a principal cause. Nationwide unrest and violence culminated in the declaration of a state of emergency for much of the country in 1985, and in 1986 the entire country was subjected to emergency rule. The emergency powers were renewed annually until 1990, when they finally were lifted.

As long as the 1983 Constitution is the pivotal statute in the South African legal order, apartheid will remain in force. In the early 1990s, this fact is recognized within and outside government. Hence, President De Klerk announced in his February 2, 1990 speech that the government aimed to achieve "a totally new and just constitutional dispensation" and directed the South African Law Commission—a body charged with the task of legal reform—to embark on a study of models of democratic constitutions.

Racial Classification

As the central feature of apartheid was the unequal allocation of political, civil, social, and economic rights on the grounds of race, legal machinery was necessary in order to divide the population into different racial groups. This was achieved by the Population Registration Act of 1950, which divided South Africa's population into three main racial categories: white, black (African), and Coloured (persons of mixed descent).[11] The Coloured group is divided, however, into a number of subgroups, the major one being the Indians.

Appearance, social acceptance, and descent are the criteria used to determine a person's racial identity. A white person is one who "in appearance obviously is a white person and who is not generally accepted as a Coloured person; or is generally accepted as a white person and is not in appearance obviously not a white person" provided that "a person shall not be classified as a white person if one of his natural parents has been classified as a Coloured person or black." In deciding whether a person is in appearance obviously white, "his habits, education, and speech and deportment and demeanour in general shall be taken into account."[12] A black (African) person is one "who is, or is generally accepted as, a member of any aboriginal race or tribe of Africa." A Coloured person is one "who is not a white person or a black."

Persons were classified by the government's Department of Home Affairs, and any appeal against classification was referred to a race classification appeal board. This system of bureaucratic race classification, which often divided families into different racial groups, inevitably caused untold suffering.

Racial classification is one of the main pillars of the 1983 Constitution. According to the Constitution, the franchise is limited to whites, Coloureds, and Indians, as defined in the Population Registration Act of 1950, and each of these groups is to constitute a separate house of Parliament.[13] Without the retention of the racial classification, the whole edifice of Parliament would collapse.

The racial foundation of the 1983 Constitution placed President De Klerk's government in a quandary. The government declared its intention to remove all vestiges of statutory race discrimination by the end of the 1991 parliamentary session. But it could not repeal the Population Registration Act without destroying Parliament itself, which would have left South Africa with no constitution until the adoption of a new one. With delays in negotiations and little prospect for the adoption of a new constitution before 1993 at the earliest, the government had little choice but to compromise. The result was the repeal in 1991 of the Population Registration Act for all purposes other than the composition of Parliament.[14]

Political, Territorial, and Social Segregation

The apartheid legal order was made up of three components. First, "grand apartheid" created separate political institutions for Africans in order to justify their exclusion from the central political process. This process was, euphemistically, given the name of "separate development." Second, the government, building on existing laws and practices, pursued policies to achieve as much territorial separation of the races as possible. Third, discriminatory segregation laws ensured that blacks were denied basic rights and treated as inferior citizens. Sometimes these laws were described as "petty apartheid" in order to distinguish them from grand apartheid, but from the perspective of the black population these laws were brutal in their design and effect and not petty at all.

Political Segregation: The Homelands. The 1983 Constitution completely excludes Africans from participation in the political system, either as voters or as legislators. When the Constitution was introduced, government spokespersons repeatedly declared that it made no attempt to regulate the political fortunes of Africans because they already had their own political institutions. Since then, the government has recognized the absurdity of this argument and accepts that negotiations between whites and blacks will inevitably lead to a constitutional system in which all races participate. Until that time comes, however, Africans will remain isolated from Parliament, so it is important to consider the political institutions established for them within the framework of apartheid.

The ideology conceived by Hendrik F. Verwoerd, prime minister from 1958 to 1966, contemplated the creation of ten independent states, known as bantustans or "homelands," to accommodate the political aspirations of Africans. This scheme envisaged that every African, wherever he or she lived, would be deemed to belong to a designated homeland that provided the closest ethnic or linguistic affiliation. Africans' right to vote and participate in political institutions would then be restricted to that homeland. They would become citizens of the homeland, losing all claim to participate in the central, white Parliament as well as their South African citizenship and nationality.[15]

The process of establishing the homelands began in 1959.[16] During the period from 1976 to 1981, four "independent" homelands were created: Transkei (1976), Bophuthatswana (1977), Venda (1979), and Ciskei (1981), often called the TBVC states. All Africans deemed to belong to these four states were deprived of their South African citizenship. Some nine million South Africans were thus arbitrarily denationalized, whether they resided in one of these entities or whether they continued to live within South Africa itself. In return, they were given the right to vote for legislative bodies established in these homelands.

The government clearly hoped that all the homelands would accept independence and thus relieve it of the moral responsibility of granting political rights to the African majority within South Africa. This expectation was spelled out in 1978 by Dr. Connie P. Mulder, then minister of Bantu Administration and Development, when he stated in Parliament:

[I]f our policy is taken to its logical conclusion as far as the black people are concerned, there will not be one black man with South African citizenship. . . .

[E]very black man in South Africa will eventually be accommodated in some independent new state in this honorable way and there will no longer be a moral obligation on this Parliament to accommodate these people politically.[17]

These hopes failed to materialize. The remaining homelands—namely, KwaZulu, Lebowa, Gazankulu, Qwaqwa, KaNgwane, and KwaNdebele—having achieved a limited form of self-government, refused to accept independence and made it clear to the National Party government that they had no intention of doing so in the future. These self-governing territories saw greater political and economic advantages in remaining part of South Africa and in pressing for African political rights within the country as a whole.

Other factors also compelled the government to revise its homelands policy. The process of denationalization was likened to the Nazi denationalization of German Jews, thereby strengthening South Africa's racist image at a time when the government was trying to remove that taint during the 1980s.

Finally, even the most ardent supporters of the independent homelands policy were unable to conceal their disappointment with the experiment. Corruption and despotism ran rife in all four independent homelands. Military regimes overthrew the civilian governments in Transkei, Ciskei, and Venda. In Bophuthatswana, South Africa had to intervene with military force in February 1988 to keep its "own man," President Lucas Mangope, in power when he was threatened by a military coup that had a measure of popular support.

Moreover, the Botha government's new policy of granting greater social and economic rights to Africans within the urban areas conflicted with Verwoerd's grand apartheid strategy, which viewed Africans as temporary sojourners in the cities who would one day return to their homelands, where they were meant to exercise their political rights.

These factors compelled the government, during President P. W. Botha's final years in power, to consider a host of new options. Although independence remained a possibility for the nonindependent homelands, it was not strongly encouraged. Instead, the government offered these homelands increased powers of self-government. It also encouraged them to enter into regional arrangements along the lines of the joint executive authority for KwaZulu and Natal, set up in 1986, to coordinate the activities of

Chief Mangosuthu Gatsha Buthelezi's KwaZulu government and the white provincial executive authority in the province of Natal.

In the cities, the government increased the powers of municipal authorities in the African townships. But these efforts were frustrated by the wave of popular opposition that swept the country in the second half of the 1980s. The government then turned, in desperation, to bringing Africans marginally closer to the central Parliament. In 1988 the Promotion of Constitutional Development Act was passed to provide for the creation of a negotiating forum for Africans. This measure created the National Statutory Council, a body consisting of several members of the government, representatives of the self-governing homelands, the chairman of each of the ministers councils in the tricameral Parliament, nine representatives elected by Africans resident outside the homelands, and not more than eight other persons appointed by the state president.

The principal function of the National Council, as it came to be called, would have been to plan and prepare a constitutional structure providing for participation by all South African citizens in the processes of government. Most African leaders rejected this proposal and instead demanded direct participation in Parliament. This demand was in turn rejected by the government, since it inevitably would have led to majority rule. In April 1987 President Botha told an election rally: "We are not prepared to have a fourth chamber [of Parliament] for blacks or a majority government."[18]

Attempts to solve South Africa's political and constitutional problems by negotiations between the government and unrepresentative African homeland and urban leaders were abandoned when F. W. de Klerk became state president in September 1989. A few months later, popular political movements such as the African National Congress (ANC), the Pan Africanist Congress (PAC), and the United Democratic Front (UDF) were unbanned, and Nelson Mandela and other prominent political prisoners were released. President De Klerk then called for negotiations between the leaders of all political groupings. At last, the idea that Africans and whites can develop politically along separate lines and within different political institutions had been abandoned.

Territorial Segregation, Land Division, and Population Removals. In 1913 the South African Parliament passed the Black Land Act, which divided the country between Africans and the other racial groups. Africans were given scheduled areas composed mainly of the so-called native reserves, which amounted to about 7 percent of the total land, and were prohibited by law from acquiring land outside those areas. In 1936 the proportion was increased to 13 percent.[19] While whites were prohibited from acquiring land in the African areas, they had free rein in the rest of the country, apart from small, mainly urban zones where Coloureds and Indians lived.

In pursuit of its policy of territorial segregation, the government forcibly moved or resettled several million Africans who lived in "black spots" in the white areas. It is estimated that between 1959 and 1988, over 3.5 million people were relocated in this way. Removals were generally accompanied by great hardship and suffering; the areas to which people were removed often lacked the necessary facilities for human habitation and were far from sources of employment.

During the 1980s the government repealed some of the laws permitting these forced removals and promised to discontinue such resettlements. Unfortunately, this promise was not always kept. Moreover, the government embarked upon a new form of forced resettlement as part of the process of homelands consolidation. Under the Borders of Particular States Extension Act of 1980, the government was empowered to transfer land to the independent homelands. Black communities settled on such land often were handed over to homeland governments without consultation and against their wishes.[20]

Similar strategies were employed to enlarge the territories of the nonindependent homelands. For instance, in 1985 President Botha arbitrarily transferred a predominantly North Sotho community of over one hundred twenty thousand people from an area called Moutse to the homeland of KwaNdebele. This was done against the wishes of the community by the simple device of redrawing the boundaries of KwaNdebele. This act, apparently prompted by the government's wish to induce KwaNdebele to opt for independence, was set aside by the Appeal Court in 1988.[21] Undeterred by this judicial setback, the government soon afterward sought to incorporate the black township of Botshabelo in the Orange Free State, with a population of about five hundred thousand, into the self-governing homeland of Qwaqwa, situated some two hundred miles away and having a population of only 157,600. Again, the Appellate Division declared this move to be unlawful.[22]

The Abolition of Racially Based Land Measures Act of 1991, which effectively repealed the 1913 and 1936 Land Acts, together with a host of related discriminatory statutes, was therefore, in the words of President De Klerk, "a historic turning point in the history of South Africa."[23] Whereas the Group Areas Act was the symbol of apartheid for the Coloured and Indian communities, the Land Acts of 1913 and 1936 were viewed by the African community as the foundational laws of South Africa's racial order. White farmers, on the other hand, saw this territorial dispensation as their sacred historical heritage. The repeal of the Land Acts consequently was bitterly opposed by the white, primarily Afrikaner, Conservative Party, which labeled the repeal as treason against the Afrikaner nation.

Unfortunately, the government failed to see this historic moment as an opportunity to address the legacy of apartheid. The injustices perpetrated by the Land Acts cannot be reversed merely by repealing these discriminatory laws. Simply legalizing land ownership for everybody may be a step in the right direction, but it ignores the fact that few Africans have the financial resources to actually purchase land. The imbalance in the present distribution of land can be truly rectified only by establishing a coherent policy that takes into account the need to restore land to those communities that were forcibly deprived of it. The Advisory Commission on Land Allocation set up by the repealing statute is not empowered to redress these historical injustices. Many groups have therefore urged that a land claims court be established to rule on the competing claims to land, with a clear authorization to restore land seized by the state for racial reasons in the apartheid era. Aninka Claassens, a human rights activist who has worked tirelessly to assist the dispossessed in rural areas for many years, sums up the position as follows:

> The present distribution of land is a major national political grievance. White conquest of land has become symbolic of black subjugation. The only way to defuse this grievance is to de-racialise the terms of land ownership. To do this we must put the hard facts of dispossession and the debased form of property relations on the table and reject these as the parameters from which to proceed.[24]

There can be little doubt that the restoration and redistribution of land will occupy a major place on South Africa's future political agenda. The United States, Canada, Australia, and New Zealand are all still embroiled in land disputes arising from claims by dispossessed indigenous communities. In South Africa, claims of this kind are certain to be asserted with great vigor. Unlike the claims of indigenous communities elsewhere, the claims of Africans in South

Africa are the result of recent history and are therefore more easily verifiable. Such claims are likely to receive a sympathetic hearing from a government representative of the majority of South African people.

Denationalization. When the pass laws were repealed in 1986, it was widely believed that all legislation restricting the free movement and residential rights of Africans had been abolished.[25] But this was not so. Under the guise of denationalization through independence for the homelands, and by a process known as "orderly urbanization," a new system of influx control was erected. Through denationalization, all Africans living in South Africa proper after the independence of the homelands would become statutory aliens in the land of their birth and relegated to the status of migrant workers. As such, they would require passports to enter South Africa and permits to seek employment in the same way that actual aliens—say, from Zimbabwe or France—do. Like other aliens, they could be deported to their country of origin, in this case to their homelands. For these millions, the passport would replace the pass.

This fantasy dominated National Party ideology for over twenty years, but was finally abandoned in the wake of fierce international criticism that labeled denationalization based on race as a violation of international law.[26] The realization that not all homelands could be persuaded to become independent led the government to modify its strategy. In 1986, amid much political fanfare, Parliament approved the Restoration of South African Citizenship Act.[27] Under this act, citizens of nonindependent homelands would remain South African nationals. The majority of those already denationalized as a result of the independence of the TBVC states would remain statutory aliens. The legislation restored citizenship only to Africans who were "permanently resident" within the national borders of South Africa.

Africans from the TBVC states who wish to regain or obtain South African citizenship must apply to the South African authorities. According to government estimates, about 1.8 million persons qualify for the restoration of citizenship, but in practice it seems highly unlikely that this figure will be reached.[28] The complicated application procedure, ignorance of the law, disputes over the meaning of the term permanently resident, and resistance from the Bophuthatswana government, which regards the change as a diminution of its status, are likely to result in less than a million people benefiting from the change in the law. Thus, the denationalization of millions of Africans, with serious consequences for their economic, civil, and political rights, will remain a reality until the TBVC states are reincorporated into South Africa.

The rest of the African population is deemed to belong to the nonindependent homelands of KwaZulu, Lebowa, Gazankulu, KaNgwane, Qwaqwa, and KwaNdebele. These people remain citizens—more correctly, nationals—of South Africa and by law are entitled to travel freely throughout the country. But they are subject to what the government calls orderly urbanization, which has, in many respects, replaced influx control.

Movement. Orderly urbanization refers to a number of laws, both racial and nonracial, that combine to prevent Africans from flooding into the towns and cities from the rural areas in the homelands. They include the Prevention of Illegal Squatting Act, the Slums Act, and the Trespass Act, which provide for the ejection of squatters and slum dwellers and the prosecution of those who enter land or buildings without the permission of the owner.[29]

In theory, these laws are nonracial: Africans and whites alike are prohibited from erecting squatter shacks on urban wastelands close to the white cities where work can be obtained. However, an appalling housing shortage exists in the African townships as a result of the authorities' refusal to provide adequate housing there, which, in the days of rigid apartheid, would have encouraged Africans to move to the cities. Consequently, it is mainly Africans who are affected by these laws, and it is clear that the laws are being used to replace the old influx control regulations.

No laws restrain the movement of Coloureds within South Africa, but Indians were at one time prohibited from residing in the Orange Free State and parts of Northern Natal without permission. These restrictions were removed in 1986.[30]

Residential Zoning. One of the most hated apartheid laws was the Group Areas Act, which zoned urban areas for exclusive occupation by different racial groups and provided for the punishment of persons occupying premises in the wrong group area.[31] As African urban areas were constituted and governed by other laws, the Group Areas Act affected mainly Coloureds, Indians, and whites. Although the act did not on the face of it permit discrimination in its interpretation, the Appellate Division of the Supreme Court, in one of its most controversial decisions, held that a discriminatory application of the law must have been envisaged by the legislature and was therefore permissible.[32] Consequently, over a hundred thousand Coloured and Indian families were forcibly moved from their homes and resettled in areas set aside for their racial groups. For example, District Six in the heart of Cape Town, an area occupied by Coloureds since 1834, with an estimated population of sixty-one thousand Coloureds and eight hundred whites, was proclaimed a white group area, and Coloureds were forcibly removed to a bleak area some ten miles from the center of Cape Town. By contrast, only two thousand white families were compelled to move as a result of the act.

In the 1980s, as the government tried to co-opt Coloureds and Indians politically for participation in the tricameral Parliament, the act was applied with less vigor. The prosecutions of Coloureds, Indians, and Africans who had moved into white group areas in large numbers decreased as the courts held that such persons might not be evicted from their homes in white areas when no accommodation in their own group areas was available.[33]

Despite the relaxation of the implementation of this law, it remained a cruel symbol of apartheid and a necessary guarantee of the maintenance of residential standards for whites. In 1988 the government allowed a minimal departure from the system of racial zoning when it introduced the Free Settlement Areas Act to provide for the establishment of selected racially open suburbs.[34]

In 1991 the Group Areas Act was finally repealed.[35] The repealing statute attempts to overcome white fears that living standards in their suburbs will drop by empowering neighborhoods to take measures to prevent the "overcrowding of residential premises," to keep such premises in a "clean and hygienic condition," and, generally, to ensure that the existing "norms and standards" of the particular neighborhood are preserved.[36] Although the law makes no reference to race, it is clearly designed to prevent neighborhood deterioration caused by the influx of black residents.

Social Segregation. Racial discrimination was a basic feature of South African society in 1948, when the National Party came to power. A plethora of laws provided for segregation in employment, social life, and most public amenities. These laws, which had been adopted in a haphazard manner over the years since 1910, were manifestations of white paternalism and the colonial heritage rather than expressions of an articulated racist ideology. Moreover, much of the discrimination at that time was based on convention rather than law.

All this changed after 1948. During the first decade of National Party rule, racial discrimination was given systematic, institutional form, so that virtually no aspect of social life was untouched by race laws. Interracial marriages and sexual relations were outlawed; rigid zoning laws were introduced to ensure both residential and business segregation; the right of Africans to visit and seek employment in the white cities was severely restricted; the reservation of many jobs for whites only was given legal backing; separate universities for Africans, Coloureds, and Indians were established, and the mission schools for Africans were taken over by the state; and segregation became the law in hospitals, hotels, restaurants, libraries, parks, transportation, sports, beaches, and almost every aspect of day-to-day life.[37]

In the 1980s, in response to both internal and external pressures, the government repealed a number of these laws and relaxed the enforcement of others. The laws prohibiting interracial marriage and sexual relations were repealed.[38] The notorious pass laws—the primary instrument of influx control—were abolished.[39] These laws had resulted in the jailing of millions of Africans whose only crime was to visit a white area without a permit, usually in search of work, or to be unable to produce an identity document or pass on demand. Job reservation was lifted, and Africans were given the right to engage in collective bargaining through the recognition of black trade unions.[40] Universities were permitted to admit persons of all races.[41] Segregation was abolished in sports, hotels, restaurants, libraries, parks, and most public amenities. Africans were given the right to own land in the townships or suburbs that adjoin the white cities.[42] The Group Areas Act, providing for racial zoning within the urban areas, was partially relaxed as a result of a number of progressive judicial decisions, and legislation was introduced to provide for the establishment of selected racially open suburbs.[43]

In February 1990, when President De Klerk announced the end of apartheid, many of the legislative pillars of apartheid were still intact. Since then all racially discriminatory statutes other than the 1983 Constitution have been repealed. But the repeal of these statutes did not mean that racial discrimination was entirely eliminated.

Public Amenities. In the first twenty years of apartheid, South Africa was a rigidly segregated society. Although a number of amenities was desegregated during the 1970s, segregation continued on buses, trains, and in public swimming pools. Many beaches were exclusively reserved for whites. This was dramatically illustrated in January 1987 when the Reverend H. J. (Allan) Hendrickse, leader of the ministers council in the Coloured House of Representatives, was severely rebuked by President Botha for swimming at a white beach and compelled to apologize publicly for this act of defiance.

Toward the end of the 1980s, the last vestiges of legally enforced social segregation were almost completely removed. South Africa's beaches were opened to all, and many public swimming pools ceased to be reserved for whites only. At this stage, a white backlash occurred in a number of Transvaal towns controlled by the reactionary Conservative Party, which had been formed after a split in the National Party in 1982. Acting on their local government powers, the towns of Boksburg and Carletonville reintroduced segregation in parks and other public amenities. Ironically, courts that had upheld the lawfulness of segregated facilities for years now held these bylaws to be invalid on the grounds that they were discriminatory and hence unreasonable.[44]

In the early years of apartheid, the reservation of public amenities for whites was protected by the Reservation of Separate Amenities Act; thus, the courts had no power to set aside unequal reservations.[45] After public authorities abandoned segregation, this statute ceased to be of much importance. The repeal of this law in 1990, however, had more than symbolic value, as it ensured that Conservative Party–controlled towns were deprived of the sole remaining statutory authorization for segregated facilities.[46]

Education and Health. Segregation was eased as well in education and health. Although each university retained its dominant racial or language character, university segregation was abandoned in law and practice.[47] No university is exclusively black or white. At the secondary and primary levels, a measure of integration occurred in both private and government schools. While most private schools had been open to all races since the mid-1970s, it was only in 1991 that some government schools were desegregated in pursuance of a new policy that allowed the parents of the children at each white school to elect to desegregate the school. In order to exercise this option, 80 percent of the parents must vote on the issue and 72 percent must favor the opening of the school. The choice to desegregate was taken mainly by the English-language schools.

School desegregation presented a special problem to the National Party government, and it was predicted that this would be the "last bastion of apartheid."[48] Two reasons accounted for this situation. First, the retention of all-white Afrikaans-language schools was seen as an essential prerequisite for the survival of the Afrikaans language and culture. Second, the quality of education in black schools was grossly inferior to that in white schools, and many feared that complete school desegregation would seriously affect the quality of white education. The discrepancy in the standard of education for whites and blacks was the result of nearly forty years of differentiated education for Africans, known as "Bantu Education," and the inadequate government funding of African education. Although the government increased its funding for African education substantially after 1976, when dissatisfaction with African schooling triggered an uprising that shook the country, the ratio of white-to-African per capita expenditure was still more than four to one. As a result, African children suffered a considerable disadvantage from poorly trained teachers, fewer educational facilities, and a higher pupil-teacher ratio than whites. The South African experience in school segregation fully demonstrated the truth of the philosophy enunciated in 1954 by the U.S. Supreme Court in *Brown v. Board of Education of Topeka* that "separate educational facilities are inherently unequal."[49]

Government-run hospitals, like schools, were strictly segregated until 1990, when they were opened to all races.

Political Repression

Throughout the apartheid era, threats to Afrikaner political hegemony—that is, to National Party rule—were vigorously repressed by a formidable arsenal of security laws. These laws, which formed an integral part of the law of apartheid, attracted as much hostile attention as the race laws. The international community, through the forum of the United Nations, probably devoted more attention to political repression in South Africa than to race discrimination. For example, the 1977 UN Security Council resolution imposing a mandatory arms embargo on South Africa was prompted not by racial discrimination but by political repression.[50]

In 1950, during the period of cold war hysteria, the South African Parliament passed the Suppression of Communism Act, which was intended to crush any attempts at basic political and economic change.[51] It not only outlawed the South African Communist Party (SACP) and the advocacy of communism, but was used against the leaders of the ANC.[52] No attempt was made initially to actually outlaw the ANC; however, drastic measures were introduced to suppress the organization's passive resistance campaign in the early 1950s. For example, heavy penalties were prescribed for civil disobedience, and the Public Safety Act was adopted to allow the government to resort to emergency rule should the existing law prove inadequate in curbing the ANC's activities (see Appendix B).[53] These emergency powers were not invoked until 1960, when a state of emergency was declared for 156 days to authorize a crackdown on political opposition following the police killing of anti-pass law demonstrators at Sharpeville. The government used the opportunity to ban both the ANC and the PAC, first for twelve-month periods only, but with permanent effect in 1963.[54]

The 1960 emergency succeeded in suppressing political opposition but had disastrous economic consequences. Foreign investors, alarmed by the acknowledgment of political instability inherent in the declaration of a state of emergency, withdrew capital, and a serious recession followed. This resulted in a change of government strategy. Rather than declaring states of emergency, the government chose to enact emergency-type laws as part of the ordinary law of the land. The period from 1963 to 1985, therefore, witnessed a program of unprecedented political repression under new security laws.

In the early 1960s, detention without trial became the lot of the dissident. Before 1960 the government had either legally charged its political opponents or imposed banning or banishment orders on them. A banning order placed severe restrictions on the personal and political freedom of an individual, while banishment resulted in exile to some desolate rural area—one of South Africa's "Siberias." In 1963 provision was made to permit detention for 90 days without trial for the purpose of interrogation; in 1965 this period was extended to 180 days; and in 1967 Section 6 of the Terrorism Act was introduced to allow indefinite detention without trial at the discretion of a senior police officer.[55] Terrorism was widely defined to cover any form of unlawful political activity.

In this environment of political paranoia, South Africa's highest court, the Appellate Division of the Supreme Court, adopted a policy of judicial restraint or abstention in its interpretation of the security laws. The result was that brutal interrogation of detainees became the rule and suspicious deaths in detention a not uncommon occurrence. It is not an exaggeration to say that during the years of the Vorster administration (1966–78), South Africa became a police state, with uncontrolled powers vested in the police force. Organizations were outlawed, political meetings prohibited, individuals banned and detained—all without having access to the courts.

* * *

In 1978 P. W. Botha, whose links were with the military and not the police, became prime minister, resulting in a political backlash against the police and demands for the curbing of police powers. In 1982, after a commission of inquiry under the chairmanship of Justice Pierre J. Rabie had examined the security laws, a new Internal Security Act was enacted.[56]

The Internal Security Act of 1982 was essentially a consolidation of earlier statutes. It introduced some reforms, such as the abolition of compulsory minimum sentences for political offenders and the institution of review tribunals—but not courts—to consider executive action. However, the act retained the main repressive features of previous enactments. Under the act, the minister of law and order was empowered to proscribe political organizations, ban newspapers, prohibit gatherings, and restrict the movement and basic rights of designated persons.[57] He was authorized to exercise these powers when he was satisfied that the security of the state was endangered—without any judicial supervision.

The 1982 Internal Security Act allowed officers of the state to order detention without trial for varying periods of time and for various purposes:

1. The attorney general, who is responsible for the prosecution, was empowered to detain a state witness for a maximum of six months.[58] No persons other than an officer of the state might have access to such a person.

2. A senior police officer might order the detention of any person when he was of the opinion that such detention would contribute to the termination of a state of public disturbance. Such a person might be held for forty-eight hours, but his detention might be extended by a more senior police officer for a maximum of six months.[59]

3. The minister of law and order might order the "preventive detention," for any period specified in his order, of any person whom he was satisfied "engages in activities which endanger or are calculated to endanger the security of the state."[60]

4. A senior police officer was empowered to order the indefinite detention for the purpose of interrogation of any person whom he had "reason to believe" had committed or intended to commit terrorism or subversion or had information relating to the commission of such an offense.[61] Such a person might be visited only

by officers of the state. This section, which succeeded Section 6 of the Terrorism Act of 1967, created the opportunity for brutal police interrogation and in effect authorized systematic psychological torture. The common-law writ of *habeas corpus* was excluded in all these cases of detention.

The Internal Security Act also created a number of substantive political crimes to supplement the common-law crime of treason. These included terrorism, subversion, sabotage, furthering the objectives of communism, and engaging in acts of civil disobedience.[62] These crimes were ambiguously defined, giving the police and prosecuting authorities a free hand to detain and try political activists.[63] A number of other statutes, described in the next chapter, buttressed the Internal Security Act.

Security laws of this kind, incorporating measures normally associated with emergency rule into the ordinary law of the land, would seem to eliminate the need for a formally declared state of emergency. An executive that enjoyed the power to outlaw opposition parties, to close down newspapers, to prohibit meetings, and to detain its political opponents without fear of judicial control would need, so it seemed, no further powers to suppress opposition. That supposition, however, proved to be flawed.

The brief period of tranquility that followed the passage of the 1982 Internal Security Act was the calm before the storm. In 1983 the government unveiled its new constitution. This event provided the impetus for the formation of the United Democratic Front, a body composed of some six hundred organizations, ranging from small rent committees to large trade unions. Apart from their opposition to the proposed constitution, the UDF's member organizations shared an allegiance to the principles of the Freedom Charter, a manifesto adopted by the ANC and other political groups in 1955 (see Appendix C). The UDF campaigned actively for a boycott of the Coloured and Indian elections to the tricameral Parliament in August 1984 and was largely responsible for the small percentage polls. The government probably would have liked to ban the UDF, as it had other popular political movements, but this would have fatally undermined the credibility of the elections. Instead, toward the end of the elections, the government began a campaign of harassment against UDF leaders.

At about the same time, on September 3, 1984, violence erupted in the townships of the Vaal Triangle, near the Transvaal–Orange

Free State border, in reaction to rent increases, corrupt local authorities, and the new Constitution. The political unrest and violence spread rapidly, and by the end of 1984, the scale of the protest and the clashes between the black community and the police recalled the Soweto uprising of 1976–77. Black schools were boycotted and closed, and a two-day stayaway in November brought industry to a halt in many parts of the Transvaal. Hundreds were killed and injured in police actions in which the police used rubber bullets, *sjamboks* (whips), and tear gas. According to a study published by the Southern African Catholic Bishops' Conference, "the police behavior in townships resembled that of an occupying foreign army."[64] In response to the uprising, the government banned political meetings, detained hundreds without trial, and called in the army to assist the police in suppressing the revolt.

On July 21, 1985, President Botha, operating under the Public Safety Act, decided that the existing law was inadequate to cope with the situation and declared a state of emergency in most areas. This emergency was lifted on March 7, 1986. But on June 12, 1986, a nationwide state of emergency was declared and was renewed annually until June 8, 1990, when it was allowed to lapse, except in the province of Natal, where it was finally lifted on October 18, 1990.[65]

During twenty-five years of political unrest and sporadic violence, the South African government had resisted the temptation to resort to emergency rule. Instead, it had chosen to suppress intensifying political demands through emergency-type measures enacted into the ordinary law of the land. These laws were clearly adequate for the government's purpose since they had been used successfully to put down the Soweto uprising and related political unrest in 1976–77. The advantage of the laws was that they avoided the necessity for a declaration of a state of emergency, which would antagonize South Africa's main Western trading partners.

When the government changed its strategy in July 1985 and opted for the wider police powers and greater political repression that a state of emergency carried, it provoked a hostile international response. In October 1986, partly in response to the imposition of emergency rule, the U.S. Congress adopted the Comprehensive Anti-Apartheid Act, which contained important though limited sanctions against South Africa. The Commonwealth and European Community also initiated sanctions against South Africa. Little doubt exists that these sanctions contributed substantially to the later reversal of National Party policy that led to the dismantling of apartheid and negotiations with the ANC.

The political situation that followed the unbanning of the ANC, PAC, UDF, and SACP in February 1990 made a thorough review of the security laws imperative. In the Groote Schuur Minute—the document that was produced as a result of the first meeting between the government and the ANC on May 4, 1990—the government undertook "to review existing security legislation to bring it into line with the new dynamic situation developing in South Africa in order to ensure normal and free political activities."[66] This undertaking was given effect in June 1991 when the Internal Security Act of 1982 was substantially amended.[67]

The 1991 amendments repealed the provisions of the 1982 act that outlawed the Communist Party and the advocacy of communism. The power of the minister of justice to proscribe an organization was severely restricted. Whereas the minister was previously empowered to outlaw an organization believed to engage in activities that endangered the security of the state, an organization now can be outlawed only if there is reason to believe that the organization is attempting to overthrow or change the authority of the state by violent means. Furthermore, the Supreme Court now has the power to review the minister's decision. The provisions in the Internal Security Act allowing for the prohibition of publications were also repealed.

The most important amendments related to the laws curtailing individual liberty. The system of banning individuals by subjecting them to house arrest or the denial of basic freedoms by executive decree was abolished, as was preventive detention. Section 29, which allowed indefinite detention without trial for the purpose of interrogation, now stated that a person suspected of terrorist activities could be held for a maximum of ten days.[68] Any extension of this period of detention required judicial approval. In the past, detainees were held incommunicado. Now they could be visited by their own doctors, families, and lawyers. The Democratic Party spokesperson for justice issues, David Dalling, commented on this amendment:

> What is left of the original Section 29 is but a pale shadow of the draconian measure we have so long abhorred. As far as is humanly possible to build in statutory protection against the physical or mental abuse of detainees, this has been done. I believe the concept of *habeas corpus* has at last made a welcome return to the body of South African law.[69]

The Courts and the Law of Apartheid

Responsibility for the violation of human rights in South Africa rests firmly with the legislature and executive. Unlike the courts of the United States, South African courts have no power to set aside acts of the legislature.[70] Courts are obliged, however, to interpret the laws of apartheid and to review administrative action taken under these laws. South African law requires courts to interpret and review laws within the context of the common-law principles of equality, individual liberty, reasonableness, and natural justice.[71] In effect, this means that courts of law may legitimately mitigate the inequality and severity of the laws of apartheid by benevolent interpretation and review.

The extent to which the courts have exercised this power is a subject of debate. While some argue that judges have correctly pursued a policy of restraint in order to avoid bringing the courts into the political arena, others claim that judges have been guilty of collaboration in the enforcement of apartheid. No study of the law of apartheid can therefore ignore the role of the courts.

South African courts are divided into lower courts (magistrates courts) and higher courts (the Supreme Court of South Africa). The former are staffed by civil servants from whom no meaningful degree of independence can be expected. Judges of the Supreme Court, on the other hand, who are appointed by the state president from private legal practice and from the ranks of court specialists or advocates (the equivalent of English barristers), model themselves on the English judiciary and pride themselves on their independence from the executive. Judges have security of tenure until the age of seventy, and although a judge may be dismissed by the state president at the request of Parliament on grounds of misbehavior or incapacity, no such action has been taken in the history of South Africa.

The Supreme Court is divided into a number of provincial divisions, which try serious cases and hear appeals from magistrates courts, and an Appellate Division, whose decisions are binding on the provincial divisions. There are some 130 Supreme Court judges, of whom fifteen are judges of appeal; the Appeal Court normally sits in panels of five judges. All but one of the judges of the Supreme Court are white, although no law prohibits the appointment of blacks; all but one are male; and the majority (about 60 percent) are of Afrikaans-speaking origin. As a result, they are prone to identify, consciously or subconsciously, with the Afrikaner government. The rest of the judges are drawn from the English-speaking community, which, in general, identifies more closely with British traditions. Afrikaner judges, however, cannot be stereotyped as sympathetic to the government, any more than English-speaking judges can be labeled as unsympathetic. While most of the judiciary is conservative by nature and outlook, a minority, including both Afrikaans- and English-speaking judges, aspire to liberal traditions and values.

When the National Party came to power in 1948, it was confronted with an Appellate Division appointed by its predecessor, the United Party government of Jan Smuts. The Appeal Court, which consisted of a number of the most liberal judges ever to grace it, refused to acquiesce meekly in the new apartheid legal order and challenged the government on two grounds. First, it set aside administrative acts providing for unequal amenities for different races, holding that the common law required an equality of treatment (akin to the "separate but equal" doctrine in the United States). Second, it obstructed the government's attempts to remove Coloured voters from the electoral roll in the Cape Province, holding that Parliament had failed to follow the correct constitutional procedure. This obstructionism so angered the government that it increased the size of the Appellate Division and set about systematically appointing lawyers sympathetic to its ideology to the Supreme Court, particularly to the Appeal Court.

By 1959 the government had brought the judiciary into line. Thereafter, restraint and abstention were to characterize judicial decisions on race and security. The unequal application of the Group Areas Act by administrative fiat was approved by the Appellate Division, despite the absence of clear statutory authority; and the detention-without-trial laws of the 1960s were made still harsher by judicial interpretations in favor of the executive.[72] The provincial divisions followed the lead of the Appellate Division and likewise refrained from challenging the legal apparatus of apartheid.

The failure of the courts to use their powers of interpretation and review to support human rights provoked criticism from academic legal quarters and led to a questioning of the judicial role.[73] It also became clear that the disenfranchised majority, who had previously looked to the courts for relief from the oppression of apartheid, had lost much of their confidence in them. This seemed to make some judges aware of the crisis facing the courts, particularly in the province of Natal.

During the 1980s the courts began to hand down more liberal judgments on racial matters. Administrative orders banishing blacks from the urban areas on the grounds that they were "idle and undesirable" were set aside until the law permitting this practice became inoperative.[74] The rights of blacks to permanent residence in the urban areas were extended in the face of administrative rules designed to compel migrant blacks to return to their rural homes.[75] A grandiose government scheme to cede parts of KwaZulu to Swaziland was halted.[76] A forced population removal was set aside and the practice judicially condemned.[77]

The enforcement of the Group Areas Act was rendered inoperative in the Transvaal by a decision requiring the state to provide evidence of alternative accommodation before a "disqualified" person (African, Coloured, Indian) might be evicted from his or her housing in a white area.[78] Finally, the practice of incorporating unwilling black communities into the nonindependent homelands was brought to an end.[79] Although these judgments were ahead of the government's reforms, the antidiscriminatory rhetoric of the government during this time no doubt encouraged judges to be more daring, particularly when they knew that it was unlikely their decisions would be overruled by Parliament.

A similar degree of judicial liberalism failed to emerge in relation to security laws. In this area, the judiciary as a whole followed the lead of the government, which gave no sign that it was prepared to relent in the implementation of its security laws during the 1980s. On the contrary, it continued to add to its legal arsenal. Nevertheless, some judges, particularly in Natal, gave bold interpretations of the security laws. They advanced the rights of an alleged political offender to be released from detention when the arresting police officer was unable to show that the detention was necessary, and the rights to protection from harsh interrogation, to bail, and to a fairer trial. In one of these cases, *S. v. Ramgobin*, Judge David Friedman declared:

> It is only through the courts exercising their powers fearlessly and impartially, that a proper balance can be achieved between the interest of the individual's liberty and the interest of the state in bringing alleged wrongdoers to justice. And the courts in this country do so exercise their powers entirely free from any direct or indirect pressure or influence from the state, the legislature or the executive branch of the government.[80]

In 1986 the Appellate Division under Chief Justice Pierre Rabie handed down two decisions on the Internal Security Act that gave rise to optimism in liberal quarters. In *Nkondo v. Minister of Law and Order*, the court declared preventive detention orders served on leaders of the UDF to be invalid, by virtue of the minister's failure to give reasons for his decision.[81] And in *Minister of Law and Order v. Hurley*, the court confirmed a Natal court decision holding that the decision of a police officer to detain a person under Section 29 is justiciable in a court of law.[82]

In 1986 Chief Justice Rabie reached the statutory retirement age of seventy, and it was anticipated that he would be succeeded by Justice M. M. Corbett, a senior judge of appeal with a liberal record on civil rights issues. But the government, for undisclosed reasons, reappointed Justice Rabie as acting chief justice for an additional two-year period. During this time, the Appellate Division retreated to its earlier policy of judicial restraint. A series of decisions on the interpretation of the emergency regulations, for example, led to renewed accusations that the Appeal Court was taking the side of the government.[83]

In 1989 Justice Corbett became chief justice. Since then the jurisprudence of the Appellate Division has undergone a significant change, and a number of important decisions in favor of individual liberty have been handed down. For instance, the court lost little time in overruling its 1988 decision in *Minister of Law and Order v. Dempsey*, in which the Rabie Court had upheld the lawfulness of an arrest under the emergency regulations by limiting the burden of proof of an arresting officer to justify such an arrest.[84] Although the power to overrule an earlier decision is exercised sparingly, the court held that an incorrect earlier decision should not be followed where individual liberty is at stake.[85] In 1991 the Appellate Division reversed a long line of Provincial Division decisions when it held that, because of the unlawfulness of his arrest, a member of the ANC arrested by security agents in Swaziland might not be tried in South Africa.[86] In this respect, South African law is more advanced than that of the United States and Britain, whose courts show little hesitation in trying persons kidnapped from abroad.[87] Decisions of this kind have done much to restore confidence in the judiciary and are probably a result of the new judicial leadership and the change in political climate.

Conclusion

Apartheid underwent changes in form and emphasis between 1948 and 1991. Before 1960 the government was preoccupied mainly with extending racial separation and consolidating white domination. During the next two decades, the emphasis shifted to territorial separation—or grand apartheid—and police repression. The 1980s are more difficult to categorize. Constitutional initiatives were aimed at politically co-opting the Coloured and Indian communities, and a number of important racial reforms were introduced. But the hopes of the early part of the decade did not materialize, and reform gave way to repression at the hands of the police and the military.

Toward the end of the decade, when the government decided to withdraw from Namibia and the National Party leadership changed hands, expectations of fundamental reform in South Africa increased. These expectations were realized in February 1990 when President De Klerk announced the dismantling of apartheid and the creation of a new democratic order as National Party policy. The repeal of the race classification laws, the Group Areas Act, and the Land Acts, as well as the radical revision of the Internal Security Act in June 1991, have virtually brought an end to institutionalized racism. In the early 1990s, South Africa embarked on the difficult task of constructing a society in which race would no longer be a determining factor in the allocation of rights or the exercise of power.

The disappearance of the legal structures of apartheid, however, does not mean that a nonracial society will emerge overnight in South Africa. Apartheid spread its roots deep and wide, and it will take years before all racist practices are brought to an end, and perhaps generations before the memory of apartheid is eradicated from the spirit of the nation. But the repeal of discriminatory laws was crucial, for only without these laws can South Africans embark on building a new society in which differentiation based on race will play no part.

Chapter II
Civil Liberties Under Emergency Rule
Gilbert Marcus

Undemocratic governments invariably rely on coercion to retain power, and the South African government is no exception. The use of the policies of apartheid to deprive selected groups of their civil rights inevitably spawned resistance, and successive governments invoked increasingly drastic powers to curb the challenge. In the words of the International Commission of Jurists' report on states of emergency, "a frequent and perhaps understandable link exists between states of emergency and grave violations of human rights."[1]

The Origin of Emergency Powers

The possibility for using emergency powers in peacetime was introduced in South Africa with the passing of the Public Safety Act in 1953. The central feature of the act was the vesting of power in the governor-general (now the state president) to declare a state of emergency if, in his opinion, "any action or threatened action by any persons is of such a nature and of such extent that the safety of the public, or the maintenance of public order is seriously threatened . . . and the ordinary law of the land is inadequate to . . . ensure the safety of the public, or to maintain public order."[2] Once an emergency has been declared, the state president is authorized to issue regulations that he feels are "necessary or expedient" for safeguarding the public or maintaining public order, and that make "adequate provision for terminating such emergency or for dealing with any circumstances" that he feels have been or could be caused by the emergency.[3] The act specifically envisages regulations authorizing summary arrest and detention without trial.[4]

In 1953 the Public Safety Act was considered a radical measure, giving the executive powers usually reserved for times of war. It bears striking similarity to the War Measures Act of 1940, which authorized the governor-general to make regulations that appeared to him to be necessary or expedient for the defense of the Union, the safety of the public, the maintenance of public order, and the effective prosecution of the war.[5] The Public Safety Act was passed in response to the defiance campaign being conducted by the then legal African National Congress (ANC), but it was not used in the 1950s. In proposing the bill to Parliament, Minister of Justice C. R. Swart (later to become the first president of the Republic of South Africa) stated that he hoped the measure "will remain purely as a deterrent to those who aim at committing violence and doing things which a peace-loving public cannot tolerate."[6]

The defiance campaign of passive resistance was directed against a number of discriminatory enactments. Political scientist Tom Lodge explains:

> The regulations disobeyed were very minor ones: use of white facilities at post offices, railway stations and on trains, breaching curfew regulations and pass laws, and entering African locations without a permit. Despite the increasingly heavy sentences handed out by magistrates (including flogging for young people), almost without exception volunteers opted to serve prison sentences which could last two or three months rather than pay the alternative fine.[7]

In 1953 the Criminal Law Amendment Act was also passed. Together with the Public Safety Act, it was intended to break the defiance campaign.[8] The measure reflected the minister of justice's preoccupations with security and race, preoccupations that typified South African society in general. In a speech to Parliament, the minister had this to say:

> Not so long ago a dance was held at a certain club in Johannesburg in support of the defiance campaign. There were about 300 non-European men and women present and 50 European men and women. They danced with one another and they carried on until 2 o'clock in the morning and they collected something like 500 pounds sterling for this defiance campaign. That is what is happening in this country. Black and White danced with each other.[9]

In essence, the Criminal Law Amendment Act prescribed increased penalties for a contravention of any law if the infringement involved "protest against the law or . . . support of any campaign for the repeal or modification of any law . . . ."[10] The penalties were severe and included fines, imprisonment for up to five years, or a whipping not exceeding ten strokes. In the case of a second or subsequent conviction, a fine had to be accompanied by a whipping or imprisonment.[11]

Together with the Public Safety Act, the Criminal Law Amendment Act effectively put an end to the campaign against unjust laws. But the causes of discontent did not disappear. Albert Lutuli, former president of the ANC and Nobel Peace Prize laureate, attached particular significance to the defiance campaign. He later wrote:

> So ended a year which changed the political complexion of South Africa. The whites took several more strides towards authoritarianism. Among Africans and Indians, and to a smaller extent among coloureds, the spirit of active opposition came alive, consent to continue being governed exclusively by the whites and for the whites was withdrawn, goals became clear.[12]

It was not until 1960 that a state of emergency was actually proclaimed, following the shooting in Sharpeville of a large group of blacks who had deliberately courted arrest by refusing to carry passes.[13] The tragedy left 69 people dead (including eight women and ten children) and 180 people wounded. The emergency endured for 156 days, during which 11,503 persons were detained.[14] Regulations promulgated pursuant to the emergency made provision for detention without trial, the prohibition of gatherings, the suppression of publications and organizations, and the creation of a variety of newly defined offenses.[15]

During the emergency, the ANC and the Pan Africanist Congress (PAC) were outlawed under the Unlawful Organizations Act.[16] Originally the ban was to be a temporary one, but in 1963 it was made permanent.[17] The prohibition continued until February 2, 1990, when President Frederik W. de Klerk made his dramatic speech announcing the unbanning of the ANC, the PAC, and all other unlawful organizations.[18]

The Genesis of Security Legislation

Sharpeville and its aftermath radically altered the political atmosphere of the country. The most immediate consequence of the banning of the ANC and the PAC was the decision by both organizations to resort to armed resistance. Nelson Mandela was to say later, at his trial in 1964, that "it was only when all else had failed, when all channels of peaceful protest had been barred to us, that the decision was made to embark on violent forms of political struggle."[19]

When the state of emergency was proclaimed in 1960, South Africa had little by way of security legislation. In an attempt to curb the activities of the ANC and the PAC, the government introduced the ninety-day detention law in 1963. This statute authorized any commissioned police officer to arrest without warrant any person whom he suspected "of having committed or intending or having intended to commit" certain specified offenses, or who, in his opinion, possessed "any information relating to the commission of any such offence or the intention to commit such offence." The detainee could be held without trial in solitary confinement for up to ninety days or until he had, in the opinion of the commissioner of police, answered all questions satisfactorily at his interrogation. Access to the detainee was specifically prohibited, save with the consent of the minister of justice. The only safeguard was the requirement that a detainee be visited "not less than once during each week" by a magistrate.[20]

The courts did little to mitigate the harshness of this measure. Three decisions of the Appellate Division substantially eroded the already meager rights of detainees. In *Loza v. Police Station Commander*, it was held that the arresting officer could renew the detention immediately upon expiration of the ninety-day period.[21] The compelling reasoning of a lower court—that arrests for the same violation would render the ninety-day limit meaningless—was rejected.[22] Instead, the Appellate Division found that a further period of detention might be justified by either a change with respect to the particular offense with which the suspect was thought to be linked or a change in the situation upon which the suspicion or opinion was based.[23]

In the case of *Rossouw v. Sachs*, the Appellate Division ruled that a detainee could lawfully be deprived of reading and writing materials in addition to being held in solitary confinement.[24] Despite recognizing that such deprivation may amount to psychological compulsion, access to reading and writing materials was regarded by a unanimous court not as a right but "as a matter of grace."[25] Finally, in *Schermbrucker v. Klindt N.O.* (*Nomine Officio*, meaning that the person is cited in an official capacity), the Appellate Division held by a majority that a detainee on whose behalf allegations of torture had been leveled could not be brought to court to testify personally to his conditions of detention.[26] The reasoning was chilling:

> [C]ompliance by a detainee with an order requiring his personal attendance in a Court would result in an interruption of his detention and interrogation designed to induce him to speak. Such interruptions, especially lengthy interruptions, may therefore clearly defeat the purpose of the detention. The purpose of the detention, though it temporarily deprives the detainee of his liberty, is intended to induce him to speak, and any interference with that detention which may negate the inducement to speak is likely to defeat the purpose of the legislature.[27]

In this trilogy of cases, the statute was silent on the issues to be decided, and the Appellate Division, South Africa's highest court, was confronted with a choice of constructions. C. Forsyth, a South African legal academic, described the court's attitude of "hands off" the security police as lending "an implicit imprimatur to the police forces to act brutally and with a licence uninhibited by legal control."[28] Effectively cut off from the outside world and bereft of any meaningful safeguards against abuse, many detainees died under suspicious circumstances while being held under the ninety-day detention law and its successors.

Fortified by the judicial endorsement of this law's drastic provisions, the legislature had little difficulty passing increasingly severe security measures. The 90-day law was never intended to be a permanent measure and was withdrawn in 1965, only to be replaced by the 180-day detention law.[29] The purpose of this provision was nominally different from the 90-day law in that it was intended as a device for protecting witnesses and securing their attendance at court. In practice, however, detainees were interrogated under it, and many were later charged with offenses. The law authorized the attorney general to order the arrest and detention of "any person likely to give material evidence for the State in any criminal proceedings" whenever he was of the view that such person might be intimidated or abscond or if he deemed it to be "in the interest of such person or the administration of justice."[30] The 180-day detention statute became a permanent feature of South African law.

In 1966 the first enactment designed specifically to combat

terrorism was introduced. Section 22 of the General Law Amendment Act was a relatively modest measure that authorized the fourteen-day detention for purposes of interrogation of a person suspected of terrorist activities. Significant safeguards were contained in the statute. The fourteen-day period could only be extended by a Supreme Court judge, who was entitled to receive written submissions from the detainee as to why the detention should not be extended. Although not repealed for many years, this provision became redundant with the passage of the Terrorism Act in 1967, the most radical provision of South African law.

The notorious Section 6 of the Terrorism Act authorized indefinite detention in solitary confinement of any person whom a senior police officer had reason to believe was a terrorist or was withholding terrorist information from the South African Police (SAP). Even harsher than the 1963 ninety-day detention law, Section 6 ensured isolation from the outside world with its provision that no one other than the minister or an officer of the state could have access to any detainee or be entitled to any information about or obtained from any detainee.[31] Even the minimal safeguard of a weekly magisterial visit contained in the ninety-day detention law was watered down. Now a magistrate was to visit a detainee once a fortnight "if circumstances so permit."[32]

The newly defined crime of terrorism, punishable by the death sentence, was made retroactive by five years. The definition bore little resemblance to offenses normally understood as constituting terrorism and criminalized activities that had little or no relationship to state security. The act also removed the courts' traditional discretion in matters of sentencing by providing for minimum periods of imprisonment upon conviction. Procedural provisions had the effect of placing the onus on the accused to rebut certain presumptions beyond a reasonable doubt. Anthony S. Mathews, a leading authority on South African security law, described the effect of this act. It was, he wrote:

> . . . certainly possible for persons to disappear without trace into detention and to remain there until they die. Even the fact of the detention itself may be suppressed, so that parents, children, husbands or wives are denied information. "Disappearance in the night," that dreaded phenomenon of the police state, is made a reality by this law.[33]

It was while being held under Section 6 of the Terrorism Act that many detainees died.

*　*　*

In 1974 the Riotous Assemblies Act, a statute that provided limited powers to prohibit gatherings, was radically amended to authorize a magistrate to prohibit any gathering for a period not exceeding forty-eight hours and the minister of justice to prohibit any gathering for an unlimited period.[34]

Following the Soweto uprising in 1976, the minister exercised his power to prohibit all outdoor gatherings except sports meetings and those specially authorized by him throughout South Africa.[35] This prohibition was renewed every year until 1991, when it was allowed to lapse. The Soweto revolt also led to the introduction of preventive detention for the first time since the 1960 state of emergency.[36] The minister of justice was authorized to arrest and detain any person whom he was satisfied "engages in activities which endanger or are calculated to endanger the security of the State or the maintenance of public order."

In 1982, following the publication of the report of the (Rabie) Commission of Inquiry into Security Legislation, most of South Africa's security laws were consolidated into one statute, the Internal Security Act 74 of 1982.[37] The new statute retained most of the obnoxious provisions of existing legislation while introducing minor safeguards. The power to detain indefinitely for purposes of interrogation was retained, as were the provisions relating to preventive detention, detention of witnesses, prohibition of gatherings, banning of organizations, prohibition of publications, and the restriction of individuals.[38] In the same year, the law of official secrecy was consolidated and amended, demonstrations in or near court buildings were proscribed, and a broad range of intimidating behavior was outlawed.[39]

Governmental control over the free flow of information had been ensured by several censorship statutes. Under the Publications Act, direct censorship was imposed by means of the banning of books, films, and public entertainment deemed to be "prejudicial to the safety of the State, the general welfare or the peace and good order."[40] The publication of "untrue" matter concerning the police and the Prisons Service was prohibited, and a tight blanket of secrecy obscured the activities of the defense force.[41]

By 1982, therefore, all the powers usually associated with states of emergency had become permanent features of the South African legal system. The full might of this security arsenal was invoked to curb the nationwide unrest that followed the introduction of the 1983 Constitution. The number of detentions recorded that year was the highest since the Soweto uprising and its aftermath during 1976–77.[42] The security forces appeared to be armed with every power for dealing with any conceivable contingency.

The Emergency: Powers of the Security Forces

On March 21, 1985, exactly twenty-five years after the Sharpeville tragedy, police opened fire on a group of mourners on their way to a funeral in the black township of Langa, near Uitenhage. Twenty people died as a result. While announcing a commission of inquiry to investigate the "incident," as it was officially called, President P. W. Botha said:

> The highest legislative and executive authorities of this country, subscribing as they do to the rule of law, should be, as a matter of principle, a shining and visible example of respect for the sanctity of law. This means that we must be seen to respect not only the letter of the law but also the spirit thereof.[43]

Within four months of making this speech, President Botha declared a state of emergency in thirty-six magisterial districts. This was lifted in March 1986 but was followed in June by a state of emergency that covered the entire country. The emergency was renewed annually until June 1990, when it was lifted everywhere except in Natal province, where it remained in force until October 1990.

Given the vast array of security laws at the state's disposal, the imposition of a formal state of emergency was surprising. Once the decision was made, however, scores of rules, regulations, and orders were promulgated that varied little from one state of emergency to another. Collectively, their sweep and severity were the absolute antithesis of the values espoused by a society predicated upon respect for the rule of law. The validity of some of these regulations was successfully challenged in the courts. But in most cases, the legislative response was swift, with amending legislation nullifying the courts' achievements.

Perhaps the most sinister provision of the emergency regulations was one indemnifying any member of a security force from civil or criminal liability "by reason of any act in good faith advised, commanded, ordered, directed or performed by any person" in carrying out his duties, exercising his powers, or performing his functions in terms of the regulations "with intent to ensure the safety of the public, the maintenance of public order or the termination of the state of emergency." Furthermore, a presumption was created that any act advised, commanded, ordered, directed, or performed was executed in good faith, until the contrary was proven.

Detentions. The most significant feature of the emergency regulations was the power vested in any member of the security force—the SAP, the South African Defense Force (SADF), and the Prisons Service—to arrest any person without warrant if he believed that the arrest was necessary for that person's own safety, for public safety, for maintaining public order, or for terminating the state of emergency.

Under the country's permanent security laws, the power to detain a person for the purposes of interrogation was vested in senior police officers. The emergency regulations, however, extended that awesome power to any member of the security forces; even a raw recruit could arrest a suspect on the basis of the most insubstantial suspicion.[44] Once in custody, the detainee could be interrogated by any member of the security force.

The person so arrested could initially be detained only for a limited period. During the 1985 and 1986 emergencies, this period was fourteen days, but it was extended to thirty days under the 1987 emergency. Thereafter, the detention could be extended by the minister of law and order for the full duration of the state of emergency.

With emergency rule taking on a permanent character, the specter of extremely long terms of detention became a reality as the minister of law and order regularly extended periods of detention. Many detainees were held for periods spanning more than one emergency, with arresting officers going through the mechanistic ritual of releasing and immediately rearresting the detainee. It was only in 1990 that limitations were eventually placed on the period of detention, restricting the total period to six months. Access to detainees continued to be tightly controlled and, until amendments to the regulations were introduced in 1990, a detainee's access to a lawyer was relegated to a privilege.

The sheer magnitude of emergency rule was reflected in the number of people detained. One of the supposed safeguards against the abuse of the sweeping powers conferred on members of the security forces was the requirement stipulated by the Public Safety Act that the names of all persons detained for more than thirty days be tabled before Parliament.[45] According to figures furnished by the minister of law and order, 7,966 people were detained during the 1985 emergency.[46] But after the declaration of a nationwide emergency in June 1986, the minister consistently refused to give the total number of people detained. In February 1987 he was asked to do so in Parliament and to specify how many of those detained were under the age of eighteen. In his reply, the minister stated that "extra-parliamentary activists and radical groups, amongst others the South African Communist Party, the ANC and the UDF, are, for revolutionary and propagandistic reasons, also interested in this information—they misuse it in the most dreadful way, to the detriment of South Africa and the majority of its inhabitants." Having "carefully evaluated" all the considerations, the minister said that he did not regard it in the national interest to supply the information requested.[47]

The Detainees' Parents Support Committee (DPSC), a private monitoring group, conservatively estimated that from the date of the declaration of the 1986 emergency on June 12 until December 31, 1986, some twenty-five thousand people had been detained. The major targets of detention were said to be children eighteen years old or younger; the United Democratic Front (UDF) and its affiliates accounted for approximately 75 percent of those detainees whose organizational affiliations were known.[48] The Progressive Federal Party put the total figure at between twenty thousand and twenty-five thousand.[49]

The detention of children was probably the most brutal facet of emergency rule. Notwithstanding the minister's reluctance to furnish statistics on the number of children in detention, papers filed before the Supreme Court indicated that 1,424 children between twelve and eighteen years of age were being held as emergency detainees as of April 15, 1987. This official figure included 2 twelve-year-olds, 19 thirteen-year-olds, 75 fourteen-year-olds, 110 fifteen-year-olds, 312 sixteen-year-olds, 461 seventeen-year-olds, and 445 eighteen-year-olds.[50] Following an outcry against the detention of children and a national campaign for their release, which the commissioner of police attempted to prohibit, many children were freed.[51]

It is estimated that from the beginning of 1984 until March 1988, approximately forty-five thousand people were detained under the permanent security laws and the emergency regulations.[52] An editorial in the *Star* made a poignant observation:

> Our nation has regressed from a country with pride in justice and the courts to a point where both are simply ignored. Any

man can be detained, can vanish and his protests of innocence never heard. Now even Parliament is refused information. So much for security of the individual. The system has become as dangerous as the chaos it is trying to prevent.[53]

As the emergency regime assumed the character of permanence, allegations of detainees, including children, being tortured became widespread.[54] The most shocking case of the systematic assault and torture of detainees emerged in the Eastern Cape. Dr. Wendy Orr, the district surgeon of Port Elizabeth, brought an application to restrain the police from assaulting detainees held under emergency regulations at the St. Albans and North End Prisons. Dr. Orr alleged that detainees whom she had examined had welts, bruises, and blisters on their bodies; some had lacerated lips and broken skin over their cheek bones, and several had perforated eardrums. Dr. Orr isolated 286 cases of complaint. She said that what had disturbed her most was that detainees had been taken out of her care for the purposes of interrogation, during which they had been "brutally" assaulted. In her application, Dr. Orr said that she had gained the impression that because police were acting under emergency powers, and because they apparently believed they enjoyed immunity under the regulations, "they, or some of them, are quite unrestrained in the abuses they inflict upon the detainees."

An interim interdict was granted, restraining the police from perpetrating further assaults. An additional ninety-three affidavits, containing further allegations of torture, were filed in the case in support of the application. Shortly after launching the application, Dr. Orr was relieved of her duties regarding the health care of detainees. In the end, the granting of the interim interdict was not opposed by the minister of law and order, who settled the matter by agreeing to pay the applicants' legal costs. Several other interdicts were granted by the Supreme Court, restraining the police from assaulting detainees.

Extensive rules governing the detention of emergency detainees were promulgated in all the states of emergency. In general, detainees were subjected to a harsh and punitive regimen that seemed largely unrelated to the purposes of securing public safety. Shortly after the declaration of the third state of emergency in 1987, new regulations were promulgated with the intention of regulating the treatment of emergency detainees on the same basis as prisoners awaiting trial. While this objective was largely achieved, certain features of the treatment of emergency detainees were considerably harsher than the treatment accorded to trial prisoners.

Both categories were subjected to a severe disciplinary code that prohibited being "insolent or disrespectful"; being "idle, careless, or negligent"; conversing or in any other manner making contact with any other person at a time when, or at a place where, it was not permissible to do so; singing, whistling, or making "unnecessary noise" or causing "unnecessary trouble" or being "a nuisance"; leaving one's cell or place of work or any other place without permission; and lodging "false, frivolous, or malicious complaints" and acting in any manner "contrary to good order and discipline."

Contravention of these vague provisions could result in a variety of punishments that included a reprimand, corporal punishment not exceeding six strokes if the detainee was a male apparently under the age of forty years and no other punishment was imposed on him in respect of the same contravention, and solitary confinement in an isolation cell coupled with a sparse diet for a period not exceeding thirty days. These provisions applied to all detainees, including children. If children were treated any differently, as was suggested by the minister of law and order and the commissioner of police, this was a privilege and not a right.[55]

During the 1989 emergency, detainees staged hunger strikes in different parts of the country. A statement issued by hunger strikers at St. Albans Prison in Port Elizabeth referred to complaints concerning inadequate medical treatment and stated:

> . . . in spite of numerous complaints registered with prison authorities, visiting judges and memoranda to the Advocate-General and even hunger strikes during the past 32 months, conditions in prison, *inter alia*, diet, health, education, recreation and sport, visits and communication have deteriorated markedly. We are left with no alternative but to take our lives into our own hands as: (1) to remind the said departments and respective officials of our plight; and (2) to herewith demand our immediate release from this dehumanizing detention without trial.[56]

In response, the minister of law and order stated that there were no grounds for complaint as to the conditions, needs, and physical treatment of detainees. His view was that the hunger strikes were being orchestrated from outside in support of extraparliamentary activities.[57] In a gesture of solidarity with the detainees, forty-two lawyers took part in a forty-eight-hour fast. They stated that their professional responsibilities required such action and that they had the support of many colleagues in all branches of the legal profession.[58] The hunger strikes spread rapidly throughout the country, with some detainees reaching the stage of irreparable physical harm. At this point, the minister of law and order received personal representations from lawyers acting on behalf of detainees. The hunger strikes were suspended and detainees were released on a large scale, although many were immediately served with restriction orders.

Control of Gatherings. The commissioner of police was given extensive powers to issue orders controlling gatherings. These powers were used repeatedly, particularly against extraparliamentary organizations. During the 1985 emergency, some ninety-four organizations were prohibited from organizing, arranging, or holding "any gathering in any building" in six specified magisterial districts in Cape Province. In 1986 a similar prohibition was imposed on 119 organizations in six magisterial districts in the Western Cape. In all the emergencies, specific gatherings to commemorate or protest particular events were prohibited. Curfews were also imposed in several magisterial districts.

Funerals, in particular, which had become highly politicized events, were singled out for special regulation. Any memorial or commemorative service in connection with the funeral of a deceased person was prohibited from being held out of doors. Only ordained ministers of religion were allowed to speak at funeral ceremonies. Public address systems were prohibited, and no "flags, banners, placards, pamphlets, or posters" could be displayed or distributed during a funeral ceremony. The number of persons allowed to attend a funeral was usually restricted to two hundred. Limitations were also imposed upon the duration of funerals. In some cases, restrictions on the content of speeches made at funerals were imposed. For example, such speeches could not "in any manner defend, attack, criticize, propagate or discuss any form of government, any principle or policy of a government of a State, any boycott action, the existence of a state of emergency or any action by a Force or a member of a Force."

Restrictions on Organizations and Individuals. In February 1988 the minister of law and order was authorized "without prior notice to any person and without hearing any person" to issue an order prohibiting an organization from carrying on or performing "any activities or acts whatsoever." An organization subjected to such a restriction was permitted to carry out only ordinary administrative functions, such as keeping its books up to date or taking legal advice. The minister was also vested with the power to place similar restrictions on individuals. In practice, a restricted organization became politically paralyzed, and the effect of the restriction was essentially the same as an outright banning.

The minister immediately exercised these powers against a variety of extraparliamentary organizations, including the UDF and several of its affiliates, as well as the Azanian People's Organization (AZAPO). Later in the year, the militant white rightwing organization, the *Blanke Bevrydingsbewiging van Suid Afrika* (White Liberation Movement of South Africa), was also restricted. By the time these restrictions were lifted by President De Klerk's government in February 1990, thirty-three organizations had been affected.

School Boycotts and Educational Matters. Special measures were taken in an attempt to prevent school boycotts. In several areas, it was decreed that, during school hours on any school day, no registered pupil could "be outside the boundaries of premises normally used for human habitation."

During the 1986 emergency, orders apparently intended to prevent persons from offering forms of education other than those prescribed by the Education and Training Act of 1979 were imposed. Control over educational matters was extended under the 1987 emergency when the director-general of education was invested with extensive powers to prohibit, among other things, the presentation on any school premises of any course or syllabus other than one officially prescribed, the wearing of specified tee shirts or other articles of clothing, and the distribution on school premises of specified publications. These emergency controls over educational institutions remained in force until 1990.

Censorship. When the 1985 emergency was proclaimed, it was specifically stated that no new controls would be placed on the media. Within days of the proclamation, however, a meeting took place between the police and press representatives at which the press was requested informally to "tone down" reports of unrest. A special committee that included members of all the forces was appointed to monitor news reports on a daily basis. In the first few months of the emergency, allegations of deliberate distortion were leveled at foreign journalists. In the months that followed, a number of foreign journalists were deported and increasingly drastic censorship provisions were implemented. The initial provisions, introduced in November 1985, seemed aimed primarily at curtailing foreign coverage of the activities of the security forces. A regulation was introduced prohibiting any person, without the requisite permission, from documenting on film or audiotape the activities of any member of the security forces. Publication or broadcast of such information outside South Africa was prohibited.

Regulations introduced with the 1986 emergency went much further. A prohibition on the making of any "subversive statement" was introduced. "Subversive statement" was broadly defined to include a statement that incited or encouraged members of the public or that was calculated to have the effect of inciting or encouraging members of the public to, among other activities, take part in boycott actions, acts of civil disobedience, and unlawful strikes. The making or publishing of a subversive statement, whether orally or in writing, or by incorporation in a television film or sound recording, was totally prohibited.

A second category of statement, although not totally prohibited, was subjected to special controls. Publications, television, film, or sound recordings containing "news or comment on or in connection with" a variety of topics, including actions of the security forces, speeches made at banned gatherings, and "the circumstances of, or treatment in, detention of a person who is or was detained" were prohibited. However, such matter could be published if authorized by a government official or if it appeared in debates or proceedings of Parliament or the President's Council, or in judicial proceedings, excluding those "in which the court concerned has not yet given a final judgment."

Other regulations prohibited taking photographs or making television or film recordings "of any unrest or security action" or of any related incident, "including the damaging or destruction of property or the injuring or killing of persons" or "of any damaged or destroyed property or injured or dead persons or other visible signs of violence from the scene [of] unrest or security action . . . or of any injury sustained by any persons in or during unrest or security action."

In 1987 an advertisement appeared in a number of newspapers coinciding with the seventy-fifth anniversary of the ANC and calling for its unbanning. Regulations were promptly promulgated in an attempt to prohibit further similar advertisements. It became an offense to publish or cause to be published any material containing an advertisement "defending, praising or endeavouring to justify" any unlawful organization's campaigns, projects, programs, actions, or policies of violence or resistance against the authority of the state.

The most bizarre censorship provision in the emergency regulations prohibited the publication of "any blank space or any obliteration or deletion of part of the text of a report or of a photograph or part of a photograph . . . if that blank space, obliteration or deletion . . . is intended to be understood as a reference" to the effect of the censorship regulations.

Further controls aimed at regulating the alternative press (community-based newspapers) were introduced in August 1987. The minister of home affairs was given the power to prohibit the publication of periodicals for a period not exceeding three months or to require prior approval for publication. He could exercise this power if, in his opinion, and based solely upon his examination of several issues of a periodical, he found a systematic or repeated publishing of matter that had or was calculated to have the effect, among other things, of threatening public safety, of "fanning revolution or uprisings in the Republic" or "fomenting feelings of . . . hostility . . . toward a local authority or a security force or toward . . . any population group" or "promoting the public image or esteem" of any unlawful organization or "promoting, fanning, or sparking boycott actions, acts of civil disobedience, stayaways, or strikes."[59]

Before the withdrawal in February 1990 of most of the emergency regulations dealing with censorship—or the Media Emergency Regulations, as they came to be known—five newspapers were temporarily closed down (*New Nation, South,* the *Weekly Mail, Grassroots,* and *New Era*) and several others faced the threat of closure. The *New Nation,* a weekly newspaper with a circulation of sixty thousand serving primarily the black community, was the first to be closed down, for a period of three months.

Censorship during the emergencies seems to have been directed primarily at foreign audiences and the domestic white electorate. Footage of brutal security force action, which South Africans did not see on the government-run television, evoked outrage and condemnation from foreign governments. The perverse solution was not to curb security force excesses, but to stifle the messenger. The clamps on reporting also had the effect of lulling white South Africans into a false sense of complacency by creating the impression that order had been restored to the townships. The greatest danger of censorship is always that those in power ultimately become seduced by their own propaganda. As the International Commission of Jurists reported in 1983:

> [I]t becomes increasingly difficult for government officials themselves to be adequately informed about the extent of abuse of authority, the gravity of social problems, and other matters which cannot be freely reported.[60]

Many of the emergency orders hinted at pathology in the body politic. For example, during the 1986 emergency, a divisional commissioner of police prohibited the possession of "any device with which a stone or any other projectile can be cast" as well as "any simulated firearm or any other object which is a copy of or which resembles any firearm, hand grenade or other explosive device." In addition, he prohibited possession of "any uniform, part of a uniform, T-shirt, flag, banner or pendant on which the name, badge or emblem" of certain specified organizations was depicted. Other regulations prohibited possession of "petrol in a container of whatever nature, excluding the petrol tank of a motor vehicle," and further prohibited the siphoning of petrol "from the petrol tank of a motor vehicle into a container of whatever nature, except with the written permission of a member of a Force."

The 1986 emergency came at a time when it was generally feared that the tenth anniversary of the 1976 Soweto uprising would provoke escalated violence throughout the country. The minister of law and order, for example, had unsuccessfully attempted to rush through Parliament amendments to the Public Safety Act and the Internal Security Act designed to bolster the already extensive powers of the security police.

These statutes were actually amended some two weeks after the declaration of the emergency, when the vetoes of the Coloured and Indian chambers blocking them were constitutionally overridden by the President's Council.[61] The Internal Security Amendment Act provided for a new form of preventive detention for a period not exceeding 180 days; it did not replace existing provisions in the act providing for both short-term and indefinite preventive detention. The principal difference between the existing preventive detention provisions and the new measure was that an order of preventive detention under the former required simultaneous provision of ministerial reasons, whereas the duty to furnish reasons under the new provision arises only after three months of detention.[62]

The Public Safety Amendment Act introduced the most far-reaching security provisions known to South African law. For the first time, an ordinary cabinet minister, the minister of law and order, was empowered to impose a state of emergency in any "unrest area." The minister was effectively given the same powers as those of the state president under the Public Safety Act, but with fewer safeguards and constraints.

Notwithstanding these amendments, the government continued to use its existing powers rather than resort to the new measures. An argument that the amendments to existing security laws rendered emergency powers unnecessary was rejected by the Supreme Court.[63]

The Emergency: Role of the Judiciary

Over one hundred years ago, the chief justice of the Cape declared that the "first and most sacred duty" of the courts is not to preserve national peace but "to administer justice to those who seek it." This function was to be performed "without fear, favour or prejudice," independently of the consequences which would ensue.[64] Few would deny that this is the proper function of the Supreme Court in a civilized legal order. The reality in South Africa during the 1980s was markedly different, however. The Supreme Court was no longer perceived to be the champion of justice. In 1968 the International Commission of Jurists observed that "in spite of a number of courageous decisions at first instance, the overall impression is of a judiciary as 'establishment-minded' as the executive, prepared to adopt an interpretation that will facilitate the executive's task rather than defend the liberty of the subject and uphold the rule of law."[65] Twenty years later, the verdict of the International Commission of Jurists was more ominous:

> Many South African judges are open to criticism not only on account of their participation in a legal system which denies basic rights of personal liberty, but also on the grounds that, in administering the ordinary laws, they have made decisions which seem inhuman and have imposed excessively harsh sentences, especially in relation to children who are charged with public violence. [W]e were not impressed by the argument that the judges are powerless in the face of government restrictions in the security area. We recognise that the judiciary is operating in a climate of severe government restrictions, but we believe the judges can choose to make an impact. If a judge remains on the Bench in such a repressive regime, there can be no excuse for failing to exercise his choice in favour of individual liberty, and whereas some judges have done justice in such cases in recent times, the majority of the South African Bench have failed to do so. We feel that it is as a result of this failure that the South African judiciary is open to the criticism of their fellow jurists in other countries.[66]

In a constitutional system predicated upon parliamentary sovereignty, the role of the courts is necessarily limited. As articulated by one judge: "Parliament may make any encroachment it chooses upon the life, liberty or property of any individual subject to its sway and it is the function of the courts of law to enforce its will."[67] Given this fundamental constitutional constraint, the role of a judge in an unjust society is inevitably controversial.

Although the function of the judiciary in a repressive legal order is limited, it does not follow that the courts are impotent. On the contrary, despite constitutional constraints, judges are able to play an important role in protecting the individual from the abuse of power. This may be achieved in a number of crucial areas: First, the Supreme Court retains the power to review the exercise of discretionary power to ensure that it is neither arbitrary nor capricious, that it is exercised for proper purposes, and that it is based upon all relevant considerations. Similarly, the Supreme Court has the power to test the validity of delegated legislation to ensure that it falls within the terms of the enabling statute, that it is not vague and uncertain, and that it does not constitute such a gratuitous interference with the rights of the individual that no reasonable person could justify it. Second, in the field of statutory interpretation, where the wording of an enactment is in any way ambiguous, judges are entitled to adopt an interpretation that avoids harshness and injustice.

The response of lawyers to the 1985 emergency was cautious. The legacy of the 1960 emergency had left them apprehensive about the scope for judicial intervention. The courts had shown a marked unwillingness to subject executive powers to judicial scrutiny. Thus, one encountered comments from the bench indicating their belief that the governor-general (i.e., the state president) was intended to have "powers of legislation equal to those of Parliament."[68]

The initial legal challenges to the 1985 emergency regulations, although largely unsuccessful, demonstrated a change in judicial temper. The unwillingness to scrutinize emergency regulations that characterized the approach during the 1960 emergency was jettisoned, with the courts showing a readiness to examine the regulations critically and, if necessary, strike them down. Litigation following the 1986 emergency was more intense. Several decisions struck down regulations on the grounds of vagueness, gross unreasonableness, or exceeding the ambit of the empowering provisions.[69] In other decisions, the court ordered the release of detainees.[70]

These decisions were greeted, particularly by the opposition press, with an almost euphoric response, indicating the public's low expectations of the judiciary. Most of the decisions were legally unexceptional. The courts were simply doing what courts of law are meant to do—curb the abuse of power.

The conduct of the judiciary during the emergencies of the 1980s was notable on two counts. First, many of the judicial victories for the opposition were short-lived. They were invariably countered with the swift introduction of amended regulations that effectively nullified the judgment in question. Such action highlighted the ultimate impotence of the judiciary in a constitutional system dominated by an executive bent on imposing its will at almost any cost.

Two decisions that would have had the effect of invalidating all detentions were remedied with indecent haste. In *Nkwinti v. Commissioner of Police*, the court held that the minister of law and order was not entitled to order the further detention of a detainee after the initial lapse of fourteen days without giving the detainee an opportunity to be heard.[71] Before judgment was delivered, however, the government amended the regulation to authorize the minister to act "without notice to any person and without hearing any person"; the amendment was made retrospective to the date of the declaration of the emergency.

In the second case, *Tsenoli v. the State President*, the court held that the regulation conferring powers of arrest and detention on members of the security force was invalid.[72] The state president had ignored a limitation on his powers that required him not simply to make regulations that provided for the safety of the public or the maintenance of public order, but also to make adequate provision for terminating the emergency. A few days later, however, another court reached the opposite conclusion.[73] The matter was finally resolved by the Appellate Division, headed by Chief Justice P. J. Rabie, in its first judgment on the validity of the emergency regulations. The court held that the interpretation adopted in *Tsenoli* was "forced and strained and not supported by the language used by the legislature."[74] Although the decision turned on a narrow compass, a unanimous court went out of its way to reaffirm the validity of the approach to interpretation in *Rossouw v. Sachs*.[75] In this case the court expressly refused to interpret security legislation restrictively so as to favor individual liberty.

The second noteworthy aspect of judicial decisions during the emergency was their highly technical nature and, barring a few exceptions, their failure to address the invasions of personal liberties created by the emergency regime. Direct challenges to the existence of the state of emergency all failed.[76]

Hopes for a more enlightened judicial interpretation of emergency powers, which had been foreshadowed by a number of decisions emanating from provincial divisions of the Supreme Court, ended with the second ruling by the Appellate Division in *Omar v. Minister of Law and Order*.[77] At issue were fundamental rights that included the right to be heard prior to an order by the minister of law and an order for the further detention of a detainee, the right of a detainee to have access to a legal adviser, and the right of a detainee to be informed of the reasons for his or her detention. In a majority judgment largely oblivious to the constitutional issues involved, the Appellate Division held that these rights had been lawfully excluded by the emergency regulations.

The emergency thus received judicial endorsement from the country's highest court. With this decision, the Appellate Division effectively emasculated judicial review as the only form of independent and external control of the emergency regulations and their implementation. The decision was described by Lawrence Baxter, a leading South African authority on administrative law, as "a political and legal disaster for South Africa, for South African lawyers, and above all, for the victims of apartheid."[78] The already marginal role played by the Supreme Court in protecting individual liberty from executive excess was thus further eroded.

The trend set by this decision was to continue. The Appellate Division held in *Minister of Law and Order v. Dempsey* that, in terms of the emergency regulations, an arrest could be justified by a mere statement that it was, in the opinion of the arresting officer, necessary for one of the prescribed purposes.[79] This ruling made it virtually impossible to challenge the validity of an arrest under emergency powers. In *Ngqumba v. Staatspresident*, it was held that under emergency powers an arresting officer's failure to consider obvious alternatives short of detention does not constitute grounds for invalidating the detention, unless the action is so drastic and unnecessary that it can be inferred that the arresting officer acted unreasonably.[80]

In *Staatspresident v. United Democratic Front*, perhaps the most perplexing decision of all, it was held that the state president is free to promulgate vague and uncertain regulations that are immune from judicial review by virtue of the "ouster clause" contained in the Public Safety Act, which provides that a proclamation by the state president cannot be set aside or questioned.[81]

These decisions caused grave disquiet in legal circles and in the human rights community generally, not only because they tampered with long-standing traditional precepts, but also because they were largely the product of a disproportionately small group of judges presided over by Chief Justice Rabie, whose tenure of office was inexplicably and possibly unlawfully extended after he had reached the compulsory retirement age. Apart from the occasional dissent, the Appellate Division in these cases showed itself unwilling to assert traditional libertarian values, preferring instead to allow the executive a free hand.

The appointment of Justice M. M. Corbett, in November 1989, as the new chief justice went some way to repairing the damage inflicted under Chief Justice Rabie. Significantly, in *During N.O. v. Boesak*, the Appellate Division overruled Dempsey's case, holding that as a matter of principle and policy, any person impinging upon another individual's freedom ought to bear the onus of justifying the legality of his or her action.

Evidence also exists of a retreat from the highly authoritarian approach that governed the conduct of the various emergencies. Although emergency powers remain at the disposal of the government, the Internal Security Act has undergone an important revision. In an explanatory memorandum accompanying the bill that introduced revisions to the act, it was stated that "the primary object of the Bill is to bring security legislation into line with the new dynamic situation developing in South Africa in order to ensure normal and free political activities."[82] The major features of the revised statute are the repeal of provisions dealing with the prohibition of publications, preventive detention, and offenses relating to communism. Detention without trial for the purposes of interrogation remains, but it is limited to ten days unless a judge of the Supreme Court orders further detention.[83] Organizations may still be prohibited, but only if they attempt to use or actually employ violent methods to achieve their aims.[84]

In a society already characterized by extreme authoritarian control, the successive states of emergency contributed significantly to an ethos of lawlessness. The scarcely disguised intention of emergency rule was to enable the executive to deal with the emergency as it saw fit. To this end, the security forces were clothed with virtually limitless powers, and officials of state were granted discretionary powers to do whatever they thought necessary. Given the reluctance of the courts to place effective controls on those responsible for executing the emergency, the abuse of power was rampant and inevitable. Not surprisingly, an already fragile legal system came to be perceived by many South Africans as both impotent and partial. As Geoffrey Budlender, a leading human rights attorney, has pointed out, when recourse to law is regarded as futile and the state appears to be beyond legal limits, those who are "alienated from the processes of social control . . . tend to exercise their own control, which is likely to be at least as arbitrary and brutal as anything they have experienced."[85]

Chapter III

The Total Strategy: The South African Security Forces and the Suppression of Civil Liberties

Nicholas Haysom

Throughout the 1980s the security forces were a central institution in South Africa, not only in implementing policy and enforcing law, but also in formulating policy and reshaping the legal landscape. The power and political influence of the security forces, which include the South African Police (SAP), the South African Defense Force (SADF), the South African Department of Correctional Services, and the police forces of the nonindependent homelands, grew considerably under the leadership of P. W. Botha. Their actions were guided by a counterrevolutionary policy known as the "total strategy," which had been developed by Botha and his generals.

The strategy had external and internal dimensions. Beyond South Africa's borders, its targets were the African National Congress (ANC), the South West Africa People's Organization (SWAPO), and the black-ruled southern African countries that gave these groups sanctuary. The tactics used by the security forces included direct military intervention, political destabilization, economic sabotage, "dirty tricks" of various kinds, and military and financial aid for surrogate forces.[1] Inside the country, the enemy consisted of the forces of opposition that rose up in the black schools, in the townships, on the factory floor, in the churches, and on university campuses.

The black revolt that broke out in September 1984 took the government by surprise, and the security establishment's strategists appeared to have no clear answer to it. The immediate reaction was a vigorous and brutal crackdown by the police, with no apparent objective other than to restore the status quo. This initial response was followed by a much more sophisticated attempt, led by the military, to destroy the leadership of the uprising while simultaneously restructuring the balance of black political forces.

In 1989, when President Botha resigned and Frederik W. de Klerk came to power, the situation changed. The security forces had demonstrated their destructive capacity but had been unable to construct lasting political solutions. At that point, the government began a process of fundamental political reform. The new strategy was implemented at the expense of the security forces, not at their behest. Thereafter, the political stature and influence of the security forces declined rapidly for a number of reasons. First, South Africa's withdrawal from Angola and the decision to grant Namibia independence were widely perceived as setbacks for the military. Second, the new president reorganized the state bureaucracy and redesigned government policy. Third, the security forces' domestic image and morale were negatively affected by damaging revelations of covert death squad activities, biased police practices, and wanton violence in the course of crowd control.

This chapter looks first at the origins of the total strategy and the rise of the security forces; it then examines the methods used to suppress civil liberties in South Africa; and finally, it traces the collapse of the total strategy and the decline of the security establishment.

The Total Strategy

The SADF establishment traditionally had been a junior partner in security management, until the SAP's brutal suppression of the student-led Soweto uprising of 1976–77. The military argued that the level of police violence was counterproductive and that South Africa needed a sophisticated strategy to deal with its racial problems, a strategy that incorporated social, economic, and political components.[2] In 1977 a Ministry of Defense white paper was prepared that introduced the concept of a total strategy in the following terms:

The resolution of a conflict in the times in which we now

live demands interdependent and coordinated action in all fields. . . . It is therefore essential that a Total National Strategy be formulated at the highest level.[3]

The paper listed numerous areas of South African society, including education, that legitimately demanded the interest, if not the intervention, of the military.

The total strategy became the conceptual vehicle for the rapid expansion of the military's role in all spheres of government and the private sector during the Botha era. The strategy called for an integrated and coordinated approach to all aspects of political, economic, and social life in order to combat the "total onslaught" being waged against South Africa—both internally and externally—by the Soviet Union and other hostile forces. General Magnus Malan, the strategy's chief advocate, often stated that the defense of South Africa was 80 percent political and only 20 percent military.

The intellectual origins of the total strategy were rooted in the counterinsurgency theory of the French military strategist, General André Beaufre. Writing about the Algerian and other counterinsurgency campaigns, Beaufre stressed the "indirect" mode of counterinsurgency warfare.[4] Such a method emphasized the psychological components of warfare and, by classifying modern warfare as all-embracing, called upon military strategists to see every aspect of social, economic, and political life as part of the battle terrain. The coordination of warfare in all these sectors, according to Beaufre, is required to prevent the development of conditions favorable to insurgency. The media, the classroom, the home, the factory, and the football field are legitimate sites for extended military engagement. In such a "war," there are no civilians.[5]

General Malan had been exposed to Beaufre's theories at the U.S. Army Command and General Staff College and in Algeria, where as a young officer he had been attached to the French forces. By 1984 Beaufre's writings, particularly his *An Introduction to Strategy*, were included in most of the courses at the SADF's Joint Defense College.[6]

At the bureaucratic level, the adoption of the total strategy was a response to the policies of Botha's predecessor, B. J. Vorster, who had been minister of police before becoming prime minister. Vorster elevated the police to key positions in the centralized intelligence agency, the Bureau for State Security (BOSS), under General Hendrik van den Bergh. BOSS appropriated some of the functions performed by military intelligence and operated as an executive secretariat for the State Security Council (SSC), a Cabinet committee consisting of police and military officers and selected senior ministers. The SSC was unable to operate effectively because of distrust between BOSS and the military hierarchy and allegations that BOSS was keeping members of the council under surveillance.[7] The rival faction in the SSC, led by P. W. Botha, then minister of defense, and General Magnus Malan, head of the armed forces, espoused a reformist philosophy that placed greater emphasis on "indirect strategies" of countering black nationalist opposition.

Vorster retired following his implication in the Information Department "Muldergate" scandal of 1977, in which the unauthorized use of public funds by government officials came to light. This development provided a political opening for P. W. Botha, who was elected National Party leader and became prime minister in September 1978. He immediately began elevating the status of the security establishment—the "securocrats," as they came to be called—and was particularly favorable toward the military component, to which he was close after having spent twelve years as minister of defense. In 1981 Botha renamed BOSS (by then called the Department of National Security, or DONS) the National Intelligence Service (NIS), trimmed its executive powers, replaced its director, and transferred some of its functions to military intelligence.[8]

Under President Botha, the SSC was upgraded so that it was no longer considered subordinate to the cabinet. In 1980 the council was described by Philip Frankel, a political scientist specializing in military affairs, as "the focal point of all national decision-making and governmental power."[9] Two years later, Botha stated that the SSC would become "the most important functional element of the proposed new executive presidency" created by the constitution that would come into force in 1984 and centralize power in the hands of the president.[10]

Although its membership was not publicly disclosed, it is believed that the SSC consisted of the state president, the ministers of law and order, defense, foreign affairs, justice, the chief of the SADF, the commissioner of police, the director of the NIS, the directors-general of foreign affairs and justice, and the secretary-general of the Office of the State President. For discussions on specific subjects, others might be invited to attend—for example, the chairman of Armscor, a parastatal body established in 1968 to manufacture armaments locally, and selected intelligence officers and ministers.[11]

The total strategy was implemented by the SSC through a

national network known as the National Security Management System (NSMS). The backbone of the NSMS comprised seventy-two regional, local, and sectional committees called Joint Management Centers (JMCs).[12] Under the control of the SADF, but responsible to the SSC, the JMCs consisted of local security officials, business leaders, and government-designated blacks who formulated local strategies and assisted in incorporating local personalities into the security system.[13] The JMCs were responsible for designing a comprehensive plan for developing black areas in line with security considerations. Four black townships were targeted as high priority for the JMCs in the late 1980s: Alexandra (Johannesburg), Duncan Village (East London), Khayelitsha (Cape Town), and Langa (Uitenhage).

The JMCs were criticized in 1986 by *The Argus* newspaper as a "political and insidious system of bureaucratic control answerable only to the state intelligence machine."[14] They were not responsible to any constituency and were widely viewed as a means of increasing the militarization of South African society.[15] This elaborate and pervasive structure created a powerful vehicle for SADF control of social and political life in South Africa until De Klerk downgraded it in 1990.[16]

Before examining how Malan and others in the security establishment applied the precepts of the total strategy to combat the black revolt of the 1980s, it will be helpful to look at the major components of the security forces: the SAP, the homeland police, and the SADF.

The Security Forces

The most important entities in South Africa's security apparatus are the South African Police and the South African Defense Force. But police forces in three of the six nonindependent homelands — KwaZulu, Lebowa, and KwaNdebele — also played a part in the government's response to the forces of black resistance and its suppression of civil liberties.

Under the total strategy, the operations of the SAP and the SADF were closely integrated, with the SADF emerging as the dominant partner. But the process was not smooth.[17] The political differences between the two organizations were reflected in the frequent accusations that the SAP, or at least many of its members, supported extreme rightwing political parties. The SADF, on the other hand, was considered to be loyal to President Botha and in line with mainstream National Party policy.

The people who made up the SADF hierarchy, however, should not be viewed as doves. Senior military officers' complaints over the "maximum force" practices of the police related to the efficacy, not the morality, of such methods. The SADF itself aggressively initiated the destabilization of the economies and infrastructure of neighboring states, which it called "proactive" action or "offensive defense."[18] Internally, the SADF, and particularly General Malan, argued for the continuation of the state of emergency, for "strong central authority" during "political adjustment," and for repression with reform.[19]

The South African Police. The SAP is a national force, controlled and directed by the Ministry of Law and Order, that has national jurisdiction regarding most alleged offenses under the laws of the land. Before 1986 the South African Transport Services (SATS) had their own police force, but this force is now part of the SAP. This leaves the traffic police and municipal guards, who are managed by municipal governments, as the only noncentralized police forces. These agencies have limited jurisdiction and have only a minor, supportive function in the policing of South Africa.

The wisdom of a national police force was questioned as early as 1961, when the Molteno Commission, a body appointed by the opposition Progressive Party to consider South Africa's constitutional future, warned:

> A centralized police force, organized on semi-military lines, is capable of being used as an engine of political oppression, and hence of presenting a threat to freedom. There is much, indeed, in the history of the South African Police, and the manner in which it has been used in the past, that illustrates the reality of this threat.[20]

The SAP was created by the Police Act of 1958, which describes its functions as follows: preservation of the internal security of the Republic, maintenance of law and order, investigation of any offense or alleged offense, and prevention of crime.[21]

Since the 1960s the SAP has regarded its first function—the preservation of the internal security of the Republic—as being of paramount importance. In South African townships, the police perform their patrolling duties in armored cars and are equipped with the same weapons as the SADF. Many township residents are therefore understandably confused over the distinction between the

SAP and the SADF. The distinctive paramilitary character of the SAP was most clearly revealed by its counterinsurgency role in preindependence Namibia; the SADF took over control of the Namibian operations from the SAP only in 1974, eight years after the start of the bush war against SWAPO, the Namibian liberation movement. The most notorious unit in Namibia, credited with 80 percent of all "kills," and a number of whose members have been charged with or convicted of rape and murder, was the crack SAP counterinsurgency unit known as *Koevoet* (crowbar).[22]

Overall responsibility for the actions of the SAP belongs to the minister of law and order. The day-to-day management of the force is in the hands of a commissioner of police based in Pretoria. The commissioner serves a nonrenewable term of two years.[23] The force is divided into nineteen regional divisions, each under the control of a brigadier.[24] Each regional division consists of various units and departments such as the Criminal Investigation Department (CID), uniformed police, vice squad, and riot squad. These regional commissioners are responsible for the 842 police stations throughout the country. Of these police stations, 64 are staffed by black personnel.[25] The SAP claims:

> In accordance with the national policy of multinational development, the aim is to have each of the population groups policed by its own people, as far as possible.[26]

Until very recently, white membership in the SAP exceeded the combined membership of all other groups. The 1989 figures, however, showed 35,254 whites, 5,879 Coloureds, 2,824 Indians, and 37,625 Africans, of whom 5,908 were special constables known as *kitskonstabels* (instant police).[27] The 1990 figures continued this trend, with whites constituting 42 percent of the total police force.[28]

Before 1984 the policing of political activities in the black townships was largely the preserve of the security branch, which operated outside of and parallel to the national structure. This branch—formerly known as the Special Branch—was until recently the most feared and influential of all police departments. The present and former commissioners of police previously were heads of the security branch. It was involved in overt and covert operations, handled a national network of informers, and was responsible for the infiltration and prosecution of anti-apartheid organizations. The security branch was dissolved in February 1991 and its staff transferred to the intelligence section of the CID, which possibly performs the same functions but less visibly.

After 1984 other branches of the SAP also were used in the

township, notably the CID and the riot squad. Riot squads were instituted as specially trained crowd-control units after the 1976–77 Soweto uprising, following which the police were widely criticized for their reliance on automatic rifles and their failure to use modern methods of crowd control.[29] At the time, the then minister of police, Jimmy T. Kruger, responded to these criticisms by saying that anti-riot equipment was "ridiculous" because "a police officer will hardly be able to handle his rifle if he is also wearing a heavy flak jacket and a face guard."[30] Nonetheless, by 1984 specialized riot squads of between twenty and two hundred members had been established, equipped with antiriot equipment, in all nineteen police divisions. After 1984 these squads were reinforced by the transfer of hundreds of policemen from other departments, and in Soweto they benefited from a R3 million expansion in facilities.[31]

In 1990 the ratio of police officers to citizens, at half of that in politically stable and geographically confined Britain, was regarded as low. The total complement of the full-time police force stood at 81,000, compared with the 1988 figure of 60,950.[32] But the force can call upon the reserve police, an active group of civilian volunteers, which in 1990 numbered 18,532, as well as the police reserve, which undertakes police duties during busy periods. The latter group, which numbered 18,917, consists of former police officers who can be mobilized in times of emergency.[33] The SAP also allows teenagers to participate in police duties through a junior reserve. In addition, since 1986 the SAP has been developing a force of full-time, though poorly trained, black auxiliary police—the *kitskonstabels,* who came under criticism for their role in the townships, where they were perceived as being violent and prone to criminal activities.[34]

The expansion of the police force had been erratic. The SAP grew rapidly between 1945 and 1960 in accordance with its security role. Thereafter, the lion's share of the budget for security was allocated to the SADF, and only in 1981 did the government begin to develop an SAP expansion program intended to bring its full-time complement from 34,271 in 1981 to 68,000 by 1990.[35] By 1985–86 the budget of the Department of Law and Order had increased to R954 million, an 800 percent increase over 1974–75.[36] By 1988–89 the budget had risen to R2,496 million.[37] By 1990 the actual complement was in excess of the projected expansion figure and did not include approximately 26,000 unfilled posts.[38]

Among the striking features of the SAP are its imperviousness to public criticism and its lack of accountability. There are no citizen review boards in South Africa. Section 27B of the Police Act 7 of 1958 inhibits exposure of police abuses in the media by placing a heavy onus on publishers to ascertain the truth of allegations of police misconduct prior to publication. The centralization of the police force and the militaristic culture it has spawned tend to enhance its closed nature.

The police have shown little inclination to discipline themselves. As Barend van Niekerk, Philip Frankel, and D. Foster and C. Luyt noted in 1971, 1980, and 1988, respectively, one of the most glaring features of the SAP disciplinary record is its failure to punish or expel members who have been guilty of assault or torture.[39] Foster and Luyt find that the annual figures for violent crimes committed by the police have not changed much over the years and usually result in two hundred to three hundred convictions. In 1990, 373 police officers were convicted of assault, out of 633 against whom prosecutions were launched.[40] Foster and Luyt comment:

[The annual figures] paint a grim picture of police violence in the ordinary business of policing criminal activities. . . . Official figures indicate that only about 10 percent of those police convicted of violent crimes are eventually discharged from the force. Furthermore, it is only a minority of those with previous convictions who are subsequently discharged. It is noteworthy, in addition, that where details are given, it is apparent that the majority of those with previous convictions hold them for similar violent crimes.[41]

The authors go on to point out that, far from facing disciplinary action, several members of the security forces who have been accused of participation in assault or torture have been promoted.[42]

More fundamentally, the police are not politically accountable to the majority of the citizens—the black population. For many years, the relationship between the police and the black community has been one of unconcealed enmity. South Africa's black citizens seldom view the police as protectors of their rights, but rather as enforcers of unjust laws that they had no part in making. Black leaders have consistently commented on the apparent inability of the police to solve crimes committed in the townships or to protect township residents from violence, rape, and theft, as contrasted with the lengths to which the police will go to prevent unlawful expressions of political dissent, to enforce discriminatory laws, and to investigate political offenses involving blacks.

Writing in 1971, Professor Barend van Niekerk contrasted the high unsolved crime rate in Soweto—where one in three adults was estimated to have been subjected to a street attack—with the prosecution of nearly one million black adults for offenses under the discriminatory influx control laws.[43] Since then the crime rate has risen and the police have been as visible in enforcing the state of emergency laws as they were in enforcing influx control laws in 1971.[44] Professor van Niekerk's concluding comment is as apt in 1990 as it was in 1971:

> In short, the "law" which ought to be the black man's protection is seen by him largely as the chief method of harassment. Symbolising the law, because they enforce it, are the police . . . [A] large part of the black population of South Africa inevitably, albeit sometimes unfairly, sees in the police force the epitome of their political and social ills.[45]

Hostility toward blacks is reflected in police training and recruitment patterns and the fact that most white police officers are "socialized into accepting coercion as an integral feature of race relations."[46] The curriculum at police colleges does little to address or alter most whites' motivation in joining the police force—the defense of white civilization. According to Philip Frankel:

> Racial brutality is, of course, an ingrained feature of South African life. Yet inasmuch as routine patrol work always allows police officials considerable informal discretion in applying the law, a specific vehicle exists for the average white policeman to displace intermeshing race and role frustrations on the subject black population . . . the result of which is a high incidence of police violence during the normal course of law enforcement in the black areas, rising to even higher levels during periods of civil disturbance, when the constraints on the use of firearms and other "hard" means of control are further lessened.[47]

In response to the ANC and the Pan Africanist Congress (PAC) going underground after their proscription in 1960, the government introduced increasingly repressive detention laws that equipped the SAP with a formidable array of powers. Between 1967 and 1982, some sixty persons held under these laws died in detention.[48] The number of such deaths increased steadily, without apparent government concern, until the death of the internationally renowned leader Steve Biko in 1977. Biko's death led to an international outcry and a public inquest. It was revealed that Biko had been kept naked for the eighteen days he was in the police cells, was manacled to the floor of the interrogation room, and was transported naked in a semicomatose condition from Port Elizabeth to Pretoria, seven hundred miles away. The inquest also revealed that the doctors who treated him subordinated his medical treatment to security interests.[49]

Prior to Biko's death, less than thirty of the deaths in detention had been followed by inquests. Some of the inquests found that death was caused by accidental falls or suicide, but the findings did not dispel the widespread belief that many of these deaths resulted from torture. Human rights organizations, in particular, were alarmed by and skeptical of findings in which six detainees were alleged to have died from jumping or falling out of windows or down stairs, two from slipping on soap in the shower, and three from accidentally striking their heads against a desk or a wall or a chair.[50] In 1976 four police officers were charged with causing detainee Joseph Mdluli's death. They refused to testify, thus making it almost impossible to determine what took place during the interrogation or which police officer delivered the fatal blow.[51]

Following the damaging revelations at the Biko inquest, in which the police were cleared of any wrongdoing, the annual number of deaths in detention dropped steadily until 1982 (there were, for example, no deaths in detention in 1981), when Neil Aggett, a white trade unionist, was found dead in his cell. At the inquest into his death, allegations were made, corroborated by Aggett's charge against the police prior to his death, that he had been driven to suicide by intense and unremitting interrogation accompanied by assaults. At this stage, the government began to recognize that the adverse publicity surrounding the deaths of detainees damaged the country's international image.

After the enactment of the Internal Security Act in 1982, which consolidated existing security laws and reinstituted the detention-without-trial provisions in a slightly modified form, the minister of law and order issued directions for the treatment of detainees in the *Government Gazette*.[52] These directions did not tamper with the essential features of the detention provisions: (1) indefinite detention without charge or trial for the purpose of interrogation and (2) no access to a legal adviser or any person other than a government official. The directions merely stated that a detainee shall not be subjected to "humiliating or degrading treatment." It granted detainees no effective methods of redress, except for their statutory right to complain to police officials, visiting magistrates, or the inspector of detainees. Other rights introduced by the directions were subject to official permission.

The inadequacy of the directions was underscored by further deaths in detention and persistent allegations that torture continued. In 1984 a kneeling detainee was shot at point-blank range by a police sergeant who became the first police officer to be convicted for the death of a detainee. By 1990 the total number of people who were known to have died in detention in South Africa had reached seventy-three.[53]

In 1983 the Detainees' Parents Support Committee (DPSC), a human rights monitoring group that was outlawed from 1988 to 1990, released a memorandum alleging widespread and systematic torture of detainees.[54] Although the police force has consistently denied that torture is practiced by its members, a comprehensive study of the treatment of detainees by the Institute of Criminology at the University of Cape Town in September 1985 claimed that torture and similar abuses were routine.[55] The study based its claims on interviews with some 176 former detainees: 75 percent reported having been beaten, 25 percent reported having been subjected to electric shock, 18 percent claimed they had been subjected to strangulation, and 14 percent alleged that they had been suspended on a pole and spun around (the "helicopter"). Other forms of alleged abuse included the use of handcuffs, chains placed around the neck, the pulling out or burning of hair, genital abuse, and beating on the soles of the feet. The most common form of physical abuse was forced exercise, including the maintenance of abnormal body positions. A higher incidence of torture was reported in the Eastern Cape than in any other area.

The study, which opposed the use of indefinite detention provisions, recommended that the interrogation of security suspects be monitored by video so long as indefinite detention provisions were in use. The police response was to introduce video monitoring of detainees' cells, claiming that the deaths in detention resulted from the psychological stress associated with confessions and not the methods used to extract confessions.[56]

Prior to 1984 concern over police conduct centered mostly around interrogation practices used on political suspects. But when the civil revolt erupted in the townships in September 1984, the police led the counterattack, and a broader range of their practices came under criticism. The police were armed not only with weapons of war but also with an ideology that justified any means, including summary execution, of dealing with the total onslaught that was perceived to be directed against the government. It was only in late 1989, after De Klerk became president, that the government exercised some restraint on the police force.

Homeland Police. The homelands play a dual function in South African society. First, they serve as a foundation for political apartheid, under which blacks are expected to exercise their political rights in their homelands in exchange for forfeiting them in South Africa itself. Second, the homelands help shift the focus of black political activism from the central government to the homeland political structures.[57] Due to overcrowding and poverty, the homelands are particularly vulnerable to political pressure, and most were affected by the civil unrest that swept through South Africa from 1984 until the end of the decade.

The devolution of powers from South Africa to its ten ethnic homelands was designed to follow a two-stage constitutional path: self-government followed by independence.[58] The four homelands that have reached the final or "independent" stage—Transkei, Bophuthatswana, Venda, and Ciskei (known as the TBVC states)—have established their own police and defense forces. In addition, three of the remaining six nonindependent homelands, KwaZulu, Lebowa, and KwaNdebele, have formed their own police forces. The security forces established by these homelands enjoy a close relationship and a similarity in their practices with their South African counterparts. For example, methods of torture that are so often associated with the SAP—electric shocks, the helicopter, hooding, and suffocation—are also prevalent in the homelands.[59] The SAP and homeland police forces frequently exchange suspects for further interrogation without any pretense of following a formal extradition process.[60]

Many of the homelands have staffed the upper echelons of their security forces with South African military or police personnel or with members of the former white Rhodesian armed forces. The full extent to which South African military personnel control Bophuthatswana was revealed during the attempted coup in that territory in February 1988. Indeed, one of the apparent reasons for that abortive military revolt was dissatisfaction over the fact that the Bophuthatswana Defense Force's senior officers and the minister of defense are white South African military officers.

Although it is possible to discern differences in the human rights records of the homeland security forces, it is clear that most of the homelands became increasingly associated with high levels of repression and unchecked police abuses. Since the homelands are largely rural and less in the public eye than the urban areas, their police practices are less visible than those of the SAP. As a result, the homeland security forces have tended to conduct themselves without concern for legal process or unfavorable publicity and have acquired a record for many of the worst police abuses in the country as a whole. The following examples during 1986, at the height of the black revolt, illustrate this phenomenon.

- In Lebowa, two prominent political activists died within hours of being taken into custody. In the first inquest, the court ruled that the deceased, Peter Nchabaleng (a United Democratic Front regional president), had died as a result of severe beatings by the Lebowa police.[61] Uncontested evidence was submitted that beatings were a regular practice in the police station. In the second inquest, Lucky Kutumela, a journalist, also was found to have been beaten to death by members of the Lebowa police.[62]
- In Bophuthatswana, an independent homeland with a bill of rights enshrined in its Constitution, the police embarked in early 1986 on a policy of detaining and assaulting youths whom they encountered in the township of Garankuwa. Assaults, confirmed by photographic evidence placed before the Bophuthatswana Supreme Court, took the form of flaying the skin from the youths' backs and buttocks.[63] A court injunction to prevent further assaults, although successful, led to the immediate detention of those who had provided evidence on affidavit. A *habeas corpus* application for their release was evaded by the immediate redetention of the deponents. This, in turn, led to a contempt of court injunction, which finally secured their release. Colonel Andrew Molope, the senior police officer involved, was also in charge of a unit called out shortly afterward to disperse an unarmed demonstration consisting mostly of women and children from the Winterveld squatter camp. Without adequate warning, the police opened fire with R4 combat rifles, killing eleven people.[64]
- In Transkei, a well-known student leader, Bathandwa Ndondo, was apprehended in the street and summarily executed. Lawyers and relatives who sought to uncover the identity of his assassins were detained or harassed. Two police officers were subsequently charged with Ndondo's death but jumped bail after their first appearance in court.[65]
- The Ciskei and KwaNdebele police, who have the worst reputation in the homelands, have been accused of perpetrating a wide range of abuses, including abducting

and assaulting opponents of the Ciskei and KwaNdebele governments.[66]

In 1989 the Transkei government was overthrown in a coup led by a popular military leader who then limited the powers of the police. In 1990 similar coups took place in Venda and Ciskei, and rebellion spread to two other homelands. In these cases, homeland security forces demonstrated that their loyalties were fickle and that they appreciated the need to keep an eye on an uncertain future.

The South African Defense Force. Like the police, the SADF is a national body. Its long-serving head, Minister of Defense Magnus Malan, led the armed forces when P. W. Botha was minister of defense (1966–78).

The main functions of the SADF are described in the Defense Act of 1957 as follows:

> The South African Defence Force or any portion or member thereof may
> (a) at any time be employed
>   (i) on service in defence of the Republic;
>   (ii) on service in the prevention or suppression of terrorism;
>   (iii) on service in the prevention or suppression of internal disorder in the Republic;
>   (iv) on service in the preservation of life, health, or property or the maintenance of essential services; and
> (b) while employed as contemplated in paragraph (a), be used on those police functions mentioned in section 5 of the Police Act, 1958 (Act No. 7 of 1958), as may be prescribed.[67]

Theoretically, the SADF and the SAP have separate roles, with the police responsible for the maintenance of internal order and the SADF responsible for the defense of South Africa's borders. Since 1960, however, the SADF also has claimed a policing role. On March 21, 1960, the then minister of defense, J. J. Fouché, stated unambiguously:

> It is the defence policy of the Union first of all to concentrate its defence organizations upon the implementation of internal security tasks. The task of the Army and the Air Force is to take action for internal security as soon as disturbances have reached a degree where the Police are unable to control them.[68]

In 1977 the definition of "service in defence of the Republic" was amended to include actions outside the republic that "in the opinion of the state president" may be a threat to the security of the republic.[69] These amendments facilitated the deployment of troops in Angola and other neighboring states without the requirement of a formal declaration of war. In the same year, Lieutenant-General J. R. Dutton expressly criticized differentiating between police and military duties:

> . . . [T]he traditional dividing line between national security and national defence would appear to have become obliterated. . . . In the new perspective, however, civil riots, strikes accompanied by violence, and urban terrorism are seen as guerrilla actions aimed at military, political, economic, or psychological objectives as part of the overall assault. . . . The role of the armed forces in the maintenance of national security would therefore appear to be a simple extension of their classical role in national defence.[70]

In pursuit of this doctrine, it has been argued that the military has a legitimate concern in all anti-apartheid activities.[71] This approach was endorsed in the *1982 White Paper on Defense and Armaments Supply* issued by the Department of Defense. In 1984 the role of the SADF was further expanded by an amendment to the Defense Act to permit its deployment in policing duties.[72] In October of that year, military personnel were deployed in conjunction with the SAP in cordoning off and searching the townships of Joza (Grahamstown) and Sebokeng (Vaal triangle). The military was then deployed regularly to man roadblocks and conduct patrols and searches in the townships, although it was kept largely in the background while the SAP assumed a more visible role. Liberal critics of the policy claimed that this politicized the function of the SADF. In a joint statement in Parliament in 1984, the ministers of law and order and defense noted about the SAP and the SADF:

> Just as the police support the Defence Force on the border, so the Defence Force is supporting the police in internal unrest situations.[73]

The army, which is the main component of the SADF and accounts for 80 percent of its strength, was organized traditionally for counterinsurgency operations. But in 1974 it began equipping and training as a conventional force. The 1975, 1979, and 1982 white papers on defense declared that this was necessary because of the independence of the former Portuguese colonies of Angola and Mozambique, the expansion of "Marxist militarism," and the growth of Soviet influence in certain southern African states.[74]

The professional core of the army is the Permanent Force, of which the overwhelming majority—85 percent in 1975—is made up of Afrikaans-speaking whites. Since 1975 the army has tried to increase its English-speaking component in order to create a new, nonsectarian image.[75] The bulk of the army is formed by the Citizen Force, which is composed of conscripts who, until 1989, served full time for a period of two years of national service (it was reduced to one year in 1990) and thereafter as reservists with annual call-ups of between thirty and ninety days. The commandos, first formed in the nineteenth-century Boer Republics, consist of men who have not undergone national service but are compulsorily required to make themselves available for service in local commando units on a part-time basis or for twelve days a year after one month's initial training.

The breakdown of the SADF in 1985 was estimated as follows:[76]

Permanent Force	43,000
Citizen Force	265,000
—National Service conscripts (67,000)	
—Reservists (198,000)	
Commandos	200,000
SADF civilians	40,000
South-West Africa Territory Force	21,000
Total	569,000

In 1980, when it became apparent that African recruitment held clear ideological and manpower advantages for the government, the SADF began to stress its multiracial character and the contribution of people of color to the defense of the country. Yet the SADF remained overwhelmingly white. In December 1985 the permanent, conscripted, reserve, and commando forces totaled well over five hundred thousand people, but fewer than five thousand were Africans, fewer than eight thousand were Coloureds, and fewer than two thousand were Indians.[77]

African troops initially were recruited into the Twenty-First Battalion, a black battalion under white officers, and more recently into segregated regional ethnic battalions in Natal and the northern Transvaal. All of the African troops served in the Namibian operational areas. The Indian component is confined to the navy, and the Coloured force principally to the "Cape Corps." Until the independence of Namibia in 1990, South-West Africa and the independent homeland forces accounted for thirteen thousand African troops.[78] Following the successful creation of a largely African army in South-West Africa during the 1980s, more Africans have been recruited into the SADF. The possibility of introducing compulsory conscription for Coloureds was raised but shelved because of anticipated resistance.

Conscription became a highly controversial issue in the latter half of the 1980s. The liberal opposition based its criticism on the argument that South Africa needed a full-time professional army instead of its part-time "amateur" army. The most prominent body opposing conscription was the End Conscription Campaign (ECC), which adopted an overtly political critique of the system of compulsory conscription. It charged that the government was engaged in an illegal and an unjust war in Namibia, and after the army moved into the townships in 1984, it criticized the use of conscripts to wage a "civil war" there. The ECC's position was that military service should be voluntary.

In 1983, responding to growing support among the churches for conscientious objection, and following the conviction of two Christians, Peter Moll and Richard Steele, for refusing to serve in the military, the government introduced amendments to the Defense Act.[79] The amendments permitted six years of alternative nonmilitary national service for religious pacifists if they could satisfy the Board for Religious Objection that they had sound religious reasons for refusing to serve in the military. In 1984 the board heard 341 applications, of which 261 were upheld.[80] The amendments also increased the penalty for political nonreligious objectors to terms of imprisonment of up to six years. From 1985 the SADF refused to release figures indicating the extent of draft dodging, although more and more cases of failure to report came before the courts. In the latter part of the 1980s, an increasing number of men failed to report for military service.

In May 1987 Phillip Wilkinson, at his trial for refusing to report for military duty, called a conscript who testified that the SADF participated in brutal policing practices.[81] In March 1988 Ivan Toms, another conscript who refused to serve, raised the unlawfulness of SADF activities in Namibia, Angola, and neighboring territories as an explanation for his decision. The following year, the ECC brought an injunction against the SADF, restraining it from pursuing a campaign of disinformation and unlawful harassment against ECC office-bearers. The SADF sought to justify its actions by claiming that in a "war" situation, such tactics were legitimate.[82] Its contention was rejected by the court.

Thus, objection to military service remained a unique moral issue for the white community and received considerable attention on both English- and Afrikaans-language university campuses. After February 1990 the issue lost some of its political edge because conscripts no longer had to serve in Namibia, the period of national service was reduced from two years to one year, and some townships, instead of demanding that the troops leave, requested that the SADF be brought in to replace the SAP.

The Government's Response to Revolt

Prior to 1984 the total strategy had provided the framework for directing public and private resources and for coordinating the various government departments in line with P. W. Botha's political program, which was designed to promote a black elite and to co-opt the Indian and Coloured communities. This process was supported and often directed by military men. It went hand in hand with legislative reforms. Botha's ability to pursue this strategy methodically was unexpectedly shaken by the political unrest that erupted in the Vaal triangle in September 1984 and spread across the country. The government's first priority was to put down the revolt as quickly as possible so that it could continue to construct a network of black urban political moderates drawn from local government structures. The SAP was entrusted with the task of suppressing the revolt and went about it with escalating levels of violence.

The government's response to the revolt came in two major phases. The first phase, from 1984 to 1986, was characterized by maximum force policing reinforced by first a partial and then a nationwide state of emergency. This was a stopgap measure, unsuccessful in its own terms. The second phase, from 1987 to 1989, was characterized by low-intensity warfare, which saw a shift in tactics from an attempt to suppress dissent to an attempt to restructure politics in the townships.

Maximum Force Policing: 1984–86. Widespread resistance to the institutions of apartheid surfaced on September 3, 1984, in the townships of the Vaal Triangle and spread rapidly through South Africa. The revolt began as a series of local township demonstrations, but gained momentum due to a number of factors: the deterioration in township living standards; the rising cost of living, caused in part by high charges imposed by community councils perceived by township residents to be unrepresentative and self-serving; the continuing crisis in black education; and opposition to the tricameral Parliament.[83]

In October 1984 the police called on the military to assist them in suppressing black opposition. But the security forces—the SAP and the SADF combined—found themselves unable to stop the revolt from spreading. In one area, the revolt took the form of an educational boycott; in another, it was manifested in a labor strike; in yet another, it was made up of demonstrations and attacks on the government-supported black municipal authorities.

On July 21, 1985, the government declared a partial state of emergency. Given the harsh and extensive nature of the laws on the statute books, especially those in the 1982 Internal Security Act, human rights lawyers questioned what the police wished to do that could not be done under the existing legislation. Three interrelated features of the ensuing states of emergency provide the answer.

- The police were given broadened executive and legislative powers. Under Section 29 of Internal Security Act 74 of 1982, only an officer of the rank of lieutenant-colonel or above could authorize the detention of a suspect. Regulation 3 of the emergency regulations extended the power to arrest and detain without trial to any member, however junior, of the security forces. Divisional police commissioners were given the power to govern black areas by decree.[84]
- The already limited judicial supervision of police powers was further curtailed. The regulations contained a clause that excluded the Supreme Court from exercising jurisdiction over members of the security forces or from setting aside orders, regulations, or actions taken in terms of the state of emergency. The regulations also gave members of the security forces an indemnity against the consequences of their unlawful actions unless the complainant could establish that the illegal act was committed in bad faith.[85] Furthermore, the regulations restricted attorneys' access to detainees, preventing lawyers from monitoring or supervising their treatment.[86] Finally, the regulations sought to frame the powers of the security

forces in the broadest manner possible to avoid legal accountability. The regulations were a prescription for law and order without the "law."

- A ban on reporting unrest events and on reporting and photographing police conduct sought to inhibit public control over police conduct.[87] The provisions were so broad and so obscure that journalists were paralyzed not only by the sweep of the regulations, but also by their inscrutability. Journalists brave enough to write on sensitive topics ran the risk of administrative punishment, as the authorities were armed with wide administrative powers to punish journalists. For example, they could deport foreign journalists, refuse to renew their work permits, or detain local journalists under the emergency regulations.[88]

The emergency regulations were therefore a prescription for unsupervised and unaccountable behavior on the part of the security forces, who were vested with substantial executive powers and armed with an array of violent weapons. The original emergency regulations gave the security forces permission to pacify the townships by engaging in an undeclared war, unconstrained by conventional limits.

The determination of the police to contain the spreading unrest in the townships found its expression in what came to be known as the "daily death rate." In answer to a question in Parliament, the minister of law and order stated that in 1986 alone, 624 adults and 92 children had been killed by the police and 1,701 adults and 387 children had been wounded.[89] A typical pattern of violence was that a demonstrator would be shot and killed, his or her funeral (which was prohibited) would follow, and in the ensuing confrontation between mourners and police, additional fatalities would be incurred—which led to more funerals and more fatalities.[90]

The police force was not able to handle crowd control in a humanitarian manner for several reasons: It was not suitably trained, it did not have the appropriate equipment, and finally, it was granted wide latitude in the use of firearms for enforcement duties. One result was that many persons killed by the police died under circumstances that did not warrant the use of deadly force. For example, a report compiled by Dr. Joe du Flou, a registrar at the University of Cape Town's Department of Forensic Medicine, based on postmortems conducted on the victims of police action, claimed that 50 percent of the persons shot by the police had been shot in the back; another 11.6 percent had wounds in their sides, suggesting that they had turned to run as police opened fire.[91] Twelve percent of the victims were younger than fifteen years old. The youngest was seven. (It has been estimated that between 1984 and 1986, over three hundred children were killed by the police.[92]) Du Flou found that birdshot was used in 40 percent of the deaths, thus strengthening claims that birdshot should not be regarded as a nonlethal form of crowd control. His findings were corroborated by a report compiled by doctors at the Empilisweni Clinic in the Crossroads squatter camp, which found that 43 percent of the 170 patients treated for shotgun wounds were under twenty years of age.[93]

Several incidents involving police conduct in the course of township patrols came under judicial scrutiny. One of the most serious occurred in Langa (Uitenhage) in the Eastern Cape on March 21, 1985. Mourners were marching from one black township to another to attend a funeral when they were confronted by police in armored vehicles who opened fire with lethal SSG shotguns.[94] SSG shot is heavy caliber, penetrates metal plate at thirty paces, and spreads one meter over thirty meters. In the course of one volley, twenty people were killed (all but one shot in the back or side) and another forty-three injured. The crowd was unarmed. In a judicial commission of inquiry into the incident, it was revealed that the police had not been equipped with official nonlethal forms of crowd control such as tear gas or rubber bullets. On the contrary, they had been instructed not to use such equipment because, as one officer testified, it did not immobilize demonstrators.[95]

The most notorious example of police brutality was the incident known as the "Trojan Horse." On October 15, 1985, police concealed themselves in boxes on the back of a truck. When a few youths began stoning the truck, the police jumped out of their boxes and opened fire, killing three persons—including an occupant of a nearby house.[96] A report by the Lawyers Committee for Human Rights provided the following eyewitness account:

> Two seconds after the door opened, the police started shooting. I saw a yellow truck with boxes on it, and I realised the police were hiding behind the boxes and shooting. As I tried to shut the door, I was shot in the shoulder. Two of the younger children were cowering on the bed just inside the door. Andrew [aged seven] was shot in the arm, leg, chest, and thigh. Michael [16 years] was shot under the arm four times. Jerry [aged 16] was one of the children who had gone outside. He came crawl-

ing back inside on all fours. We didn't realise it then, but he had been shot in the head. He staggered into the other room and collapsed on the bed where he died seconds later. A nine-year-old child who had been playing in the street on his bicycle was also shot dead. I slammed the door shut, but four policemen came to the house and kicked it open. They dragged Jerry's body roughly off the bed and across the floor. Then the police went around the house and picked up all the shot pellets and left.[97]

Supreme Court judges condemned the conduct of the security force officials responsible for the killing of black township residents and commented in particular on the inadequate training of the police and their "shoot first" policy. The criticism directed at the police for their use of lethal weapons in the course of crowd control was also extended to the use of supposedly "nonlethal weapons."[98] Tear gas, rubber bullets, and birdshot were all used by the police with fatal results.[99] As in Northern Ireland, the use of such non-lethal weapons led to their more indiscriminate and reckless usage, and not necessarily to a decrease in fatalities. The police response to accusations that it did not utilize European riot control methods was to state that such equipment was unsuitable in South Africa.[100] In the official SAP journal, *Servamus*, Helmoed-Romer Heitman stated:

> In present circumstances, there are probably only two ways in which the number of fatal casualties can be reduced: Either the rioters must exercise firmer control over their own activities or the police will have to act far more strongly earlier in the proceedings. . . .[101]

In the same issue, it was claimed that the number of children killed by police could be attributed to the agitators' policy of placing women and children in the front line of riots.[102]

During the first three years of the state of emergency, the police fully exercised their wide powers of detention. It is estimated that by August 1987, over twenty-six thousand people had been detained, many of them belonging to youth organizations, trade unions, and political organizations.[103] Of those detained, the Human Rights Commission has calculated that only 2 to 4 percent will ever be convicted of an offense.[104] While the police sought to neutralize popular municipal and labor organizations by detaining their leaders, most of the police action was directed at young people, who were viewed as having provided the backbone of township-based resistance. In 1987 the DPSC estimated that 40 percent of those detained were children eighteen years of age and under, some as young as twelve years of age.[105] Incessant campaigning took place for the release of children under age eighteen. The government, to reduce the figures, released statistics only for the number of children under the age of sixteen held in custody under the emergency. Allegations have also been made that in cases where a person sought by the police was not available, "hostages" were taken into custody on the understanding that they would be released once the wanted family member had reported for detention.[106] These allegations were denied by the police.

Police attempts to restore law and order in the townships during the early stages of the black revolt were essentially defensive. They were confined to protecting the targets of community rage, disrupting community organizations, and detaining community leaders. By mid-1985 it had become clear that maximum force policing on its own had had little impact on the main currents of township politics and was insufficient to restore the authority of the municipal governments.

The daily death rate, according to an official index of unrest, had continued to escalate. Maximum force policing methods had further politicized the black community and had reinforced social cohesion among township residents. Regular security force patrols confirmed township residents' perceptions that they were under siege by an occupying army. Confronted by increasingly intense and diverse forms of popular resistance, the security establishment recognized the need for a new approach that would disorganize the anti-apartheid rebellion, not merely suppress it. This led to the second phase of the government's response: manufacturing "violent stability" through a low-intensity civil war.

Low-Intensity Warfare: 1986–89. By the mid-1980s, South African strategists appeared to have come under the influence of the more practical theories of Colonel John J. McCuen, an American who developed his ideas on counterinsurgency warfare in Vietnam.[107] McCuen focused on low-intensity conflict, operating on the premise that there should be little or no direct security force intervention.[108] If the security forces have to intervene in a conflict situation, McCuen argued, they have already lost the strategic initiative. Military involvement can win battles, but it will lose counterinsurgency wars. Foreign forces, he wrote, cannot "win over" the local population by waging war on them.

Low-intensity conflict postulates that there are no battlefields, that victory is measured in terms of attitudinal changes in a target group, and that pacification has population, not territory, as its objective.[109] The redefinition of victory means that even where no outright military victory has occurred, enough physical and political damage will ensure that the revolutionaries cannot win either.

Low-intensity conflict is a war of counterorganization that seeks to utilize or create groups composed of grass-roots civilians to wage "revolutionary violence." The role of the military is to coordinate the distribution of economic aid to targeted social groups and to supply logistic and informational support to its surrogate groups. Where the security forces do become involved, it is on a covert basis, through either assassination or other types of clandestine operations. Once the premises of total strategy have been accepted—that South Africa is at war within its borders and that civilians are the targets—the shift to implementing low-intensity conflict logically follows.

What is apparent in McCuen's theory, and in the speeches of its South African advocates, is that the creation of a political solution requires not a commitment to political bargaining, not even top-down reform, but a bottom-up reconstruction of political forces. In 1986 McCuen's theory was summarized in a seventy-five-page document entitled "The Art of Counter-Revolutionary Warfare" and distributed throughout the NSMS.[110]

Dr. David Webster, a human rights monitor who was assassinated in 1989, described this new policy as one of proactive policing. It included such measures as prior restriction on the right to assemble rather than belated violent intervention, and the use of vigilantes rather than security forces to disrupt political activities.[111] The state of emergency was maintained only to facilitate the introduction of a more long-term, penetrating strategy.

Mark Phillips and Mark Swilling date the shift from maximum force policing to low-intensity warfare as occurring in 1986.[112] The shift is plainly evident in the policing and security responses to the civil revolt. The process, which was controlled and directed by the military, provided the foundation for the withdrawal of troops from the townships. Broadly, the following tactics were utilized to restructure black townships politically and economically:

- Community leaders were detained and vigilantes and assassins were used to disrupt popular organizations. When released, detainees were isolated from their organizations by vigilantes or the police. In extreme cases, potential troublemakers were surgically removed—that is, assassinated.

- The organizational vacuum created in this way was filled by personalities and groups favorable to government development programs. The local JMC coordinated financial and infrastructural development in support of the local community councils, with a view to reestablishing a black elite and embarking on a "winning hearts and minds" campaign, known to some securocrats as WHAM.
- In order to strengthen the hand of the community councillors and to formalize the vigilante groups, the state embarked on a national program to introduce black municipal guards and auxiliary police—the *kitskonstabels*. These groups received crash courses in police instruction and, in the case of the municipal guards, were armed and placed at the service of the community councils.

By assuming the management of the low-intensity civil war, the military had claimed a right to influence decision making at all levels. Although purporting to exercise only a technocratic security function—a role described by Chester Crocker, former U.S. assistant secretary of state for African affairs, as "buying time for domestic political evolution"—the military was well placed to control the nature and direction of reform.[113]

If the injection of finances and the upgrading of townships constituted the "soft" elements of the strategy, vigilante violence and covert assassination squads were the "hard" elements. Soft methods, the securocrats calculated, could not succeed on their own.

Vigilantes. In the latter part of 1985, a new pattern of aggressive, extralegal violence emerged in the black townships. The authors of the violence were vigilantes. Their targets were the same as those of the security forces, namely, anti-apartheid civic and youth organizations. By August 1987 vigilante violence had become the single largest cause of fatalities in the revolt.

A survey of vigilante groups throughout the country showed that, at a minimum, they operated with the connivance of the police or the SADF.[114] Police lethargy or reluctance to curb vigilante violence was sufficient to leave the victims of vigilante groups vulnerable to potentially fatal attacks. In the homelands, the vigilantes enjoyed overt state sponsorship, but in the urban areas, the motivation and composition of the vigilante groups varied.[115] In some cases, different vigilante groups emerged at approximately the same time, and examples of the police encouraging their formation suggested a coordinated strategy.

The vigilantes succeeded in creating a condition that, from the perspective of the security forces, could be termed "violent stability." Vigilante violence, once initiated, became a self-generating cycle of attacks and retaliation, with the conflict often paralyzing entire communities.

The vigilantes' activities helped the government in several additional ways. First, the violence that resulted from their attacks, which was categorized as "black-on-black" violence, gave credence to government claims that vigorous and harsh policing was necessary to protect black township residents. Second, the vigilantes were able to target groups in a way that military or police patrolling could not. Third, the level of violence and terror that the vigilantes generated was greatly disruptive but did not attract much international or domestic attention. Many communities that had continued to support civic associations or popular leaders throughout the emergency lost cohesion and direction after the emergence of vigilantes in their areas. In some cases, civic and youth leaders simply fled the area, abandoning their organizations and communities. This created a political vacuum that was often filled by persons favored by the government.[116] Fourth, the vigilantes were "cheap," as one homeland leader, Lennox Sebe, pointed out.[117]

The following examples of vigilantes in action illustrate their value to the government:

- On January 1, 1986, a large group of vigilantes from KwaNdebele, known as the *mbhokoto*, abducted over four hundred men from the Moutse district, an area that was resisting the jurisdiction of the KwaNdebele homeland authorities. The men were beaten for several hours before being released. The chief minister of KwaNdebele personally supervised these assaults. Some of the victims identified their attackers to the police the same day, but the police never apprehended any of the assailants.[118]
- In the Crossroads squatter camp near Cape Town, vigilantes known as *witdoeke* accomplished in less than a week what government pressure had failed to do in ten years.[119] In May 1986, in the presence of the police, they demolished the squatter camp, rendering twenty thousand people homeless. Residents claimed damages

against the SAP on the grounds that they instigated and failed to prevent this action by the vigilantes.[120] The civil suit was settled out of court by payment of monies to a trust representing the interests and welfare of the former residents of these squatter camps.

The most dramatic and far-reaching instance of vigilante violence and the police role in it took place in Natal. In mid-1987 violence erupted in the black townships of Pietermaritzburg. By March 1990 an estimated three thousand persons had been killed in the province and sixty thousand persons displaced from their homes. To place the number of deaths in context, it should be noted that in 1988 nearly twice as many persons died in the Pietermaritzburg townships as were killed in Beirut.[121] By March 1988 nearly two-thirds of the persons killed nationwide in unrest-related events had been killed in the Pietermaritzburg district.[122] In other words, vigilante violence and countervigilante violence in Pietermaritzburg had become the most prevalent cause of death in South Africa under the state of emergency.

The conflict was between supporters of Inkatha, headed by Chief Mangosuthu Gatsha Buthelezi, the chief minister of KwaZulu, and supporters or members of groups that favor the ANC, such as the United Democratic Front (UDF) and the Congress of South African Trade Unions (COSATU). The essential catalyst for the violence was the conflict over political superiority in the region. Inkatha blamed the violence on attempts by ANC–supporting groups to render the areas ungovernable; the UDF/COSATU forces claimed that the violence was a result of Inkatha's determination to root out any alternative political presence in a region it claims as its own fiefdom.

Political competition alone, however, does not explain the intensity and scale of the violence. Nor is sufficient explanation offered by Natal's socioeconomic conditions, which also prevail in other areas. The nature of the violence can be explained only by two factors: the role of the SAP and the relationship of Inkatha to the KwaZulu and South African governments. Partisan policing by the SAP was a necessary condition for the extent and duration of the violence. Both the UDF and COSATU complained that it was the failure of the police to intervene impartially, or at all, in the conflict that caused its rapid escalation. Attorneys for the two groups stressed that it was not only partisan support for Inkatha that fueled the violence, it was policing practices that left both sides with the impression that violence goes unpunished, and that it is more effective to take the law into one's own hands than to seek legal remedies.

A second necessary condition for the violence in Natal was Inkatha's easy access to arms and logistical and other support as a result of its connections with the KwaZulu and South African governments. The "Inkathagate" scandal that erupted in mid-1991 provided documentary evidence of Pretoria's financial support for Inkatha and its associated trade union movement, as well as a degree of paramilitary training. What made Natal, and several townships in the Transvaal, so appropriate for low-intensity conflict strategies was that Inkatha, through the skillful use of ethnic tensions and tribal chauvinism, was capable of being transformed into an organized, aggressive force. Were government resources to be withdrawn from Inkatha, however, and the perpetrators of the violence—on both sides—jailed, the conflict, it was argued, could not endure.

In January of 1989, COSATU attorneys, believing that their informants' statements revealed a pattern of police collaboration with Inkatha "warlords," made a study of incidents of violence in the district of Imbali Stage I.[123] According to their report, the majority of the monitored attacks were perpetrated by Inkatha members, whereas the majority of the persons arrested after the attacks were COSATU or UDF supporters. The police, who had detained well over a thousand UDF or COSATU members but only a handful of Inkatha members since 1987, were alleged to have shown a differential response to suspects by attempting first to identify whether a suspect was a member of the UDF/COSATU alliance or of Inkatha. Inkatha warlords were not apprehended, despite identification by witnesses and judicial findings by inquest magistrates that they had been responsible for certain murders. The police also tolerated the illegal carrying of arms by Inkatha members.

The COSATU lawyers' report also suggested that Inkatha members were less likely to be held in custody if apprehended. Only a handful of successful prosecutions had followed the estimated five thousand murders since 1987. According to the attorneys, police investigations were lackadaisical.[124] The report stressed, however, that the conduct of the police was not the result of their laziness or roguery, but rather the result of their partiality toward Inkatha. The minister of law and order, on the other hand, claimed that Inkatha was the innocent party and that blame for the conflict should be laid squarely at the door of COSATU.[125]

On numerous occasions, communities accused the police of

standing by when Inkatha *impis* (warriors) attacked them, but of intervening when the community assembled to repulse a mass attack.[126] The KwaZulu police force, under the authority of Buthelezi himself, became a special target for criticism. Evidence was given in open court that KwaZulu police members were instructed to join the Inkatha movement upon their recruitment. In the Transvaal, where the violence spread in July 1990, the pattern of Inkatha attack–police passivity repeated itself. Of 146 incidents of violence, 66 percent were initiated by Inkatha compared with 6 percent initiated by the ANC.[127] Furthermore, Inkatha aggressors carried firearms much more frequently, notably the Soviet-made AK47s.

Until 1990 the minister of law and order persisted in discouraging the involvement of church and other establishment groups in peace initiatives. As a result of the shift in the political climate in 1990, the minister of law and order and the police hierarchy began to change their approach and to respond to their critics in Natal. Police headquarters appointed a brigadier to investigate complaints against the police, and the minister met with representatives of UDF/COSATU in an attempt to reverse the deteriorating stature of the SAP and to halt the social and economic effects of the violence, which threatened to engulf the region.

The SADF also began to play a larger role. In Imbali and two other townships, community residents requested that the SAP be replaced by military units. After March 1990 SADF units began to perform policing duties in some of the townships.

Assassinations. The vigilante phenomenon tended to obscure the growing frequency of assassinations of anti-apartheid activists, especially in the latter half of the 1980s, at a time when the SADF developed a covert "dirty tricks" bureau closely linked to Military Intelligence. The Human Rights Commission, a nongovernmental monitoring agency, released figures showing that between 1977 and August 1989, at least forty-nine activists had been assassinated and another ten had disappeared.[128] Some of the more prominent activists assassinated during the 1980s were:

- *Griffiths Mxenge.* In 1981 Griffiths Mxenge, a civil rights lawyer, was assassinated.
- *Matthew Goniwe.* In July 1985 the bodies of Matthew Goniwe and three other respected township leaders were found.
- *Victoria Mxenge.* In August 1985 Victoria Mxenge, a well-

known civil rights attorney and the wife of Griffiths Mxenge, was assassinated in her house near Durban in Natal.
- *Dr. Fabian Ribiero.* On December 5, 1986, Fabian Ribiero, a political leader in the Mamelodi township near Pretoria, was assassinated by unknown gunmen. The car allegedly used in the getaway was subsequently linked to a former Rhodesian Selous Scout.
- *Dr. David Webster.* Early in May 1989, a white academic, David Webster, was shot dead by assassins outside his house.

The SAP's failure to identify or apprehend the assassins contrasted with the rapid identification and prosecution of persons alleged to have committed acts against the state.

In addition to assassinations, other tactics against activists included poisoning, letter and parcel bombs, and the killing of household pets. Numerous anti-apartheid activists had their homes and offices firebombed and ransacked. Bombings caused the destruction of the office block belonging to COSATU in Johannesburg on May 6, 1987; the demolition of a group of offices housing anti-apartheid organizations (including COSATU) in Cape Town on August 29, 1987; the destruction of the head offices of the South African Council of Churches in Johannesburg in 1988; and the destruction of the head offices of the Southern African Catholic Bishops' Conference in 1988.

By 1989 human rights groups had begun to accuse elements in the security forces of these acts. After the assassination of Anton Lubowski, a leading member of SWAPO, on September 12, 1989, the Human Rights Commission stated that these acts received "if not the official sanction then at least a less than enthusiastic investigation." Speculation about the assassinations came to an end on October 19, 1989, when a former security policeman, Butane Nofomela, claimed that he had been part of an officially constituted police death squad.[129] Nofomela, himself on death row for a murder unrelated to the activities of the death squad, claimed to have killed Griffiths Mxenge. His version of the death squad's activities tallied with evidence presented earlier at a political trial and was confirmed by two former colleagues, Captain Dirk Coetzee and David Tshikalanga.[130] Coetzee's extensive allegations about SAP death squads were published in a radical Afrikaans-language newspaper, *Vrye Weekblad*, in Johannesburg in late 1989.

Shortly afterward, police revealed they were investigating another death squad—an SADF covert Special Forces unit known as the Civil Cooperation Bureau (CCB)—controlled by Military Intelligence, which was linked to the deaths of David Webster and Anton Lubowski.[131] In response to the public furor that followed these revelations, President De Klerk appointed a judicial commission of inquiry in February 1990, headed by Justice Louis Harms, a provincial supreme court judge.[132] Nofomela and Coetzee had implicated eleven police officers. Among those named was Major Eugene de Kock, who, in separate inquest proceedings during 1989, had been implicated in the alleged execution of ANC suspects.

The Harms Commission began and ended in controversy. A major problem was its mandate, which was to investigate only "murders and other unlawful acts of violence" committed in the Republic of South Africa. The terms were later broadened to include an investigation of whether assassinated SWAPO leader Anton Lubowski was an agent of the South African Military Intelligence. The terms thus excluded hit squad raids into neighboring states, the assassination by parcel bomb of several prominent ANC members, and, indeed, the actual assassination of Lubowski.

The commission's evidence primarily concerned the existence of two networks: an SAP "antiterrorist" death squad based at Vlakplaas, as revealed by Nofomela and others, and the CCB, which had also been linked to assassinations. Evidence linked the unit to at least one attempted assassination, but the inquiry into the CCB was hampered by the deliberate removal or destruction of CCB files and records. The CCB was disbanded in July 1990. For the purposes of this survey, only the evidence implicating the SAP unit is reviewed.

In summary, Coetzee, Nofomela, and Tshikalanga alleged that an SAP hit squad unit was based at the Vlakplaas Farm outside Pretoria.[133] It utilized the services of members of the SAP, former members of the ANC who had been captured and "turned," and other persons recruited directly into the unit. The unit was alleged to have assassinated pro–ANC individuals inside the country, such as civil rights lawyer Griffiths Mxenge and Japie Maponya, the brother of an ANC guerrilla. The unit also stole and destroyed cars and property belonging to activists and trade unionists and was involved in cross-border raids to assassinate ANC members.

The commission's investigating team produced little or no evidence to prove or disprove these allegations, which were denied by the police. Justice Harms indicated that he doubted the veracity of Coetzee and Nofomela. However, a private agency, the Independent Board of Inquiry into Informal Repression (IBIIR), acting on its own, managed to produce hard evidence corroborating aspects of

Nofomela's and Coetzee's statements and indicating that at least some of the police witnesses had lied to the commission.[134]

At the conclusion of the inquiry, Justice Harms chose to accept only those aspects of Nofomela's and Coetzee's evidence that were corroborated by indisputable proof. He suggested that the unlawful activities carried out by the two men were performed "unofficially."[135] Notwithstanding the poor record of the SAP unit—only twenty persons arrested or captured in six years—Justice Harms found no need for its disbandment. He did, however, recommend that it should conform to certain procedural and operational guidelines.

The commission was handed a list of 265 incidents of hit squad–type violence against anti-apartheid activists or their organizations. The offices of COSATU and its affiliates sustained fifty-one attacks or bombings between 1985 and 1989. Various church bodies endured seventeen such attacks. The commission, in line with its passive understanding of its role and a restrictive interpretation of terms of reference, chose not to investigate these incidents unless evidence was placed before it by some other agency or party.

Hit squad–type violence continued during and after the Harms Commission, although it was frequently associated with the ultra-rightwing. In Bophuthatswana, however, a member of that territory's police force claimed that a police hit squad had been operating with the full knowledge of the SAP, but the IBIIR questioned the veracity of this claim.[136] Irregular police practices in KwaNdebele were the subject of the Parsons Commission of Inquiry. Evidence before the commission indicated that the KwaNdebele Police, under the SAP's Brigadier Hertzog Lerm, were a law unto themselves and inter alia refused to investigate killings of activists that were allegedly perpetrated by police or vigilantes.[137]

A sequel to the publication of Dirk Coetzee's allegations was a civil suit against the *Vrye Weekblad* for R1.5 million by the head of the SAP's forensic laboratories, General Lothar Neethling. Coetzee had claimed that General Neethling had supplied him with poison to kill ANC activists. Testimony was taken from Coetzee in London, where he had fled. In the ensuing court case in South Africa in early 1991, the presiding judge found in favor of the newspaper, declaring that the story was both in the public interest and also was probably true.[138] The judge specifically found that Neethling had misled the Harms Commission and, by implication, that the Harms Commission's negative findings on the veracity of Coetzee's allegations were incorrect.

Meanwhile, in a bizarre coda to these events, in March 1990 it was revealed that a Military Intelligence/CCB-linked group had infiltrated the Johannesburg City Council's security department. Unknown to the city's Management Committee, the department had established a network of spies and informers to collect information on ANC sympathizers and white opposition groups. A combined SADF–City Council team had embarked on operations such as assaults on activists (including an actor in an anti-apartheid play) and sabotage of activists' homes. A commission of inquiry, under Justice Victor Hiemstra, was appointed by the administrator of the Transvaal to investigate the activities of this group. The commission uncovered a military operation guided by the total onslaught theory and an outlandish spy-versus-spy farce in which City Council agents bugged not only their own employers but also the SADF and each other.

The SADF's prominence in these operations was not accidental. As early as 1977, Helmoed-Romer Heitman, an SADF captain who later became South African correspondent for the prestigious Western defense journal, *Jane's Defence Weekly*, had offered detailed advice to members of the intelligence services on how to carry out "extralegal operations."

> Operations can include the sabotage or doctoring of discovered arms or supply caches. The resultant difficulties will sap confidence and morale, as well as creating distrust between the insurgency and its suppliers. Such operations should not, however, be overdone so as to avoid creating suspicion. They could range from doctored foodstuffs, via mixing petrol with paraffin for lamps and tampering with medical supplies, to the placing of instant detonation fuses in, for example, every tenth hand grenade, etc. The preference here would be for the infliction of illness or injury, not death, the former having the added advantage of sapping morale and straining logistics. The intelligence services can also create some havoc by the supplying of false information, particularly the type to create mistrust. Thus a leader of the insurgency could be made to appear as a police-informer by, for instance, paying him more or less secretly, or less subtly, by rewarding him publicly. . . . *Further, some extralegal operations may prove beneficial both in eliminating certain key members of the insurgency and in sowing suspicion* [emphasis added]. Needless to say such operations would need to be suitably disguised. . . .[139]

Low-intensity warfare proved effective in its repressive and disorganizing component, but it achieved little in winning the hearts and minds of township residents. Vigilantes, for example, were not able to generate popular support; by 1989 they had managed only to create a violent stability. A Philippine commentator on a similar phenomenon in that country has aptly remarked, "If vigilantes are a formula for peace, then my country can only be headed for more war."[140] In the context of the highly charged and politicized schools and townships, even infrastructural development could not make any headway. The recognition of this fact by political rather than security leaders led to a distinct shift in political and, subsequently, policing strategies at the end of 1989.

The total strategy had inverted Von Clausewitz's celebrated dictum that war was merely politics by other means. By 1989 it had become clear that the security strategy could manage the political crisis, but could not end it.

The De Klerk Era and the Demise of the Securocrats

While previous governments had turned a blind eye to abuses by the security forces, President De Klerk, who took office in September 1989, allowed public inquiries into these allegations. Opting for a political rather than a military solution to continuing black resistance, De Klerk legalized the ANC, the PAC, and the South African Communist Party (SACP). He also downgraded the influence of the security forces in determining local and national strategies. He did this by elevating his political advisers at the expense of the security establishment, by trimming the legal powers and financial resources of the security forces, and by limiting police authority to control political meetings and demonstrations.

This significant change of heart by the government did not, however, prepare the police for the political changes that were to occur within South Africa during the latter half of 1989. On September 5, 1989, two weeks before F. W. de Klerk was sworn in as state president, the SAP became the focus of international attention when a Coloured police officer, Lieutenant Gregory Rockman, publicly criticized the methods of crowd control used by the riot police. Describing police action during a protest in Mitchell's Plain, a Coloured township outside Cape Town, he stated publicly:

> They were just hitting people. They didn't care if they were innocent bystanders or not. They were running after them even when they were fleeing, hitting them. It seemed to me that they were enjoying themselves, feasting on the people. The squad stormed the kids like wild dogs. You could see the killer instinct

in their eyes. The cause of the riots in Mitchell's Plain were [*sic*] due to the unprofessional doings of the riot unit at Mitchell's Plain schools which I witnessed with my own eyes.[141]

Rockman's allegations led to requests for a commission of inquiry into police violence and eventually to the prosecution of two senior riot control policemen.[142] The police who participated in the Mitchell's Plain assault on demonstrators were not charged, but their commanding officers were. The magistrate, in acquitting the officers on the grounds that they had not participated in the assault, described the police assault as "utterly despicable."[143]

The police adopted a different approach to protest gatherings in the last quarter of 1989. For the first time in decades, political rallies and marches took place in all the major cities without any police intervention. On September 12, 1989, the SAP announced that the use of *sjamboks* (whips) would be stopped immediately.[144] The announcement stated that the use of *sjamboks* promoted a negative image nationally and internationally.

Shortly thereafter, the police stated their intention to improve their image by developing a more nonpolitical role in South Africa. In November 1989 President De Klerk released eight leading political prisoners, including the ANC's Walter Sisulu. Large public demonstrations and rallies were allowed to take place to celebrate their release. While the image of the police force improved as a result of this new approach, the morale of the force was reported to be low.[145] Moolman Mentz, the opposition Conservative Party spokesperson on law and order, reported that police officers had informed him that they were expected

> . . . to act like missionaries instead of police. The government is losing the loyalty of its security forces. When that happens, they are more than halfway to losing the fight. A senior security police officer told me he had to stand and look as nine laws were broken in front of his eyes and he could do nothing.[146]

In December 1989 it was announced that the state president had downgraded the NSMS.[147] This step appeared to signal a determined attempt to reduce the local as well as national influence of the SADF, and it was accompanied by an increase in the influence and stature of political figures outside the security system such as Dr. Gerrit Viljoen, then minister of education and development aid, and Hendrik J. ("Kobie") Coetsee, minister of justice. President De Klerk stated that this reform was aimed at reconfirming the cabinet as the country's highest policy-making power. Furthermore, government support for Armscor, the state-run armament industry, was drastically reduced, and in 1990 the SADF budget was cut in real terms for the first time in three decades. These moves constituted a marked break with the past.[148]

The capacity of disgruntled elements in the SADF to move against this new and more open political culture was inhibited by the public disclosures that both the SAP and the SADF had been involved in death squad activity. Nofomela's disclosures relating to an SAP hit squad, and the detention without trial of two former policemen, allegedly working for a military intelligence death squad responsible for the death of Anton Lubowski, placed enormous pressure on the highest echelons of the SAP and the SADF.

In early 1990 De Klerk announced the formation of the Harms Commission to investigate these death squads and a commission to examine the circumstances of the death of a detainee in John Vorster Square Police Station.[149] These investigations were followed by the announcement of further commissions of inquiry into the police shootings of demonstrators in Sebokeng on March 26, 1990, and a spy network operated by the Johannesburg City Council's traffic and security department. In both commissions, the chairmen made highly critical remarks about the performance and attitude of the security forces. Justice Richard Goldstone, who heard evidence on the shooting of demonstrators in Sebokeng, which resulted in twelve deaths and the wounding of 281 persons, found that the "force used was quite immoderate and disproportionate to any lawful object sought to be attained." Use of SSG shot was completely unjustified, and the police commanding officer had disobeyed all proper procedures in the manner that he had armed, controlled, and instructed his men.[150] The majority of the persons who were shot had sustained wounds on their backs or on the back of their heads.

Furthermore, the police were subjected to continuing public criticism of their role in the vigilante violence in Natal and in townships in other parts of the country. This outcry was underscored by repeated demands from several black communities that the SAP be replaced by the SADF as a peacekeeping force in the townships.

On February 2, 1990, President De Klerk announced the unbanning of the ANC, the SACP, and the PAC, organizations that the police and army had committed themselves to destroying for three decades. On February 11, Nelson Mandela, the founder of the ANC's military wing and its most charismatic leader, was released from life imprisonment.

The police response to the rising political temperature that followed De Klerk's initiatives was uneven. In some areas, the police exercised restraint in the face of provocative conduct by demonstrators; in other areas, notably Sebokeng in the Vaal Triangle, the police opened fire. The shooting of demonstrators at Sebokeng provoked direct criticism from Mandela that the police were attempting to sabotage the new political reforms.[151] At the highest levels of the SAP, notably from the commissioner of police, there were public statements of support, if not for President De Klerk's new political direction, at least for the notion that the police should not intervene in politically charged situations.

On January 17, 1990, President De Klerk had summoned the top structure of the SAP to Pretoria and advised them that it was his intention to "remove the police from the political battlefield," adding: "We will not use you any longer as instruments to attain political goals."[152] He asked the police to understand his decision to relax restrictions on demonstrations and marches and to show restraint in the exercise of their powers. The commissioner of police, General J. van der Merwe, echoed these sentiments later the same week, stating that the police would be retrained to carry out their policing duties impartially, with "understanding, insight and even pity."[153]

In line with the new approach, the *casspir* armored personnel carriers used in the townships were replaced with patrol cars, a police community relations department was established, and the dreaded security branch was dissolved and its personnel accommodated within the CID. The SAP appointed a national network of senior officers to act as ANC liaison officers. Political education courses were conducted within the SAP to assist members in "understanding their role in a new South Africa."[154] A police spokesperson denied that the courses were designed to prevent SAP rank-and-file support for a rightwing coup. Throughout 1990 the SAP arrested various white rightwing extremists and, in a display of impartiality, held such persons under the detention-without-trial provisions of the Internal Security Act 74 of 1982.

Notwithstanding these and other measures to project the police as a user-friendly community service committed to the new South Africa, the SAP was haunted by past practices, and its community outreach was bedeviled by serious doubts about its present intentions. The busiest man in the SAP appeared to be public relations officer, Brigadier Leon Mellet, who was called upon repeatedly to explain the gap between promise and practice.

It remains unclear how widely the commitment to a "new South Africa" is held by ordinary members of the SAP. In April 1990 it was reported that police were resigning from the force at the rate of twenty-two persons per day.[155] The minister of law and order ascribed their resignations to the poor conditions of service in the police force and sought to remedy the drop-out rate by improving police salary scales. Speculation existed, however, that many members of the SADF and the SAP were linked to far rightwing groups. The theft of a variety of combat weapons from an SADF armory by a rightwing group fueled this speculation, as did a comment by an unnamed police source indicating that the SAP, when probing offenses of this kind, could not guarantee that its investigating officers were not linked to such groups.

Conclusion

The security forces remain a central institution in South African political life. In any period of political transformation, the legitimacy and the conduct of the institutions that have a monopoly on the use of legalized force are critical to the success of the process. Although these institutions will be crucial in defending and implementing new reforms, elements operate within the security forces that have the capacity, and perhaps the inclination, to sabotage the political initiatives. Ensuring proper implementation of the reform initiatives may involve the vigorous policing of rightwing groups to which security force members are sympathetic by virtue of their background and the institutional culture of these forces.

The transformation of South Africa's political system requires a commitment from these institutions because it is highly unlikely that the transition will be supervised by an outside agency, such as the British troops in Zimbabwe or the UN forces in Namibia. Members of the security institutions are militarily trained, have access to arms and to information, have witnessed and participated in the enormously destructive civil wars in the region, and understand their own disruptive potential. As long as rightwing elements within the security forces remain under scrutiny, demoralized and disorganized, a backlash against the De Klerk reforms remains improbable. F. W. de Klerk and his cabinet undoubtedly appreciate the fine line between pressure that serves to neutralize the rightwing elements in these forces and pressure that provokes rebellion. For this reason, it is likely that any amnesty offered to fighters in the armies of the national liberation movement will be extended to those officers in the security forces who have contributed to its woeful human rights record.

For the same reason, it is unlikely that F. W. de Klerk will use a new broom to sweep the security forces clean. Herein lies, perhaps, the potentially most damaging legacy of total strategy. For what is required of the security forces is not merely a political passivity, but an active engagement in professional and impartial policing. During 1990 and 1991, the several initiatives undertaken by the security forces, notably by the SAP, to project themselves in this mold glaringly failed to win them the popular legitimacy they seek.

The reasons for this failure can be traced to the institutional history of the forces. First, the security forces continue to be haunted by revelations of the unlawful overt and covert activities that total strategy spawned. Second, old ways of thinking die slowly when the institutional structure remains unchanged. The security forces have performed their function within a set of political objectives for so long that it would be unrealistic to assume that old loyalties and old enmities were extinguished overnight on February 2, 1990. Moreover, any move toward a new mode of consensus policing requires an appreciation of the relationship of accountability between the police and the policed. Such a notion is the very antithesis of the attitudes and ideas that informed total strategy. Total strategy was premised on totalitarian social manipulation, which places a premium on ends rather than means and understands no boundaries between legitimate and illegitimate areas of operation. Its most insidious legacy may prove to be the Machiavellian cop-culture that it shaped and that lingers on.

Chapter IV

Blacks and the Administration of Justice

John Dugard

The apartheid state has never completely excluded blacks from participating in the administration of justice or, indeed, in most government departments. Blacks have served as police officers, soldiers, doctors, magistrates, and bureaucrats within the system, but have never risen to senior positions outside the homeland structures. Despite their limited participation, blacks have become increasingly alienated from a system of law and administration whose principal aim has been the denial of their rights and the restriction of their advancement. In this process, respect for the law and the courts has suffered. To many blacks, the law is simply an instrument for the maintenance of white domination. As South Africa enters a new era, one of the most important issues will be the restoration of legitimacy to the legal system. This chapter considers the extent to which blacks today participate in the administration of justice, current black attitudes toward the law, and possible remedies for the future.

Black Participation in the Administration of Justice

Blacks have participated actively in the implementation, albeit not the formulation, of the structures of apartheid. The four "independent" homeland states of Transkei, Bophuthatswana, Venda, and Ciskei (TBVC states), created to further "grand apartheid," are led and administered by blacks, with the support of white advisers in key roles. The nonindependent homeland states of KwaZulu, Lebowa, Gazankulu, Qwaqwa, KaNgwane, and KwaNdebele are likewise led and administered by blacks. Outside the homelands, black-led local councils govern the lives of blacks. Black children in segregated black schools are taught by black teachers, and black educators supervise this system. More than half the police force is black, but the army remains predominantly white.[1]

A number of reasons may be advanced to explain the willingness of blacks to participate in the structures of apartheid. Economic reasons are no doubt paramount. Personal ambition, particularly on the part of some—but not necessarily all—homeland and local government leaders, is also an explanation. But altruism cannot be discounted: Many teachers have continued to work in a system of which they strongly disapprove in order to prepare the youth for a future South Africa, and doctors have not denied their services to the sick, despite their principled objections to segregated hospitals. Some black political leaders have chosen to work within the system of apartheid in order to undermine its development. The homeland leaders who have vigorously opposed independence for their territories may take much of the credit for the breakdown of the principal aim of grand apartheid—ten ethnic independent homelands—as their obstructionism made it impossible for the National Party government to proceed with its plans. Therefore, the morality of participation cannot be judged easily.

In the discussion that follows, attention is focused on the extent to which blacks participate in South Africa's judiciary and legal profession, and on the debate over the morality of participation in those spheres of public life. Many of the issues raised in the context of this limited study, however, have broad implications and may be applied to other areas of human endeavor.

South African courts are divided into lower courts (magistrates courts) and higher courts (the Supreme Court of South Africa). Magistrates are civil servants appointed from the ranks of the prosecutors in the Department of Justice. They have limited jurisdiction over both criminal and civil matters. At present, there are some 965 magistrates in South Africa, excluding the homelands.

As explained in Chapter I, judges of the Supreme Court are appointed by the state president from private legal practitioners—that is, from the ranks of court specialists or advocates (the counterpart of English barristers). Modeled on the English judiciary, they are independent from the executive. The Supreme Court is divided into a number of provincial divisions, which try serious cases and hear appeals from the magistrates courts, and an Appellate Division, whose decisions are binding on the provincial divisions. There are 130 Supreme Court judges, of whom 15 are judges of appeal.

Judges. In South Africa, as in Britain, judges are appointed by the executive—that is, by the state president acting on the advice of his cabinet. The appointment of blacks is not legally prohibited, but until mid-1991 no black person had been appointed to judicial office.[2] In August 1991 Ismail Mahomed S.C., a prominent human rights lawyer, became the first black person to be appointed to the South African bench. Until recently, no South African government would have contemplated appointing a black person to the bench, as most whites would probably not have tolerated being tried by a black judge. Two factors have traditionally inhibited such appointments.[3]

First, judges in South Africa, as in Britain, are by strict tradition chosen from the ranks of the senior advocates or barristers, known as senior counsel. Attorneys and academic lawyers are not, in practice, eligible for judicial appointment. The bar, which views itself as the elite branch of the legal profession, has attracted fewer blacks than the "side-bar," or attorneys' profession, as it is more difficult for a black person to make a career at the bar. Consequently, there are today only four black senior counsel—three Indians and one African—who are eligible for judicial appointment.

The second inhibiting factor is the legal system itself. Black advocates are understandably reluctant to apply laws that discriminate against their own people or nondiscriminatory laws in whose making they—and their people—play no part. For this reason, black lawyers have actively discouraged the few black senior counsel from considering judicial appointment.

In February 1987 a black senior counsel, Hassan Mall S.C. of Durban, was appointed for one month as an acting judge—normally a prelude to a full judicial appointment. This provoked an outcry from black legal and political organizations. The Democratic Lawyers Association announced that it regretted that Mr. Mall had accepted an acting judicial appointment and declared that "the association is of the firm view that, having regard to the present political, social, and economic structures existing in the country and the vast number of repressive laws, it is not proper for any of its members to serve in any judicial capacity."[4] This outcry had the desired effect: Mr. Mall has not accepted any further judicial appointment. Since this experience, the opposition of black lawyers to judicial appointment has hardened further and, in some quarters, judicial service is viewed as collaboration.[5]

A related issue here is that of "tokenism." Black lawyers generally are unwilling to accept judicial appointment as long as they are likely to remain tokens on a predominantly white bench. It is unlikely, therefore, that black lawyers will accept judicial appointments without an assurance that the government will embark on an affirmative action policy to ensure that more blacks are brought into the judicial system.

Judges in the TBVC states are mainly white males of South African or Rhodesian origin. In Bophuthatswana, however, there is a single black judge.

Magistrates. The lower courts consist of regional magistrates courts and district magistrates courts. Regional magistrates have criminal jurisdiction only and are limited in their sentencing powers to imposing ten years' imprisonment, a fine of R10,000, or a whipping. District magistrates have both civil and criminal jurisdiction. In civil matters, they are limited in the kind of orders that they may make; in criminal matters, their jurisdiction is limited to imposing imprisonment for one year, a fine of R1,000, or a whipping.[6]

In South Africa proper (excluding the TBVC states and self-governing territories), there are 144 regional magistrates, all of whom are white. Of the 821 district magistrates, 807 are white, 3 are Coloured, and 10 are Indian.[7] There is one African magistrate. There are, however, a number of African magistrates in the self-governing territories and the TBVC states.[8]

The Prosecution. Like England and the United States, South Africa has an adversary system of criminal justice, but unlike England, the prosecution of criminal offenses is vested in the hands of professional prosecutors. An attorney general is attached to each provincial division, charged with the prosecutions in that division. Each attorney general has a staff, operating in the Supreme Court and lower courts, which conducts prosecutions. All attorneys general are white and, with one exception, all the prosecuting advocates in the Supreme Court are white. In the magistrates courts, however, there are a number of black prosecutors. In 1990, of the 994 prosecutors in both regional and district magistrates courts, 28 were African, 61 Coloured, 34 Indian, and 871 white.[9]

Juries and Assessors. South Africa inherited its jury system from England.[10] As jurors were by law drawn exclusively from the white population, racially biased verdicts were commonplace.[11] This resulted in the gradual replacement of trial by jury with trial by a judge sitting alone or trial by a judge and two legally trained assessors. By 1969, when the jury system was finally abolished, the number of jury trials held in South Africa had dropped below 1 percent.[12]

Under the terms of the Criminal Procedure Act, judges of the Supreme Court may, at their discretion, request one or two assessors to sit with them in any criminal trial. Where the death penalty is a possible sentence, however, judges are obliged to sit with two assessors.[13] While the judges retain the power to decide on all questions of law when they sit with assessors, the assessors enjoy an equal status with the judge in deciding on matters of fact. Consequently, assessors may outvote the judge on the factual aspects of the verdict. For instance, in a recent trial involving African National Congress (ANC) "soldiers" charged with murder, the two assessors outvoted the judge on his finding in favor of mitigating circumstances, thereby compelling the judge to impose the death sentence. The law permits a judge to summon as an assessor any person who, in that judge's opinion, "has experience in the administration of justice or skill in any matter which may be considered at the trial."[14] In practice, most assessors are lawyers.

The Criminal Procedure Act does not prohibit the appointment of black assessors. Initially, conventional attitudes about race on the part of many white judges, coupled with the paucity of black legal practitioners, virtually ensured that blacks would not be requested to sit as assessors. In recent times, however, this practice has changed. On a number of occasions over the past few years, judges have appointed black assessors from the ranks of advocates, attorneys, and academic lawyers. In 1985 the judge president of Natal, Justice A. J. Milne, appointed two assessors—one African and one Indian—to sit with him in a major treason trial involving the leadership of the United Democratic Front (UDF). For some years this practice was welcomed by black lawyers, but in the late 1980s, the same arguments that were raised against blacks accepting judicial appointments were invoked against the appointment of assessors.[15]

The Legal Profession. Black lawyers have made an important contribution to the advancement of justice in South Africa. Mohandas Gandhi, who practiced as a lawyer during his twenty-one-year stay in South Africa (1893–1914), used his legal skills to oppose the discriminatory measures to which Indians were subjected.[16] Later, Gandhi's strategy of passive resistance, which he had initiated in South Africa, was adopted by Nelson Mandela and Oliver Tambo, themselves lawyers, when they mobilized the defiance campaign against apartheid laws in 1952–53.[17] Other black lawyers have played a prominent role in South African public life, either as lawyers or as political activists.[18]

Until recently black lawyers were obliged to contend not only with discriminatory practices in the profession and the courts, but also with laws that obstructed their legal practice. The Group Areas Act, for example, was used to prevent black advocates from keeping offices (called chambers) in the same building as their white colleagues and to prohibit black attorneys from occupying offices within the precincts of the courts.[19] Moreover, in 1960 the Appellate Division endorsed a magistrate's ruling that black lawyers were obliged to sit at separate tables in magistrates courts. The organized legal profession did little to overcome these injustices.[20] The Johannesburg Bar acquiesced in the ban on black members occupying chambers with other advocates, while the Law Society of the Transvaal, representing the attorneys' profession, took steps, albeit unsuccessfully, to disbar Nelson Mandela for inciting people to disobey unjust laws during the defiance campaign.[21] Today, black lawyers are free from legislative restraints in the practice of their profession. The structure and organization of the profession, however, continues to place black lawyers at a disadvantage vis-à-vis their white colleagues.

The South African legal profession is modeled on that of England and is divided into advocates (barristers) and attorneys (solicitors). Advocates, who are court specialists, have the sole right of audience before the Supreme Court; attorneys, on the other hand, give legal advice on all issues, draft agreements and wills, effect the transfer of land, and have the right of appearance before the magistrates courts. Clients may consult directly with an attorney, but not with an advocate. Advocates must be instructed (briefed) by an attorney to advise a client or to appear in court.

Advocates view themselves as the senior branch of the profession and constitute an elitist group. They practice only in the major cities where divisions of the Supreme Court are located. Black lawyers have found it difficult to penetrate this branch of the profession, with its higher professional qualifications, geographical limitations, lack of access to the lay public, and elitist traditions. Wittingly or unwittingly, these traditions have imposed obstacles for aspiring black advocates. Consequently, most black lawyers have had little choice but to practice as attorneys.

Thirty years ago, forty-four of the three thousand attorneys in South Africa were black.[22] There were no African advocates. Today, the number of black advocates and attorneys has increased considerably, but they are still outnumbered by their white colleagues. In 1987 the *African Law Review* reported that there were over six thousand attorneys in South Africa, of whom 651 were black (300 Africans). Of the 871 advocates at that time, 77 were black (26 Africans).[23] In the last few years, a substantial number of blacks has entered both branches of the profession, but the black-white ratios of one to ten (attorneys) and one to twelve (advocates) have probably not changed significantly.

Before 1984 blacks were confined to seven exclusively black universities in South Africa proper and the TBVC states, unless they obtained government permits to enroll in the "white universities." Since then they have been permitted to enroll at the other twelve universities, but, in fact, few have entered the Afrikaans-language universities.[24] As a result, since 1984 the annual number of black law graduates has increased substantially. A law degree is not, however, a complete professional qualification. An aspiring attorney must also complete a two-year period of apprenticeship with an attorney, known as articles of clerkship, while an aspiring advocate must serve a four-month period of pupilage with an advocate. As most attorneys are white, it follows that blacks wishing to become attorneys will have to serve their articles of clerkship, in most cases, with white attorneys. Unfortunately, many black law graduates have difficulty in completing their professional training because of their inability to find a qualified attorney who will provide them with articles.

Until recently, all attorneys' firms were racially divided. Today, however, there are a small number of racially integrated firms, most notably those specializing in human rights work.

Black lawyers tend to have practices limited to criminal law, small commercial transactions, matrimonial matters, political trials, and motor vehicle accident work. Corporate tax law remains the preserve of the successful white lawyer. Inevitably, exclusion from this lucrative form of work creates bitterness on the part of black lawyers.

Black legal practitioners have serious complaints about both branches of the profession. White attorneys are accused of obstructing the professional training of aspiring black attorneys by their failure to provide opportunities for articles of clerkship. There are also allegations that the attorneys' admission examination is manipulated by white examiners to restrict the number of blacks entering the profession. The bar, too, has come under criticism. In 1987 a black attorney, Dolly Mokgatle, said the following of the bar:

Educational, financial, and professional reasons account for the small number of black advocates. Today, however, many liberal white advocates express dismay over the present whiteness of the bar and argue that something must be done to remedy the situation. Despite such protestations of concern, there is little evidence that any steps are currently being taken to attract blacks to the bar. The system of pupilage and the bar admission examination, both introduced within the past decade, have placed new hurdles in the way of blacks joining the bar.

Moreover, the bar seems quite content with the retention of the present Latin requirement for admission to the bar, despite the fact that this requirement is known to deter blacks from qualifying as advocates. Worse still, there is no institutional encouragement given to blacks to join the bar. While attorneys regularly visit law schools in order to recruit students as attorneys and some firms make a deliberate effort to employ black articled clerks, there is no such attempt on the part of the bar to encourage blacks to join their ranks.

Generally, blacks are left with the impression that the bar is determined to resist any change that might threaten the cherished traditions it has inherited from England—even if this may seriously jeopardize the long-term interests of the South African legal system. That rigid adherence to its "old ways" will result in the continued exclusion of blacks from the bench does not seem to disturb the bar unduly.[25]

Dissatisfaction with the response of the various professional bodies to the needs and aspirations of black lawyers led to the formation of the Black Lawyers' Association (BLA) and the National Association of Democratic Lawyers (NADEL). The former, which is restricted to African lawyers in the Transvaal and Orange Free State, is concerned primarily with the professional interests of African lawyers, while the latter, a nonracial national body (with a predominantly black membership), is more concerned with political-legal issues affecting the role of lawyers.

Black Attitudes Toward the Law and Its Institutions

Many whites in South Africa seem to be unaware of the resentment and anger that blacks feel toward the legal system. Whites have shared in establishing this legal system, which has served to protect their property and to govern their personal and employment relationships in an equitable manner. For them, it is a fair system of rules and principles administered by fair-minded, erudite judges. For blacks, it is something totally different: an unfair system of rules designed to maintain white privilege and domination, administered by whites for blacks. It was inevitable that blacks would lose confidence in this system of law. Consequently, for the majority of the population, the law is not legitimate.

In 1988 Professor Charles Dlamini of the University of Zululand, one of South Africa's foremost black legal scholars, described the attitudes of blacks toward the South African legal system:

> [E]mpirical studies reveal that blacks have the least confidence in the legal system of South Africa. This is largely due to the government's policy of apartheid, which has created the impression in the minds of many blacks that the law is working against them. Relative ignorance also contributes to this. Not every aspect of South African law discriminates on the basis of race. For instance, South African private law is largely fair and reasonable: It is what may be termed the "law of apartheid" which singles out blacks for discriminatory treatment.
>
> But whatever the quality of South African private law, it is not by this law that the South African legal system is generally judged, but rather by the laws relating to race and state security. Distrust and suspicion of the legal system often leads to refusal to apply for legal aid. Moreover, people put their faith in persons rather than systems. While whites are well represented in the legal profession, blacks are not. Seen from this perspective, therefore, South African law faces a crisis of legitimacy in the black community.[26]

A number of factors are responsible for this alienation from the legal system, for this lack of confidence in the law. The following are probably the most important.

The Absence of Black Participation in the Making of the Laws. Both Robert Sobukwe, the founder of the Pan Africanist Congress (PAC), and Nelson Mandela emphasized the absence of black participation in lawmaking in their trials in the early 1960s. When Sobukwe was tried in 1960 on a charge of incitement to disobey apartheid laws, he refused to recognize the competence of the court and stated that he felt "no moral obligation whatsoever to obey the laws made exclusively by a white minority."[27] He was jailed for three years.

In 1962, when Mandela was charged with inciting workers to strike and leaving South Africa unlawfully, he challenged the competence of the court to try him on two grounds: first, that he, as a black person, could not be given a fair and proper trial; and, second, that he considered himself "neither legally nor morally bound to obey laws made by a Parliament in which he had no representation."[28]

The Discriminatory Nature of the Laws. The laws of apartheid were designed to secure white privilege and domination and to stifle black advancement. Thousands of blacks have been jailed for the most technical of statutory offenses (particularly under the much-hated pass laws), evicted from their homes (under the Group Areas Act and population removal laws), denied a proper education, subjected to the indignity of race discrimination, confined to 13 percent of the land, deprived of their nationality, and denied a say in the making of laws—all in pursuance of apartheid. It is hardly surprising, therefore, that blacks should see the laws of apartheid as an instrument of oppression. However, this perception is not confined to the laws of apartheid. It has extended to the entire legal system, including the liberal Roman-Dutch common law, and to the institutions and officers of the law.

The Virtual Exclusion of Blacks from the Administration of Justice. While South African commercial and private law may not in theory discriminate against blacks, in practice blacks are seldom equal parties in civil disputes. Given the fact that there are no black judges, few black magistrates, and a disproportionately low number of black lawyers, it is not surprising that the officers and institutions of the law are viewed as alien and hostile. In his statement to the court in 1962, Nelson Mandela declared:

> It is true that an African who is charged in a court of law enjoys, on the surface, the same rights and privileges as an accused who is White insofar as the conduct of this trial is concerned. . . .
> In its proper meaning, equality before the law means the right to participate in the making of the laws by which one is governed, a constitution which guarantees democratic rights to all sections of the population, the right to approach the court for protection or relief in the case of the violation of rights guaranteed in the constitution, and the right to take part in the administration of justice as judges, magistrates, attorneys general, law advisers, and similar positions.
> In the absence of these safeguards, the phrase "equality before the law," insofar as it is intended to apply to us, is meaningless and misleading. All the rights and privileges to which I have referred are monopolized by Whites, and we enjoy none of them.

The White man makes all the laws, he drags us before his courts and accuses us, and he sits in judgment over us.

I feel oppressed by the atmosphere of White domination that lurks all around in this courtroom. Somehow this atmosphere calls to mind the inhuman injustices caused to my people outside this courtroom by the same White domination.[29]

The Conduct of the Police. From the beginning of the colonization of South Africa, blacks have been the victims of police rudeness, roughness, and brutality. The enforcement of the pass laws, the population removal laws, and the security laws, in particular, have left a legacy of fear and bitterness. This legacy, which features prominently in the folklore and literature of blacks, will take years to overcome.[30]

The Shortage of Legal Representation. South Africa's legal aid system is hopelessly inadequate. It has been estimated, for example, that one hundred thousand to one hundred fifty thousand people go to jail each year following trials in which they were not represented by a lawyer.[31] The overwhelming majority of those unrepresented are black. As many whites can afford to hire lawyers, but many blacks cannot, a perception is created that the legal system is deliberately rigged against blacks. The shortage of black lawyers creates a problem even for those blacks who can afford legal representation but prefer to hire a black lawyer or have trouble finding a suitable white lawyer to represent them.

Judicial Conduct. Most judges and magistrates are careful not to exacerbate already poor race relations by injudicious comment or conduct in cases involving blacks. Unfortunately, there are exceptions to this rule, which, when given publicity, serve to shape black perceptions of the administration of justice. Professor Dlamini, examining some of these incidents of judicial indiscretions, has observed:

There are a number of pronouncements which have emanated from the bench that seem to betray a racial bias, or at least the absence of total impartiality. These belong to what has been dubbed "racial mythology." They include unsubstantiated statements such as that made in *R v. Tusini* where the trial judge had taken judicial notice of the "fact" that blacks can and do recognize people they know in comparative darkness in circumstances in which it would be almost impossible for a white person to do so. In *R v. A* and *S v. M* judicial notice was taken at trial that black women submit to rape without protest, while in *S v. Sihlani* a magistrate stated that a black woman will generally not support the evidence of her husband against her lover. In the older case of *Mcunu v. R* the court remarked that black witnesses who gave evidence of an alibi were generally liars. . . .

Many of these apparently discriminatory comments and attitudes are not based on conscious prejudice, but on unconscious racial attitudes which judicial officers have picked up during the formative years of their lives. Indeed, few openly racist utterances emanate from the bench today. In many cases, the discrimination is more subtle and unconscious and this may account for the denial that race is a factor in the administration of justice. The case of *S v. Magwaza* is such an example. The judges both in the trial court and on appeal referred to a middle-aged white woman, who was one of the witnesses, as "Mrs. Momple," while the black witnesses were referred to by their first names irrespective of their age. There is no doubt that these differentiations were made along racial lines. They may be perceived as racially motivated, as evidence of the fact that white judges associate with blacks mainly on a master-servant level and therefore treat black persons in court in a similar fashion. This might be regarded as petty discrimination, but the thoughtless use of language in this manner by the courts has a negative effect upon the black community's perception of the courts and the law.

In the light of cases of this kind, the black public must be pardoned if it has the impression that the portrayal of justice as a blindfolded woman with scales and a sword is a caricature that has nothing to do with what sometimes happens in practice. Also, blacks must be forgiven if they perceive justice as favouring the fairer colour.[32]

Sentencing. Sentencing is a highly individualistic exercise. Cases are never identical, as the judge or magistrate must consider both the facts of the crime and the personal circumstances of the accused before sentence is passed. Individual differences notwithstanding, however, it is still possible to compare sentences passed and to draw certain conclusions from these sentences.

South African judges and magistrates are generally sensitive to the issue of racial disparities in sentencing and have often warned that the appearance of one law for whites and another for blacks should be avoided.[33] Unfortunately, however, South African criminal justice provides ample evidence of racial disparities in sentencing.

Until 1990, when the state president declared a moratorium on the implementation of the death penalty, pending legislation, to limit it to extreme cases, South Africa was among the three highest executing states in the world.[34] Since 1910 over forty-two hundred persons have been executed, of whom a disproportionately high number have been black.[35] Inevitably, this has led to accusations of racial bias in the execution of the death penalty. While it may be difficult to substantiate such accusations in cases of murder, it is clear that race has often played a determining factor in the sentences imposed for rape. For instance, Barend van Niekerk, a white campaigner against the death penalty, wrote in 1979:

> Since 1911, for instance, more than 150 blacks have been executed for rape, in the vast majority of instances so it would seem (but the statistics are less than enlightening) for the rape of white women; not a single white (according to my enquiries and information and available statistics) has ever been sentenced to death, let alone executed, for the rape of a black woman. In the same period, it seems as if only three executions took place of whites, all for the rape of white children of tender age. It is interesting to note that there is reason to believe that more black women are raped by white men than vice versa.[36]

The killing of whites by blacks has frequently resulted in the imposition of the death penalty; but the same cannot be said of the converse situation. Whites found guilty of killing blacks are rarely sentenced to death, although there have been a number of notable exceptions in recent years.[37] In many cases, whites convicted of killing blacks have been sentenced to extremely lenient sentences, as shown by the following incidents listed in the 1985 issue of the *South African Journal on Human Rights*:[38]

- A twenty-year-old white youth who beat a black man to death with karate sticks was sentenced to twelve hundred hours in prison, to be served on weekends. The youth was walking down a street with his girlfriend and bragged that he was going to kill a *houtkop* (wooden head). He killed the next black man he encountered.

- Three young white men who kicked a black man to death because they thought he was tampering with their car were sentenced to five cuts (lashes) each.

- A national serviceman, twenty-two-year-old Stephanus

Jooste, murdered a fifteen-year-old black girl by knocking her down with a stone and running over her twice with his car; he also assaulted three other innocent black pedestrians. Jooste was jailed for an effective ten years by the Pretoria Supreme Court. Jooste's companion, Jan Welgemoed, who took part in the girl's killing, was sentenced to five lashes. In addition, Acting Justice A. P. Myburgh sentenced Welgemoed to five years in jail, all of which was suspended, for assaulting two of the other pedestrians.

- Five schoolboys who beat and kicked two black men to death at their school sports ground in August 1984 were sentenced by Justice D. Curlewis to work for fifty-two consecutive weekends in a hospital. The fifteen- and sixteen-year-old boys were found guilty of culpable homicide after the battered body of William Nkosi, age thirty-six, was discovered on the sports field and Solomon Kuna, age sixty-eight, died of multiple wounds and bruises in the hospital.

- Three young white immigrants who went on a rampage of racial revenge were sentenced in the Witwatersrand Local Division to an effective ten years' imprisonment by Justice T. T. Spoelstra. Two of their victims died as a result of blows inflicted by a pick handle, a hammer handle, and a knobkerrie (a short, wooden club with a knob at one end). Two others were severely beaten. Mark Elliot Macedo, age twenty-two, Richard Gary Kegel, age twenty-two, and João dos Santos Loureiro, age twenty-one, assaulted the four innocent black pedestrians as retribution for the stabbing of a close friend by three unidentified black men. The accused pleaded guilty to and were convicted on two counts of murder with extenuating circumstances and two of assault with intent to do grievous bodily harm.

- A Johannesburg policeman, Neil Harker, age twenty-one, was fined R30 or fifteen days' imprisonment by a magistrate following the death of a Coloured dancer, Benito Holmes. Harker was convicted of assaulting Holmes outside an all-night café in Hillbrow after he saw Holmes with a white woman. Harker, with two others, abused the couple. Then he summoned Holmes out of the café to fight. It was found that Harker had punched Holmes in the mouth, knocking him to the pavement. But he was acquitted on a charge of culpable homicide because the court accepted medical evidence that the fall, not the blow, was the cause of death.

- Four policemen from Dirkiesdorp police station at Volksrust were charged with culpable homicide. They had arrested Absolom Manana and his son, Themba, on suspicion of stock theft, and had tortured them with electric shocks and suffocation by hooding. Mr. Manana senior told the court he had screamed, sweated, cried, and writhed on the floor as the shocks were administered. He could tell the policemen nothing about the cattle thefts. Mr. Themba Manana was found dead in his cell some time afterward, and evidence was that he had died of asphyxiation, probably caused by electrocution. The police officers—except for one who was found to be present as an interpreter—pleaded guilty to one or both of these assaults, including the administering of electric shocks, but stated that it was not their intention to seriously injure Mr. Manana. The trial judge stated that those who had tortured Themba Manana could not have foreseen his death, and they were acquitted. As they did not have the intention to kill, they could not be convicted of murder. The accused were found guilty of assault. It was observed that they had not been acting out of self-interest. All the men were given suspended prison sentences and fined.

Racial bias in sentencing was highlighted in 1989 by a case heard by the Louis Trichard circuit court. A white farmer brutally assaulted one of his farmworkers, who had accidentally killed the farmer's dog. The farmer then chained the worker to a tree and assaulted him again with sticks. He was left chained to the tree, where he died of a brain hemorrhage resulting from the beating. The farmer was sentenced to a fine of R3,000. In addition, he was ordered to pay compensation of R130 per month for sixty months to the worker's widow. A five-year prison sentence was suspended. A petition for the judge's impeachment on grounds of racist bias in sentencing was presented to Parliament by Helen Suzman, M.P., and was rejected by the speaker of Parliament.[39]

Although sentences of the kind described above are not necessarily representative of the sentences imposed in most cases, they have contributed substantially to the perception that racial bias exists in sentencing.

The average black layperson is not able to systematically assess the manner in which judges have interpreted the laws of apartheid, since most people's perceptions depend on press reports of sentencing and judicial demeanor. Black lawyers who have carefully followed the performance of the judiciary in the interpretation of the laws of apartheid have substantial grounds for disquiet. They know of seminal cases in which the Appeal Court, faced with a choice in the interpretation of a law or ruling, chose the interpretation that most favored white interests. They know of the decision in *Minister of the Interior v. Lockhat,* in which the Appellate Division held that the Group Areas Act represented a "colossal social experiment" and therefore "must have envisaged" unequal implementation—despite the fact that the statute itself failed to authorize unequal treatment of the different races.[40] They know of the decisions in *R. v. Pitje,* in which the Appellate Division approved the "reasonableness" of separate court tables for black legal practitioners—despite the absence of any law prescribing such a separation.[41] They know of the many occasions on which the Appellate Division has exercised its choice in favor of the executive in the interpretation of the security laws and emergency regulations.[42] Decisions of this kind have influenced the attitude of black intellectuals toward the judiciary and added fuel to the debate over the illegitimacy of the judicial system.

The lack of confidence in the legal system requires urgent redress if a future South Africa is to be governed by the rule of law. The abolition of racist and repressive laws will go a long way toward developing black confidence in the law, but on its own will not be enough. It also will be necessary to bring more blacks into the administration of justice at all levels. The legal profession will have to make concerted efforts to train more black attorneys and advocates. Blacks will have to be appointed to the bench, even if this involves a break with the tradition of appointing judges from the ranks of senior counsel only.[43] Blacks will have to be involved in the administration of justice in other ways too, as assessors or as jurors. The urgency of this matter is stressed by Professor Dlamini:

[S]erious consideration should be given to the appointment or increase in the appointment of blacks as prosecutors, magistrates, and judges. . . . It may be contended that it is difficult to appoint blacks as judges because of the lack of suitably qualified blacks.

Indeed, this may be so, but steps should be taken to remedy the situation. This could be done by offering more bursaries for blacks to study law and by opening up opportunities for them after completing their studies.

Affirmative action should be adopted in the appointment of black judges. This in itself is nothing new, but . . . it may convince many blacks that race has no influence on the administration of justice.[44]

If the inherited traditions of the legal profession, such as the division between advocates and attorneys and the practice of judicial appointments, obstruct the process of expanding black participation in the justice system, these traditions will have to be abandoned. In order to achieve a new society under law, respect for the law, its institutions, and its officers will have to be restored. This will be possible only when the majority of the population feels that the legal system is theirs and not some alien system prescribed by a minority, for the majority.

Chapter V
Looking Ahead
John Dugard

Rapid and profound changes occurred in southern Africa as the 1980s gave way to the 1990s. Namibia moved smoothly to independence under the joint supervision of South Africa and the United Nations, bringing an end to a forty-year dispute. In 1988 the African National Congress (ANC) published a set of constitutional guidelines for a democratic South Africa (see Appendix D), and in 1989 issued a statement of its preconditions for negotiations, which was endorsed by the Organization of African Unity in the Harare Declaration. The South African Law Commission, a government-appointed body charged with the task of law reform, recommended the adoption of a bill of rights for South Africa. P. W. Botha retired as state president and was replaced by F. W. de Klerk. Prominent political prisoners were released, the strict ban on political gatherings was relaxed, and South Africa experienced a unique outpouring of political expression.

On February 2, 1990, in his address at the opening of Parliament, President De Klerk announced the lifting of the thirty-year-old ban on the ANC, the Pan Africanist Congress (PAC), and the South African Communist Party (SACP) and called for negotiations aimed at achieving "a totally new and just constitutional dispensation in which every inhabitant will enjoy equal rights." He stated:

> The agenda is open and the overall aims to which we are aspiring should be acceptable to all reasonable South Africans.
> Among other things, those aims include a new, democratic constitution, universal franchise, no domination, equality before an independent judiciary, the protection of minorities as well as of individual rights, freedom of religion, a sound economy based on proven economic principles and private enter-

prise; and dynamic programmes directed at better education, health services, housing and social conditions for all.

In this connection, Mr. Nelson Mandela could play an important part. The Government has noted that he has declared himself to be willing to make a constructive contribution to the peaceful political process in South Africa.[1]

Soon after De Klerk made this speech, Nelson Mandela was released from prison after twenty-seven years.

The unbanning of the ANC and the release of Nelson Mandela were followed by the return of prominent political exiles who had been granted special immunity from prosecution in order to participate in negotiations. Voices that had been silenced and ideologies that had been suppressed for over thirty years were again heard throughout the land. Political life was transformed as the search for a new national order began.

F. W. de Klerk's commitment to a "just constitutional dispensation" was confirmed by talks held between the government and the ANC in May 1990, at Groote Schuur in Cape Town. This meeting led to the adoption of the Groote Schuur Minute, in which both parties agreed "to a peaceful process of negotiations" and to the establishment of a working group to consider the definition of "political offense" in order to facilitate the release of political prisoners and the granting of indemnity to exiles.[2] At the same time the government began to review security legislation and to work toward lifting the state of emergency in order to remove the legislative obstacles in the way of open political activity. In June 1990 the state of emergency was lifted in all parts of the country except Natal and KwaZulu, where it was ended in October.

In August a second round of talks between the government and the ANC was held that resulted in the Pretoria Minute, in which "the ANC announced that it was suspending all armed actions with immediate effect."[3] A joint working group report on the definition of political offense was approved by both parties, and April 30, 1991, was set as the target date for the release of political prisoners.[4] Deep concern was expressed about the violence in the country and both parties committed themselves to a peaceful resolution of the conflict through negotiations.

The new relationship between the government and the ANC did not bring peace to the country. On the contrary, the violence in Natal escalated and spread to the black townships around Johannesburg in the Transvaal. Although the causes of and motives for the violence are unclear, it mainly took the form of conflict between the ANC and Inkatha, which transformed itself from a cultural movement into a political party—the Inkatha Freedom Party (IFP)—in July 1990. Calls for peace from ANC Deputy President Nelson Mandela and IFP president Chief Mangosuthu Buthelezi, after a meeting in January 1991, had little impact on the violence, particularly in the Witwatersrand, where a virtual state of war developed between Zulu migrant workers accommodated in all-male hostels and township residents sympathetic to the ANC. To aggravate matters, the police were accused of siding with Inkatha supporters or, at least, of taking inadequate steps to quell the violence.

The violence slowed down the negotiation process as the ANC repeatedly expressed its lack of confidence in the government's determination to suppress the warlike behavior of Inkatha supporters. In addition, disagreement surfaced over the proper procedure for the adoption of a new constitution. While the ANC favored the adoption of a constitution by an elected constituent assembly, of the kind that approved the Namibian Constitution of 1990, the government insisted that negotiations for a new constitution should initially be undertaken by a multiparty conference consisting of those political organizations that have proven support in the country.

In his opening address to Parliament in 1991, F. W. de Klerk rejected the idea of an elected constituent assembly and of an interim government for the transitional period consisting of the major political parties (see Appendix E).[5] The government's attitude was understandable, as it would lose its position as a principal actor in negotiations for a new constitution if this task were handed over to a democratically elected constituent assembly. The ANC seemed to be sensitive to this political reality and agreed to participate in a multiparty conference as a first step toward the adoption of a new constitution.

A new constitution would require the approval of either a referendum or an elected constituent assembly if it was to enjoy legitimacy. This was not denied by the government, whose insistence on a multiparty conference seemed to be aimed at ensuring that the government played a major role in the adoption of the basic principles of a new constitution, even if these were later fleshed out by a constituent assembly. In Namibia, the constituent assembly was guided by principles approved by the Security Council of the United Nations. It seemed likely that the government envisaged that a multiparty conference would play a similar role in the drafting of the new South African constitution.

By mid-1991 no progress had been made in constitutional negotiations, despite the repeal of the remaining discriminatory laws and the drastic amendment of the security laws. The lack of progress was due largely to concerns about the role of the police in the confrontations between Inkatha and ANC supporters and the failure of the government to release all persons claimed by the ANC to be political prisoners. The postponement of the election of a new national executive committee by the ANC probably also contributed to the ANC's delay in embarking on negotiations.

Nevertheless, during 1990–91 a number of conferences and workshops on the form of a new constitution were held. The ANC's Constitutional Committee played a particularly important role. In April 1991 it published *A Bill of Rights for a New South Africa* and *A Discussion Document on Structures and Principles of a Constitution for a Democratic South Africa*, which stimulated open debate both within and outside the ANC (see Appendix F). Government spokespersons from time to time expressed themselves on the new constitution in a manner that suggested the government was actively rethinking its attitude toward the constitutional protection of minorities, or group rights. Both principal political actors—the government and the ANC—seemed determined to press for a constitution that would serve them well in government or in opposition. This spirit augured well for the adoption of a democratic and nonracial constitution for South Africa.

This concluding chapter does not attempt to forecast the new constitutional system that will emerge from the ashes of the apartheid state. Instead, it examines the constitutional options for South Africa and the current debate over these options, the future of human rights and the likely mechanisms for protecting them, the redress of present injustices by means of affirmative action and the redistribution of wealth, and the role of the legal order in structuring a post-apartheid society.

Constitutional Options and Issues

When he resigned from Parliament and from his position as the leader of the Progressive Federal Party in February 1986, Frederik Van Zyl Slabbert told Parliament:

> The tricameral Parliament is a hopelessly flawed and failed constitutional experiment. It does not begin to solve the problem of political domination; in fact, it compounds it.[6]

In the early 1990s, few would disagree with this assessment. By excluding Africans completely, and by failing to give Coloureds and Indians any real power in Parliament, the 1983 Constitution sealed its own fate. After 1984 South Africa became a society in violent conflict, and in large measure the blame must be laid at the door of the Constitution. There was, therefore, an almost universal demand for its abolition. Even those who conceived and nurtured it recognized that it had failed; hence, President De Klerk's call for negotiations leading to a just constitution with equal rights for all (see Appendix G).

There is little doubt that all major political groups in South Africa—the National Party, the ANC, the PAC, Chief Mangosuthu Gatsha Buthelezi's IFP, the homeland governments, the Democratic Party, the Labor Party, the other political parties in the House of Representatives, and even the white Conservative Party—endorse President De Klerk's call for a just constitution.

Until mid-1991, there was little serious debate, as compared to political posturing, about constitutional programs. However, the debate assumed realistic proportions as a result of the talks about negotiations between the National Party government and the ANC. In all probability, the following issues will feature prominently on the negotiations agenda:

- the nature of the state: unitary, federal, confederal, or partitioned;
- constitutional checks and balances to protect minorities;
- a bill of rights, including the redistribution of land and wealth, and affirmative action.

Nature of the State

The primary political groups disagree fundamentally over what type of constitutional order will best advance justice and guarantee equality. Options range from territorial partition (Conservative Party) to majority rule in a unitary state (ANC), with federalism (Democratic Party), confederalism, and a wide range of consociational models in the middle.

Partition. For many years, the idea of a South Africa partitioned into a whites-only Afrikaner state and a multiracial, predominantly black state has been advocated by Afrikaner extremists. While the National Party itself pursued a policy of territorial fragmentation aimed at relocating blacks politically, if not physically, in the homelands, the question of partition became submerged in the homelands policy. Now that the National Party has abandoned the homelands scheme as unrealistic, and the prospect of a nonracial state has become a reality, partition has again surfaced as a political policy among white rightwing groups.

The extent of the territorial demand varies from group to group. Whereas one Afrikaner faction claims the Transvaal, Orange Free State, and northern Natal as historically Afrikaner territory, another, more realistic claim envisages the creation of a *boerestaat* (Afrikaner state) in the barren reaches of the northern Cape and Orange Free State.

Partition is improbable, however, since no clearly demarcated whites-only territory exists. The wealth of the country is concentrated in the Witwatersrand in the Transvaal, where integration is more advanced than elsewhere in South Africa. Partition is therefore rejected by most whites (both Afrikaans- and English-speaking) and blacks as a dream of the "lunatic right." At present, the extent of white, particularly Afrikaner, opposition to a nonracial society is hard to gauge. If, however, this factor becomes an obstacle to the creation of a nonracial democracy, and Afrikaner extremists would be satisfied with a separate state in the underpopulated northern Cape, partition may well be considered. Memories of the traumatic partitioning of India and Palestine must, however, surely deter any serious consideration of this option, except as a final resort.

Confederation. As long as the National Party accepted the concept of independent ethnic homelands as the solution to South Africa's racial problems, the party favored a confederation of sovereign states consisting of South Africa and the independent homelands. In the early 1990s, the confederal option has virtually no support.

Three of the independent homelands—Transkei, Ciskei, and Venda—seem to be willing to reincorporate into South Africa; and the government, acknowledging the failure of the homelands policy, seems to be prepared to negotiate their return. This is a fortuitous development, as it is clear that the ANC, which has consistently opposed the homelands policy, will not accept the continuation of a fragmented South Africa and is determined to return to the pre-1976 borders.

Bophuthatswana alone remains committed to a separate existence. On February 20, 1990, President Lucas Mangope declared that Bophuthatswana would "be an independent state 100 years from now."[7] It is difficult to take this claim seriously, however, since Bophuthatswana's "independence" depends largely on South African military and economic support. If South Africa's support were withdrawn, Bophuthatswana could not survive. Since Bophuthatswana, the last supporter of confederalism, lacks credibility, the confederal option is probably no longer on the agenda of South Africa's political negotiations.

Federation vs. a Unitary State. In 1909, when the Union of South Africa was being planned, support for federation came both from Natal, which feared Afrikaner domination, and from white liberals, who argued that the interests of the black majority would be more secure in a federation than in a white-dominated unitary state. These forces were, however, too weak to withstand the strong demand for a unitary state by leaders such as Jan Smuts and John X. Merriman, who saw in a union of the four British colonies—the Cape of Good Hope, Natal, the Orange River Colony, and the Transvaal—an opportunity for the unification of Afrikaner and Briton and the formulation of a uniform policy to deal with the "native question."[8] As a sop to the federalists, the four colonies were allowed to retain their identity as provinces, with limited regional powers. Since 1910, therefore, South Africa has been a unitary state with a powerful central Parliament, modeled on that of Westminster. Under this system, Afrikaner and Briton united to maintain white domination and to deny black political advancement.

In the 1960s a white opposition party, the Progressive Party, started to advocate federalism in reaction to the injustices perpetrated by a central Parliament in a unitary state and in the belief that racial justice could be best achieved under a federation.[9] The successor to the Progressive Party, the Democratic Party, remains committed to a federal solution.

The Democratic Party advocates a territorial federation based largely on the four provinces. Other federalists advocate different forms of federalism; notably, a "race federation" based on ethnic groupings rather than territorial divisions or "segmental autonomy," a territorial federation in which the units would be largely ethnically determined.[10]

The ANC has consistently opposed federalism. In its constitutional guidelines, published in 1988, the organization declared:

a. South Africa shall be an independent, unitary, democratic and nonracial state;
b. (i) Sovereignty shall belong to the people as a whole and shall be exercised through one central legislature, executive and administration.
   (ii) Provision shall be made for the delegation of the powers of the central authority to subordinate administrative

units for purposes of more efficient administration and democratic participation.

Federalism is seen by the ANC as a device to deny majority rule, to obstruct national unity, and to give constitutional recognition to ethnicity. The ANC's attitude was summed up by Nathaniel M. Masemola, a member of the ANC Legal and Constitutional Committee, in the following way:

> South Africa has had a unitary constitution since the establishment of the Union of South Africa in 1910. The unitary structure (as distinct from the colour-bar clauses of the Union of South Africa Act 1909) has served the country well since that date and has never been seriously questioned by the mass of the people. However, now that white power seems to be seriously threatened, loud voices are clamouring from inside the white laager, calling for change from unitarianism to federalism or even confederalism. This call is clearly based on fear of majority rule rather than on a rational judgment of the real interests or needs of the people of South Africa.[11]

These concerns have substance with respect to proposals for a race federation or segmental autonomy—that is, a territorial federation in which the independent homelands of Transkei, Bophuthatswana, Venda, and Ciskei and the self-governing homelands are accorded the status of federal units.

Similar objections may be raised to suggestions that South Africa be transformed into a cantonal system. One of the most popular suggestions of this kind envisages a Swiss-style federation, with 306 cantons based on the present 306 magisterial districts, each with an average population of eighty thousand.[12] Such fragmentation cannot be considered seriously, as it inevitably would promote ethnicity and undermine national unity.

A territorial federation based on historical divisions—that is, the four provinces of 1910—is less easy to dismiss.[13] Such a federation would not perpetuate ethnicity or deny majority rule, as blacks comprise the majority in all four provinces. Nor would it stifle national unity any more than the present provincial system, which has stimulated healthy regional rivalry without detracting from a sense of national purpose. A federation of this kind, however, would weaken the power of the central government and, in so doing, would arguably provide greater protection for individual liberty and minority rights.

The ANC's continuing opposition to federation is clear from the

Discussion Document on Structures and Principles of a Constitution for a Democratic South Africa. Part 2 of this document states that "South Africa should be reconstructed as a nonracial, nonsexist, democratic and unitary republic," which is to include Transkei, Bophuthatswana, Venda, and Ciskei. The ANC is, however, sensitive to the dangers of centralization and to the need for some degree of regional autonomy. The commentary of the *Discussion Document* declares that "a unified South Africa shall not be an over-centralised, impersonal and over-bureaucratised country" and that regional governments should be established provided they are not "devised as a means of perpetuating privilege, ethnic or racial divisions along territorial zones" but instead are "based upon the distribution of population, availability of economic resources, communications and urban/rural balance."

Whether South Africa is to remain a unitary state, including Transkei, Bophuthatswana, Venda, and Ciskei, or to become a federation is one of the most important issues in the constitutional negotiations. In mid-1991 the Democratic Party was the only committed proponent of territorial federation, but other groups, such as Inkatha and the (Coloured) Labor Party, have shown support for such a solution in the past.[14] Moreover, the independent homeland states will probably feel more comfortable about reincorporation into a federation than into a unitary state. The attitude of the National Party remains unclear. In the past, it was against federalism because it was the policy of an opposition political party. As National Party policy draws closer to that of the Democratic Party, it is possible that the party will urge a federal solution.

It seems, therefore, that the differences between federalists and unitarists is narrowing. If the ANC can accept some form of autonomy for regions that have a historical or economic—but not ethnic—identity of their own, it is probable that a compromise of the kind reached in 1910 will be repeated, with federation rejected but a measure of regional autonomy accepted.

Constitutional Checks and Balances

Universal adult franchise—or one person, one vote—is a minimum precondition for any viable political compact in South Africa. In a unitary state modeled on the Westminster pattern, this would result in a winner-takes-all government and open the door to domination by the majority party; hence, the minority political and ethnic groups oppose such a system. Although some type of federation would reduce the likelihood of majoritarian domination, there are also demands for additional constitutional techniques to tame the power of the majority. The checks and balances most frequently suggested in South Africa are the instruments of consociational engineering advocated by American scholars such as Donald L. Horowitz and Arend Lijphart—namely, government by coalition, the minority veto, proportional representation, vote pooling, and a powerful upper house.[15]

Several of these schemes are premised on the recognition of ethnic minorities in the constitution. The notion of a minority veto presupposes the vesting of a veto power in designated minority groups; some forms of vote pooling require members of the executive or legislature to win the support of a substantial portion of each designated ethnic group in order to be elected. Although schemes of this kind are incorporated in the constitutions of several ethnically divided societies, such devices would probably not be acceptable in a post-apartheid South Africa because of the deep antagonism that apartheid has engendered toward any form of ethnic engineering. This antagonism was also a factor in Namibia, where the independence constitution studiously refrained from any recognition of ethnic minorities, despite the ethnic pluralism of the country.[16] The KwaZulu-Natal Indaba Constitutional Proposals of 1986, which sought to create a regional constitution for Natal, include a minority veto in a scheme that explicitly recognizes the ethnic groups of that province. Much of the hostility toward these proposals was caused by these provisions.

The separate voters' roll is another ethnic-based strategy for minority protection that enjoys some support in South Africa. An extreme form involves completely separate rolls for the different groups, while a more moderate proposal is for a common voters' roll for one legislative chamber and racially separate rolls for another chamber. Neither proposal is likely to gain support from any organization opposed to ethnicity in the constitution.

Proportional representation ensures a fairer representation of minorities in the legislature than the single-member constituency system that prevails in South Africa, Britain, and the United States. Moreover, it frequently results in a system of coalition politics that secures some protection for minorities. This is illustrated by the 1989 Namibian election, in which proportional representation resulted in all major political parties obtaining representation in the constituent assembly that drafted the Namibian Constitution and led to a positive process of consensus politics between the South West Africa People's Organization (SWAPO) and the representatives of minority groups. Proportional representation, a prominent feature in the Namibian Constitution, has acquired political legitimacy within South Africa itself.[17]

Initially, both the National Party and the ANC favored retention of the existing electoral system, which, by recognizing only one winner in each constituency, entrenches a two-party system and makes it virtually impossible for minority parties to enter the legislature or to obtain any influence in government. The principal actors, however, have shifted their positions and both now favor proportional representation. In its April 1991 *Discussion Document*, the ANC Constitutional Committee justified proportional representation on the grounds that it encourages participation in the political process of all groups with significant support and leads to a more exact political reflection of the popularity of parties. In addition, the committee might have said, proportional representation allows minority ethnic groups to organize themselves into political parties and to achieve representation in the legislature as political parties rather than as ethnic groups. As Namibia has shown, proportional representation dispenses with the necessity for recognizing minority groups in the constitution itself.

Implicit in the ANC and National Party endorsement of proportional representation is the recognition that a coalition government is likely in a new South Africa. Their acceptance of such an approach is confirmed by the manner in which both parties seem determined to expand their power base by forging links with other political parties.

In some quarters, an upper house or senate is viewed as an instrument that will limit the powers of a popularly elected lower house. The National Party's plan for the composition and powers of the upper house is as yet unknown, but there are suggestions that the plan envisages an upper house composed of representatives of different regions or special interest groups with powers similar to those of the U.S. Senate. While the ANC *Discussion Document* accepts the need for an upper house, it contemplates a body very different from that apparently preferred by the National Party. It states:

> The second house of Parliament will be the Senate, which will also be elected according to universal suffrage without regard to race, gender, colour, ethnic origin, language or creed. The Senate will neither be a corporatist chamber made up of interest groups (youth, labour, women, or business or other groups) nor will it represent ethnic or so-called "community" interests. The electoral system will, however, be different from that adopted for the elections of the National Assembly, and will make provi-

sion for representation on a regional but not on an ethnic basis. The Senate will be the guardian of the constitution, with power to refer any dispute concerning the interpretation or application of the constitution to the appropriate court for its decision and the power to review. Where appropriate, the Senate may delay the passage of legislation passed by the National Assembly, but it will not have the power to veto legislation.[18]

Both the National Party and the ANC seem to agree that a post-apartheid constitution will contain checks and balances aimed at decentralizing power, securing fair representation for minority groups, and protecting individual liberties. But such goals will have to be achieved without any reference to ethnicity.

A Bill of Rights

South Africa's human rights record is well known. After World War II, when the community of nations began to invoke the instrument of the law to protect and advance human rights, South Africa introduced the policy of apartheid, which used the legal process to promote racial privilege and injustice. Internationally, South Africa refused to accept emerging human rights norms. It declined to endorse the Universal Declaration of Human Rights of 1948 (together with the Soviet bloc and Saudi Arabia), and like the United States, it is not a party to any international human rights convention. Domestically, the South African government refused to restructure its constitution to provide for the protection of human rights and instead used the law relentlessly to enforce race discrimination and suppress opposition. A constitution that gave Parliament unbridled power and contained no bill of rights rendered the courts virtually powerless against apartheid.

Dissenting voices were raised in support of human rights. In 1955 a "Congress of the People," convened by the Congress Alliance, in which the ANC played a dominant role, adopted the Freedom Charter. This document, which remains a manifesto of the liberation struggle, has been described by Albie Sachs as "amongst the most advanced documents of its time, spelling out in clear and coherent language economic and social rights that were to become internationally agreed upon only in the 1960s and people's rights that were only to be formulated in the 1970s and 1980s."[19] (A leading ANC lawyer, Sachs endured a quarter-century of exile and in 1988 sustained serious injuries in Mozambique from a car bomb believed to have been planted by agents of the South African government.) The Freedom Charter was followed in 1960 by a more orthodox proposal by the Progressive Party for a bill of rights aimed at protecting principal civil and political rights.[20] However, successive governments under Prime Ministers Hendrik F. Verwoerd and B. J. Vorster ensured that a human rights culture did not develop. The security police harassed and detained human rights activists, and severe curbs were placed on the advocacy of human rights.

In 1961 and again in 1983, the National Party government expressly rejected proposals to include a bill of rights in the Constitution. The ideological reason for this position was spelled out by the President's Council, a constituent body of the South African Parliament, when it declared that a bill of rights was unacceptable because of the humanist emphasis it placed on individual rights vis-à-vis the authority of the state, "whereas particularly the Afrikaner with his Calvinist background is more inclined to place the emphasis on the state and the maintenance of the state."[21]

The 1980s brought a new interest in the legal protection of human rights. New organizations, both within and outside the legal professions, were created to monitor human rights violations and to educate the South African public about the methods employed to protect human rights in other countries. Individual judges began to speak out in favor of a bill of rights. The founding of the United Democratic Front (UDF) resulted in a revival of interest in the Freedom Charter. A regional conference in the province of Natal, in which the principal white and black political actors participated, proposed the adoption of a bill of rights for that province, and in 1985 the South African government enacted a declaration of rights for Namibia.[22]

In 1985 the government declared a state of emergency, and new arbitrary police powers were introduced to cope with the "unrest" that resulted from the enactment of the 1983 Constitution. In the face of these developments, the prospect of a bill of rights seemed more remote than ever. Then, with no explanation, the minister of justice, Hendrik J. Coetsee, announced in Parliament on April 23, 1986, that he had requested the South African Law Commission, whose members are appointed by the government, to investigate the role of the courts in the protection of group rights and individual rights and to consider the desirability of introducing a bill of rights.[23]

Why this sudden about-face? Was it because the government had genuinely changed its attitude toward human rights? Or was it because the government realized that such an instrument might protect whites, particularly Afrikaners, against a future black government? Or was it to forestall imminent U.S. sanctions by sending out a belated signal that South Africa was prepared to model itself constitutionally on the United States in order to promote human rights?

The fact that the National Party, which is historically hostile to a bill of rights, instructed a statutory body appointed by the state president to report on the issue inevitably led to suspicion and cynicism about the motives for the study and its likely outcome. It was widely believed that the Law Commission would produce a report that exalted group rights and, by implication, Afrikaner group rights over individual rights. Opponents of the government were unenthusiastic about a bill of rights for a second reason. They argued that the South African situation was a liberation struggle and not a human rights problem.[24] Consequently, the priority was liberation and not the protection of human rights.

Attitudes toward the need for a bill of rights underwent a profound change as a result of the publication of the ANC Constitutional Guidelines in 1988 and the South African Law Commission's *Working Paper on Group and Human Rights* in March 1989. The ANC Constitutional Guidelines pay homage to the 1955 Freedom Charter and declare that it "must be converted from a vision for the future to a constitutional reality." According to the guidelines:

> The constitution shall include a Bill of Rights based on the Freedom Charter. Such a Bill of Rights shall guarantee the fundamental human rights of all citizens irrespective of race, colour, sex, or creed, and shall provide appropriate mechanisms for their enforcement.

The rights to be guaranteed include the freedoms of association, expression, thought, worship, and the press. But nothing further is said about the mechanisms for enforcement.

Since the publication of these guidelines, a bill of rights has featured prominently in ANC constitutional pronouncements. The Harare Declaration of August 1989 provides that in the post-apartheid society, "All shall enjoy universally recognized human rights, freedoms and civil liberties, protected under an entrenched Bill of Rights." ANC spokespersons have also extolled the virtues of a bill of rights and accepted the need for the protection of these rights by an independent, nonracial judiciary exercising powers of judicial review.[25] The commitment of the ANC to human rights is stressed by Albie Sachs:

For those of us who have suffered arbitrary detention, torture and solitary confinement, who have seen our homes crushed by bulldozers, who have been moved from pillar to post at the whim of officials, who have been victims of assassination attempts, and state-condoned thuggery, who have lived for years as rightless people under states of emergency in prison, in exile, outlaws because we fought for liberty, the theme of human rights is central to our existence.[26]

The South African Law Commission's report contains a draft bill of rights and a discussion of the various methods by which such an instrument might be implemented. The draft bill is not intended as a final statement, but as a working paper designed to elicit comment. Its emphasis is on individual rights. The basic civil and political rights to be found in most international instruments and bills of rights receive endorsement. It proclaims the right to life (but fails to outlaw capital punishment), liberty, privacy, and fair trial; guarantees the freedoms of speech, assembly, association, and movement; and condemns torture and cruel, inhuman, or degrading treatment. Equality before the law is recognized, and discrimination on grounds of race and gender is outlawed. Most important, the draft bill asserts "the right of all citizens over the age of eighteen years to exercise the vote on a basis of equality in respect of all legislative institutions at regular and periodical elections and at referendums." In the interest of the security of the state or other public interests, the rights granted in the bill may be altered, "but only in such measure and in such manner as is acceptable in a democratic society."

The ANC's Constitutional Guidelines and the Law Commission's report have transformed the nature of the debate over human rights in South Africa and produced widespread agreement that, whatever form the new constitution takes, it should include a justiciable bill of rights. Namibia's adoption of a bill of rights in its independence constitution has given additional support to this consensus.

The commitment to a bill of rights received additional endorsement in November 1990 when the ANC Constitutional Committee published a substantial *Working Document on a Bill of Rights for a New South Africa*. Although this document reveals much common ground with the Law Commission's working paper, it highlights a number of areas of disagreement, particularly in the social and economic fields. In essence, these problems, which are examined separately here, are a legacy of forty years of apartheid.

The Judiciary. In the Law Commission's draft bill of rights, the existing divisions of the Supreme Court are entrusted with the task of judicial review and are empowered to set aside any legislation or administrative act that violates any of the rights contained in the bill. Critics, however, raise two objections to the present judiciary as guardians of a bill of rights. First, with one exception, all the judges are white and it is feared they will inevitably reflect the racial attitudes of the white community. A prominent ANC lawyer has said that "the South African revolution will be incomplete if it leaves the present judiciary in place because it is invidiously intertwined with the present state."[27] Second, their interpretations of race and security laws suggest that they are not qualified to exercise the value-oriented role required of judges empowered to review acts of Parliament against the provisions of a bill of rights.[28]

It has therefore been suggested by the ANC Constitutional Committee that a constitutional court be created "that draws on the experience and talents of the whole population."[29] In order to overcome the objection, raised by the Law Commission, that such a court would be too politicized, the ANC Constitutional Committee suggests that it should be "appointed by the President on the recommendation of a judicial service commission, or by other methods acceptable in a democracy, comprising judges, practitioners and academics."[30]

Individual or Group Rights. Both the ANC guidelines and the Law Commission's draft bill contemplate a traditional bill of rights guaranteeing the civil and political rights of the individual. The guidelines denounce the constitutional protection of group rights on the grounds that this would perpetuate the status quo, but at the same time declare that "the state shall recognize the linguistic and cultural diversity of the people and provide facilities for free linguistic and cultural development."

This approach is endorsed by the ANC Constitutional Committee in its documents on both a bill of rights and constitutional principles. In the *Discussion Document* it declares that "all languages of South Africa will have equal status" and that "the state shall take all reasonable and necessary steps to protect, promote and enhance the language rights of all the people of South Africa in relation to education and culture and in the functioning of the state at local, regional and national levels."[31]

The Law Commission correctly indicates that group rights should be secured in the electoral provisions of a constitution and not in a bill of rights. Its draft bill refuses to provide for group rights on the grounds that South African law is "orientated toward the individual" and "does not recognize the legal subjectivity of an amorphous group such as, for example, a racial group, an ethnic group, or a cultural group." On the other hand, cultural, religious, and linguistic rights attaching to particular groups are protected by means of individual rights.

Although group rights are not directly protected, some recognition is given by the Law Commission to the rights of groups by a provision recognizing "the right of every person or group to disassociate himself or itself from other individuals or groups." Where such disassociation results in racial, religious, linguistic, or cultural discrimination, however, no public funds shall be allocated to such an enterprise. Racially exclusive private schools with no public financing are therefore anticipated.

The initial response of the National Party government to this aspect of the Law Commission draft bill was predictable. While the government accepted the necessity for the protection of individual rights, it was dissatisfied with the refusal of the Law Commission to accord equal status to the protection of group rights. This disagreement was made clear by President De Klerk in his opening address to Parliament on February 2, 1990, when he stated:

> The Government accepts the principle of the recognition and protection of the fundamental individual rights which form the constitutional basis of most Western democracies. We acknowledge, too, that the most practical way of protecting those rights is vested in a declaration of rights justifiable by an independent judiciary.
>
> However, it is clear that a system for the protection of the rights of individuals, minorities and national entities has to form a well-rounded and balanced whole. South Africa has its own national composition, and our constitutional dispensation has to take this into account. The formal recognition of individual rights does not mean that the problems of a heterogeneous population will simply disappear. Any new constitution which disregards this reality will be inappropriate and even harmful.
>
> Naturally, the protection of collective, minority and national rights may not bring about an imbalance in respect of individual rights. It is neither the Government's policy nor its intention that any group—in whichever way it may be defined— shall be favoured over or in relation to any of the others.[32]

The National Party appears to have changed its attitude toward group rights since February 1990. Demands that the bill of rights be employed to protect both group and individual rights have stopped, as have suggestions that the constitution include a veto for each racial group and that the members of the upper house be elected on racially separate voters' rolls.

It seems that the National Party has come to appreciate the unacceptability of any form of express protection for ethnic groups in either a new constitution or the bill of rights and believes that the best way for an ethnic minority to protect its interests politically is by forming a coalition with other similar groups. The National Party therefore seems to contemplate the formation of a "rainbow coalition" or "alliance of moderates" comprising itself, the IFP, the Coloured Labor Party, and other groups opposed to the ANC, which might together form either the government or a powerful opposition. Since the National Party has abolished statutory discrimination and admitted blacks to the party and its parliamentary caucus, the strong animosity to the party among blacks is fast disappearing. A rainbow coalition is therefore a real possibility in a post-apartheid South Africa.

Freedom of Speech. The U.S. Bill of Rights, as interpreted by the U.S. Supreme Court, adopts a libertarian approach to free speech that tolerates even the most offensive and discriminatory utterances. It is unlikely that a post-apartheid South Africa will display the same measure of tolerance toward free speech. The National Party government has placed so many restrictions on freedom of expression over the past years that generations of South Africans have grown up in a society in which this fundamental principle is unknown. Furthermore, blacks have been subjected to racial abuse for so long that there is an understandable desire to outlaw the expression and propagation of racist ideologies.

This context explains why both the ANC guidelines and the ANC Constitutional Committee's working document on a bill of rights, while reaffirming freedom of expression, provide that the advocacy or practice of racism or the incitement of ethnic or regional exclusiveness or hatred shall be outlawed.[33] The same legacy accounts for Article 23(1) of the 1990 Namibian Constitution, which, in order to express the revulsion of the people of Namibia to apartheid, authorizes the legislature to pass laws punishing the propagation of apartheid.

Social and Economic Rights. The debate in South Africa over the inclusion of social and economic rights in a bill of rights has followed the traditional pattern. One argument is that these rights, generally known as second-generation rights, have no place in a bill of rights, as they are nonjusticiable. In support of this view, which is endorsed by the Law Commission, Justice J. M. Didcott, one of South Africa's foremost liberal judges, declared:

A bill of rights is not a political manifesto, a political programme. Primarily, it is a protective device. It is a shield, in other words, rather than a sword. It can state, effectively and quite easily, what may not be done. It cannot stipulate, with equal ease of effectiveness, what shall be done. The reason is not only that the courts, its enforcers, lack the expertise and the infrastructure to get into the business of legislation or administration. It is also, and more tellingly, that they cannot raise the money.[34]

The Law Commission took the same view. It argued that socioeconomic rights asserting the right to work, to holidays, to proper pay, to favorable working conditions, and to education, as contained in the Universal Declaration of Human Rights and the International Covenant on Economic, Social, and Cultural Rights of 1966 are nonjusticiable and therefore belong to a political manifesto rather than a bill of rights.

On the other hand, there are those who insist that a South African bill of rights should break with the Anglo-Saxon tradition of restricting rights to what is justiciable and that such an instrument should, in line with the African Charter on Human and Peoples' Rights, seek to advance not only second-generation rights, but also third-generation rights, such as the right to peace, development, and a clean environment.[35] This view is preferred by the ANC's guidelines, which give special attention to social and economic rights. According to these guidelines, the state would be obliged to protect the right to work, to guarantee education and social security, and "to take active steps to eradicate speedily the economic and social inequalities produced by racial discrimination." A Worker's Charter, protecting the right to strike and collective bargaining, would be incorporated into the constitution.

The solution to this dispute is to be found in the Namibian Constitution of 1990, which, in this respect, is modeled on the Indian Constitution of 1949. It contains a justiciable bill of rights limited to civil and political rights ("first generation rights") only. But in addition, in a separate section on "principles of state policy," it requires the state to promote economic and social rights and to maintain the environment.[36] These principles are not legally enforceable by the courts but are intended to guide the government in making and implementing laws and the courts in interpreting them.

Property Rights. Perhaps the most difficult problem that will face a post-apartheid society is the redistribution of land and wealth. An absolute prohibition in a bill of rights on the expropriation of land or on the nationalization of industries without proper compensation would severely obstruct the movement toward a just society. At present, the white minority owns nearly 90 percent of the land; probably 95 percent of the country's productive capacity is vested in the white community. It would be a strange bill of rights that ensured that 80 percent of the population renounced its right to own land because to do so would violate the acquired rights of 20 percent.

This is an emotive issue on which positions have already been adopted. On the grounds that it is socialistic, President De Klerk has expressed opposition to any form of the redistribution of wealth. At the other end of the spectrum, the PAC persists in demanding the return of the land to the black majority. The ANC guidelines adopt a moderate position by merely advocating "the abolition of all racial restrictions on ownership and use of land" and the "implementation of land reforms in conformity with the principle of affirmative action, taking into account the status of victims of forced removals."[37] More strident voices within the ANC, however, propagate the nationalization of rural land.

The Law Commission's draft bill seeks to curb the redistribution of wealth by recognizing

> . . . the right to private property, provided that legislation may in the public interest authorize expropriation against payment of reasonable compensation which shall in the event of a dispute be determined by a court of law.

This provision is uncontroversial as far as property for personal use is concerned, as the ANC guidelines declare that "property for personal use and consumption shall be constitutionally protected." Problems arise, however, in relation to property that is owned for the purpose of production and not for personal use and consumption, as it is this property that a government of a post-apartheid South Africa may wish to expropriate in order to achieve a more equitable distribution of land and wealth without the obstacle—which in practice might prove insurmountable—of reasonable compensation.

While a bill of rights cannot be employed to entrench white property rights, it is equally clear that some protection against a majority government will have to be given to property holders.[38] The Namibian Constitution offers a solution that may prove satisfactory. It accepts the right to retain property but provides that the state may expropriate property in the public interest subject to the payment of just compensation, in accordance with the procedures and requirements laid down by the legislature.[39] In substance, this is the approach adopted by the ANC Constitutional Committee.[40]

Economic Policy. The history of the U.S. Supreme Court shows clearly that it is the function of the legislature and not the courts to regulate economic policy. As Justice Holmes declared in his dissenting opinion in *Lochner v. New York*, "a constitution is not intended to embody a particular economic theory."[41] It follows that it is not the function of a bill of rights to lay down a particular economic policy, be it socialist or capitalist.

The Law Commission ignores the lesson of the United States in its draft bill, which recognizes

> . . . the right, freely and on an equal footing, to engage in economic intercourse, which shall include the capacity to establish and maintain commercial undertakings, to procure property and means of production, to offer services against remuneration and to make a profit.[42]

This attempt to provide constitutional backing for a policy of free enterprise, which enjoys the support of the National Party government, will be unacceptable to the ANC, which, in its guidelines, declares that the state shall ensure that the entire economy serves the interests and well-being of all sections of the population "and that the economy shall be a mixed one, with a public sector, a private sector, a cooperative sector and a small scale family sector."[43] Moreover, a provision such as that of the Law Commission will lead to endless litigation and bring the courts into the same type of confrontation with the legislature as that experienced by the U.S. Supreme Court.

Affirmative Action. The U.S Supreme Court has been compelled to qualify the principle of equality before the law in order to take account of historical injustices to minority groups and women.[44] The legacy of racial injustice in South Africa runs deeper than in the United States and has affected the majority rather than the minority. The need for redress by means of affirmative action is therefore much greater.

Affirmative action is a controversial issue in contemporary South Africa. The civil service has not only retained its predominantly white character but also persists in a policy of favoring the employment and advancement of Afrikaners. The business community and some universities, however, already practice affirmative action on a voluntary basis.[45] They have studied the experience of the United States and modeled their own programs on it. South African whites outside the civil service are therefore probably more prepared for affirmative action than the United States was when it first embarked upon this course.

The Law Commission adopts a cautious approach toward affirmative action, which it has considered only within the areas of education and employment. It finds that affirmative action "is recognised in international law as being non-discriminatory, so long as it is temporary and is not enforced against the will of the minority." It goes on to say that the legislature should be permitted "to make certain laws to grant a minority group which has been discriminated against certain advantages temporarily with the object of achieving equality."[46] The draft bill qualifies the requirement of equality before the law with the proviso that legislation shall be permissible on a temporary basis for the improvement of the position of persons or groups who find themselves to be disadvantaged "for historical reasons."[47] This measure echoes provisions in the International Convention on the Elimination of All Forms of Racial Discrimination, the Canadian Charter of Rights and Freedom, and the Indian Constitution.[48]

In South Africa, the problem is not how to redress historical injustices for a minority, as the South African Law Commission suggests, but rather for a group comprising 70 percent of the population. Nor is the need for redress confined to education and employment.

Albie Sachs, who is in the forefront of ANC constitutional planning, states in *Protecting Human Rights in a New South Africa*:

> It is not just individuals who will be looking to the bill of rights as a means of enlarging their freedoms and improving the quality of their lives, but whole communities, especially those whose rights have been systematically and relentlessly denied by the apartheid system. If a bill of rights is seen as a truly creative document that requires and facilitates the achievement of the rights so long denied to the great majority of the people, it must have an appropriate corrective strategy.[49]

This "corrective strategy," he argues, will have to be directed at every aspect of South African society, including "the restoration of land, wealth, and dignity to the people."[50]

The ANC's guidelines, although not explicit on this subject, also contemplate a much wider form of affirmative action than that practiced in the United States and accepted by the Law Commission.

The guidelines see affirmative action as a way of redressing past inequalities based on both race and gender. They require the state "to take active steps to eradicate, speedily, the economic and social inequalities produced by racial discrimination" and to implement land reforms "in accordance . . . with affirmative action."[51]

The ANC Constitutional Committee's working document on *A Bill of Rights for a New South Africa* addresses this question more fully:

> Nothing in the Constitution shall prevent the enactment of legislation, or the adoption by any public or private body of special measures of a positive kind designed to procure the advancement and opening up of opportunities, including access to education, skills, employment and land, and the general advancement in social, economic and cultural spheres, of men and women who in the past have been disadvantaged by discrimination.[52]

The document furthermore obliges all organs of the state to "pursue policies and programmes aimed at redressing the consequences of past discriminatory laws and practices," particularly with respect to the public service, defense and police forces, and the prison service.[53] The state is also empowered, in terms of this document, to "take steps to overcome the effects of past statutory discrimination in relation to the enjoyment of property rights," a position that appears to approve the notion of affirmative action with respect to the redistribution of land.[54]

Affirmative action will have a major political role to play in a post-apartheid society, and it would be unacceptable to place unreasonable restraints on this process by means of an equality-before-the-law provision in a bill of rights. Opinions differ, however, as to what affirmative action should include. Will it merely cover rectification in the fields of education and employment, as the Namibian Constitution has done, or will it be used to embark on a radical program of redistribution of land and wealth as well?

The Future of the South African Legal Order

In this book, we have sought to show how discriminatory race laws and repressive security and emergency laws have damaged South African law and legal institutions, undermined the reputation of the judiciary, and destroyed respect for the law among the majority of the population. The apartheid legal order that governed South Africa for over forty years has been likened to the legal systems of slavery, fascism, and colonialism. For many South Africans, law is no longer seen as an autonomous system of inherited rules, principles, values, and traditions designed to regulate society and to curb governmental excesses, but as an instrument to further the ideology of the National Party.

One of the major tasks facing a post-apartheid South Africa will be the restoration of respect for the law and its institutions. This can best be achieved, first, by an unequivocal repudiation of the law of apartheid and, second, by the creation of political institutions premised on the rule of law and respect for human rights.

Repudiation of the past presents a serious problem. Had the liberation movements defeated the National Party government militarily, the major exponents and enforcers of apartheid would undoubtedly have been brought to trial on charges of crimes against humanity before courts modeled on the Nuremburg Tribunal, which prosecuted Nazi war criminals. Following the Nuremburg precedent, a likely scenario is that those accused would have been unable to plead that they had acted in accordance with the law in force at the time—that is, the law of apartheid—on the grounds that this legal order fell so far short of civilized notions of law that it failed to qualify as law at all. Trials of this kind would probably have repudiated most dramatically the legitimacy of the law of apartheid. But this has not happened.

Instead, the government—weakened politically by internal dissent and economically by external sanctions—and the ANC—weakened militarily by the South African security forces and materially by the collapse of its main supporters in Eastern Europe—abandoned armed confrontation and agreed to negotiate a nonracial political order. In pursuance of a policy of national reconciliation, the government released political prisoners and extended immunity from prosecution to returning ANC guerrillas; in return, the ANC appeared to abandon the idea of Nuremburg-type trials.

Reconciliation is of paramount importance in South Africa. But the recent experience of countries such as Argentina, Uruguay, and Chile suggests that the granting of amnesty to those guilty of human rights violations is unlikely to encourage respect for the law and its institutions or to promote a return to the rule of law.[55] Similarly, the postwar German experience shows the need for the denunciation of the law under which human rights were grossly violated.[56] Justice requires that the apartheid legal order be denounced as statutory injustice and that the principal apartheid criminals be exposed. The need for reconciliation may render the punishment of such persons politically unwise, but this does not justify the failure to publicize the full horrors of the apartheid state by judicial proceedings or by some special commission of inquiry. Without this fidelity to historical truth, it will not be possible to deter the new order from perpetrating similar atrocities or to restore the integrity of the law.

The second requirement for the restoration of the law's credibility is the creation of new institutions, based on the rule of law and respect for human rights, that demonstrate a commitment to personal liberty, racial and gender equality, and the sharing of resources. Fortunately, there are indications that the major actors in the South African political drama share a common commitment to such a constitutional order.

South Africa entered the final decade of the twentieth century in a new spirit of reconciliation and negotiation. Establishing a new political order will not be an easy task, since important differences in outlook and expectations exist. Both the National Party government and the ANC, however, have committed themselves to an order in which equality before the law and respect for basic rights are to be protected. This consensus is the starting point for a new system to arise from the ashes of apartheid.

APPENDICES

APPENDIX A

Address by State President F. W. de Klerk,
February 2, 1990

**ADDRESS BY STATE PRESIDENT F. W. DE KLERK, DMS,
AT THE OPENING OF THE SECOND SESSION
OF THE NINTH PARLIAMENT
OF THE REPUBLIC OF SOUTH AFRICA
FRIDAY, 2 FEBRUARY 1990**

Mr Speaker, Members of Parliament.

The general election on September the 6th, 1989, placed our country irrevocably on the road of drastic change. Underlying this is the growing realisation by an increasing number of South Africans that only a negotiated understanding among the representative leaders of the entire population is able to ensure lasting peace.

The alternative is growing violence, tension and conflict. That is unacceptable and in nobody's interest. The well-being of all in this country is linked inextricably to the ability of the leaders to come to terms with one another on a new dispensation. No-one can escape this simple truth.

On its part, the Government will accord the process of negotiation the highest priority. The aim is a totally new and just constitutional dispensation in which every inhabitant will enjoy equal rights, treatment and opportunity in every sphere of endeavour—constitutional, social and economic.

I hope that this new Parliament will play a constructive part in both the prelude to negotiations and the negotiating process itself. I wish to ask all of you who identify yourselves with the broad aim of a new South Africa, and that is the overwhelming majority:

- Let us put petty politics aside when we discuss the future during this session.
- Help us build a broad consensus about the fundamentals of a new, realistic and democratic dispensation.
- Let us work together on a plan that will rid our country of suspicion and steer it away from domination and radicalism of any kind.

During the term of this new Parliament, we shall have to deal, complementary to one another, with the normal processes of legislation and day-to-day government, as well as with the process of negotiation and renewal.

Within this framework I wish to deal first with several matters more closely concerned with the normal process of government before I turn specifically to negotiation and related issues.

1. Foreign Relations

The Government is aware of the important part the world at large has to play in the realisation of our country's national interests.

Without contact and co-operation with the rest of the world we cannot promote the well-being and security of our citizens. The dynamic developments in international politics have created new opportunities for South Africa as well. Important advances have been made, among other things, in our contacts abroad, especially where these were precluded previously by ideological considerations.

I hope this trend will be encouraged by the important change of climate that is taking place in South Africa.

For South Africa, indeed for the whole world, the past year has been one of change and major upheaval. In Eastern Europe and even the Soviet Union itself, political and economic upheaval surged forward in an unstoppable tide. At the same time, Beijing temporarily smothered with brutal violence the yearning of the people of the Chinese mainland for greater freedom.

The year of 1989 will go down in history as the year in which Stalinist Communism expired.

These developments will entail unpredictable consequences for Europe, but they will also be of decisive importance to Africa.

The indications are that the countries of Eastern and Central Europe will receive greater attention, while it will decline in the case of Africa.

The collapse, particularly of the economic system in Eastern Europe, also serves as a warning to those who insist on persisting with it in Africa. Those who seek to force this failure of a system on South Africa, should engage in a total revision of their point of view. It should be clear to all that it is not the answer here either. The new situation in Eastern Europe also shows that foreign intervention is no recipe for domestic change. It never succeeds, regardless of its ideological motivation. The upheaval in Eastern Europe took place without the involvement of the Big Powers or of the United Nations.

The countries of Southern Africa are faced with a particular challenge: Southern Africa now has an historical opportunity to set aside its conflicts and ideological differences and draw up a joint programme of reconstruction. It should be sufficiently attractive to ensure that the Southern African region obtains adequate investment and loan capital from the industrial countries of the world. Unless the countries of Southern Africa achieve stability and a common approach to economic development rapidly, they will be faced by further decline and ruin.

The Government is prepared to enter into discussions with other Southern African countries with the aim of formulating a realistic development plan. The Government believes that the obstacles in the way of a conference of Southern African states have now been removed sufficiently.

Hostile postures have to be replaced by co-operative ones; confrontation by contact; disengagement by engagement; slogans by deliberate debate.

The season of violence is over. The time for reconstruction and reconciliation has arrived.

Recently there have, indeed, been unusually positive results in South Africa's contacts and relations with other African states. During my visits to their countries I was received cordially, both in private and in public, by Presidents Mobutu, Chissano, Houphouet-Boigny and Kaunda. These leaders expressed their sincere concern about the serious economic problems in our part of the world. They agreed that South Africa could and should play a positive part in regional co-operation and development.

Our positive contribution to the independence process in South West Africa has been recognised internationally. South Africa's good faith and reliability as a negotiator made a significant contribution to the success of the events. This, too, was not unnoticed. Similarly, our efforts to help bring an end to the domestic conflict situations in Mozambique and Angola have received positive acknowledgement.

At present the Government is involved in negotiations concerning our future relations with an independent Namibia and there are no reasons why good relations should not exist between the two countries. Namibia needs South Africa and we are prepared to play a constructive part.

Nearer home I paid fruitful visits to Venda, Transkei and Ciskei and intend visiting Bophuthatswana soon. In recent times there has been an interesting debate about the future relationship of the TBVC countries with South Africa and specifically about whether they should be re-incorporated into our country.

Without rejecting this idea out of hand, it should be borne in mind that it is but one of many possibilities. These countries are constitutionally independent. Any return to South Africa will have to be dealt with, not only by means of legislation in their parliaments, but also through legislation in this Parliament. Naturally this will have to be preceded by talks and agreements.

2. Human Rights

Some time ago the Government referred the question of the protection of fundamental human rights to the South African Law Commission. This resulted in the Law Commission's interim working document on individual and minority rights. It elicited substantial public interest.

I am satisfied that every individual and organisation in the country has had ample opportunity to make representations to the Law Commission, express criticism freely and make suggestions. At present, the Law Commission is considering the representations received. A final report is expected in the course of this year.

In view of the exceptional importance of the subject of human rights to our country and all its people, I wish to ask the Law Commission to accord this task high priority.

The whole question of protecting individual and minority rights, which includes collective rights and the rights of national groups, is still under consideration by the Law Commission.

Therefore, it would be inappropriate for the Government to express a view on the details now. However, certain matters of principle have emerged fairly clearly and I wish to devote some remarks to them.

The Government accepts the principle of recognition and protection of the fundamental individual rights which form the constitutional basis of most Western democracies. We acknowledge, too, that the most practical way of protecting those rights is vested in a declaration of rights justifiable by an independent judiciary. However, it is clear that a system for the protection of the rights of individuals, minorities and national entities has to form a well-rounded and balanced whole. South Africa has its own national composition and our constitutional dispensation has to take this into account. The formal recognition of individual rights does not mean that the problems of a heterogeneous population will simply disappear. Any new constitution which disregards this reality will be inappropriate and even harmful.

Naturally, the protection of collective, minority and national rights may not bring about an imbalance in respect of individual rights. It is neither the Government's policy nor its intention that any group—in whichever way it may be defined—shall be favoured above or in relation to any of the others.

The Government is requesting the Law Commission to undertake a further task and report on it. This task is directed at the balanced protection in a future constitution of the human rights of all our citizens, as well as of collective units, associations, minorities and nations. This investigation will also serve the purpose of supporting negotiations towards a new constitution.

The terms of reference also include:

- the identification of the main types and models of democratic constitutions which deserve consideration in the aforementioned context;
- an analysis of the ways in which the relevant rights are protected in every model; and
- possible methods by means of which such constitutions may be made to succeed and be safeguarded in a legitimate manner.

3. The Death Penalty

The death penalty has been the subject of intensive discussion in recent months. However, the Government has been giving its attention to this extremely sensitive issue for some time. On April the 27th, 1989, the honourable Minister of Justice indicated that there was merit in suggestions for reform in this area. Since 1988 in fact, my predecessor and I have been taking decisions on reprieves which have led, in proportion, to a drastic decline in executions.

We have now reached the position in which we are able to make concrete proposals for reform. After the Chief Justice was consulted, and he in turn had consulted the Bench, and after the Government had noted the opinions of academics and other interested parties, the Government decided on the following broad principles from a variety of available options:

- that reform in this area is indicated;
- that the death penalty should be limited as an option of sentence to extreme cases, and specifically through broadening judicial discretion in the imposition of sentence; and
- that an automatic right of appeal be granted to those under sentence of death.

Should these proposals be adopted, they should have a significant influence on the imposition of death sentences on the one hand, and on the other, should ensure that every case in which a person has been sentenced to death will come to the attention of the Appellate Division.

These proposals require that everybody currently awaiting execution be accorded the benefit of the proposed new approach.

Therefore, all executions have been suspended and no executions will take place until Parliament has taken a final decision on the new proposals. In the event of the proposals being adopted, the case of every person involved will be dealt with in accordance with the new guidelines. In the meantime, no executions have taken place since November the 14th, 1989.

New and uncompleted cases will still be adjudicated in terms of the existing law. Only when the death sentence is imposed will the new proposals be applied, as in the case of those currently awaiting execution.

The legislation concerned also entails other related principles which will be announced and elucidated in due course by the Minister of Justice. It will now be formulated in consultation with experts and be submitted to Parliament as soon as possible.

I wish to urge everybody to join us in dealing with this highly sensitive issue in a responsible manner.

4. Socio-Economic Aspects

A changed dispensation implies far more than political and constitutional issues. It cannot be pursued successfully in isolation from problems in other spheres of life which demand practical solutions. Poverty, unemployment, housing shortages, inadequate education and training, illiteracy, health needs and numerous other problems still stand in the way of progress and prosperity and an improved quality of life.

The conservation of the physical and human environment is of cardinal importance to the quality of our existence. For this the Government is developing a strategy with the aid of an investigation by the President's Council.

All of these challenges are being dealt with urgently and comprehensively. The capability for this has to be created in an economically accountable manner. Consequently, existing strategies and aims are undergoing a comprehensive revision.

From this will emanate important policy announcements in the socio-economic sphere by the responsible Ministers during the course of the session. One matter about which it is possible to make a concrete announcement is the Separate Amenities Act, 1953. Pursuant to my speech before the President's Council late last year, I announce that this Act will be repealed during this Session of Parliament.

The State cannot possibly deal alone with all of the social advancement our circumstances demand. The community at large, and especially the private sector, also have a major responsibility towards the welfare of our country and its people.

5. The Economy

A new South Africa is possible only if it is bolstered by a sound and growing economy, with particular emphasis on the creation of employment. With a view to this, the Government has taken thorough cognisance of the advice contained in numerous reports by a variety of advisory bodies. The central message is that South Africa, too, will have to make certain structural changes to its economy, just as its major trading partners had to do a decade or so ago.

The period of exceptionally high economic growth experienced by the Western world in the sixties was brought to an end by the oil crisis in 1973. Drastic structural adaptations became inevitable for these countries, especially after the second oil crisis in 1979, when serious imbalances occurred in their economies. After considerable sacrifices, those countries which persevered with their structural adjustment programmes recovered economically so that lengthy periods of high economic growth and low inflation were possible.

During that particular period, South Africa was protected temporarily by the rising gold price from the necessity of making similar adjustments immediately. In fact, the high gold price even brought prosperity with it for a while. The recovery of the world economy and the decline in the price of gold and other primary products brought with them unhealthy trends. These included high inflation, a serious weakening in the productivity of capital, and stagnation in the economy's ability to generate income and employment opportunities. All of this made a drastic structural adjustment of our economy inevitable.

The Government's basic point of departure is to reduce the role of the public sector in the economy and to give the private sector maximum opportunity for optimal performance. In this process, preference has to be given to allowing the market forces and a sound competitive structure to bring about the necessary adjustments.

Naturally, those who make and implement economic policy have a major responsibility at the same time to promote an environment optimally conducive to investment, job creation and economic growth by means of appropriate and properly co-ordinated fiscal and monetary policy. The Government remains committed to this balanced and practical approach.

By means of restricting capital expenditure in parastatal institutions, privatisation, deregulation and curtailing government expenditure, substantial progress has been made already towards reducing the role of the authorities in the economy. We shall persist with this in a well-considered way.

This does not mean that the State will forsake its indispensable development role, especially in our particular circumstances. On the contrary, it is the precise intention of the Government to concentrate an equitable portion of its capacity on these aims by means of the meticulous determination of priorities.

Following the progress that has been made in other areas of the economy in recent years, it is now opportune to give particular attention to the supply side of the economy.

Fundamental factors which will contribute to the success of this restructuring are:

- the gradual reduction of inflation to levels comparable to those of our principal trading partners;
- the encouragement of personal initiative and savings;
- the subjection of all economic decisions by the authorities to stringent financial measures and discipline;
- rapid progress with the reform of our system of taxation; and
- the encouragement of exports as the impetus for industrialisation and earning foreign exchange.

These and other adjustments, which will require sacrifices, have to be seen as prerequisites for a new period of sustained growth in productive employment in the nineties. The Government has also noted with appreciation the manner in which the Reserve Bank has discharged its special responsibility in striving towards our common goals.

The Government is very much aware of the necessity of proper co-ordination and consistent implementation of its economic policy. For this reason, the establishment of the necessary structures and expertise to ensure this co-ordination is being given preference. This applies both to the various functions within the Government and to the interaction between the authorities and the private sector.

This is obviously not the occasion for me to deal in greater detail with our total economic strategy or with the recent course of the economy.

I shall confine myself to a few specific remarks on one aspect of fiscal policy that has been a source of criticism of the Government for some time, namely State expenditure.

The Government's financial year ends in only two months' time and several other important economic indicators for the 1989 calendar year are still subject to refinements at this stage. Nonetheless, several important trends are becoming increasingly clear. I am grateful to be able to say that we have apparently succeeded to a substantial degree in achieving most of our economic aims in the past year.

In respect of Government expenditure, the budget for the current financial year will be the most accurate in many years. The financial figures will show:

- that Government expenditure is thoroughly under control;
- that our normal financial programme has not exerted any significant upward pressure on rates of interest; and

- that we will close the year with a surplus, even without taking the income from the privatisation of Iscor into account.

Without pre-empting this year's main budget, I wish to emphasise that it is also our intention to co-ordinate fiscal and monetary policy in the coming financial year in a way that will enable us to achieve the ensuing goals—namely:

- that the present downturn will take the form of a soft landing which will help to make adjustments as easy as possible;
- that our economy will consolidate before the next upward phase so that we will be able to grow from a sound base; and
- that we shall persist with the implementation of the required structural adaptations in respect, among other things, of the following: easing the tax burden, especially on individuals; sustained and adequate generation of surpluses on the current account of the balance of payments; and the reconstruction of our gold and foreign exchange reserves.

It is a matter of considerable seriousness to the Government, especially in this particular period of our history, to promote a dynamic economy which will make it possible for increasing numbers of people to be employed and share in rising standards of living.

6. Negotiation

In conclusion, I wish to focus the spotlight on the process of negotiation and related issues. At this stage I am refraining deliberately from discussing the merits of numerous political questions which undoubtedly will be debated during the next few weeks. The focus, now, has to fall on negotiation.

Practically every leader agrees that negotiation is the key to reconciliation, peace and a new and just dispensation. However, numerous excuses for refusing to take part are advanced. Some of the reasons being advanced are valid. Others are merely part of [a] political chess game. And while the game of chess proceeds, valuable time is being lost.

Against this background I committed the Government during my inauguration to giving active attention to the most important obstacles in the way of negotiation. Today I am able to announce far-reaching decisions in this connection. I believe that these decisions will shape a new phase in which there will be a movement away from measures which have been seized upon as a justification for confrontation and violence. The emphasis has to move, and will move now, to a debate and discussion of political and economic points of view as part of the process of negotiation.

I wish to urge every political and community leader, in and outside Parliament, to approach the new opportunities which are being created constructively. There is no time left for advancing all manner of new conditions that will delay the negotiating process.

The steps that have been decided are the following:

- The prohibition of the African National Congress, the Pan Africanist Congress, the South African Communist Party and a number of subsidiary organisations is being rescinded.
- People serving prison sentences merely because they were members of one of these organisations or because they committed another offence which was merely an offence because prohibition on one of the organisations was in force will be identified and released. Prisoners who have been sentenced for other offences such as murder, terrorism or arson are not affected by this.
- The media emergency regulations as well as the education emergency regulations are being abolished in their entirety.
- The security emergency regulations will be amended to still make provision for effective control over visual material pertaining to scenes of unrest.
- The restrictions in terms of the emergency regulations on 33 organisations are being rescinded. The organisations include the following:
    National Education Crisis Committee
    South African National Students Congress
    United Democratic Front
    Congress of South African Trade Unions
    Blanke Bevrydingsbeweging van Suid-Afrika (White Liberation Movement).
- The conditions imposed in terms of the security emer-

gency regulations on 374 people on their release are being rescinded and the regulations which provide for such conditions are being abolished.

- The period of detention in terms of the security emergency regulations will be limited henceforth to six months. Detainees also acquire the right to legal representation and a medical practitioner of their own choosing.

These decisions by the Cabinet are in accordance with the Government's declared intention to normalise the political process in South Africa without jeopardising the maintenance of the good order. They were preceded by thorough and unanimous advice by a group of officials which included members of the security community.

Implementation will be immediate and, where necessary, notices will appear in the Government Gazette from tomorrow.

The most important facets of the advice the Government received in this connection are the following:

- The events in the Soviet Union and Eastern Europe, to which I have referred already, weaken the capability of organisations which were previously supported strongly from those quarters.
- The activities of the organisations from which the prohibitions are now being lifted no longer entail the same degree of threat to internal security which initially necessitated the imposition of the prohibitions.
- There have been important shifts of emphasis in the statements and points of view of the most important of the organisations concerned, which indicate a new approach and a preference for peaceful solutions.
- The South African Police is convinced that it is able, in the present circumstances, to combat violence and other crimes perpetrated also by members of these organisations and to bring offenders to justice without the aid of prohibitions on organisations.

About one matter there should be no doubt. The lifting of the prohibition on the said organisations does not signify in the least the approval or condonation of terrorism or crimes of violence committed under their banner or which may be perpetrated in the future. Equally, it should not be interpreted as a deviation from the

Government's principles, among other things, against their economic policy and aspects of their constitutional policy. This will be dealt with in debate and negotiation.

At the same time I wish to emphasise that the maintenance of law and order dare not be jeopardised. The Government will not forsake its duty in this connection. Violence from whichever source will be fought with all available might. Peaceful protest may not become the springboard for lawlessness, violence and intimidation. No democratic country can tolerate that.

Strong emphasis will be placed as well on even more effective law enforcement. Proper provision of manpower and means for the police and all who are involved with the enforcement of the law, will be ensured. In fact, the budget for the coming financial year will already begin to give effect to this.

I wish to thank the members of our security forces and related services for the dedicated service they have rendered the Republic of South Africa. Their dedication makes reform in a stable climate possible.

On the state of emergency I have been advised that an emergency situation, which justifies these special measures which have been retained, still exists. There is still conflict which is manifesting itself mainly in Natal, but as a consequence of the countrywide political power struggle. In addition, there are indications that radicals are still trying to disrupt the possibilities of negotiation by means of mass violence.

It is my intention to terminate the state of emergency completely as soon as circumstances justify it and I request the co-operation of everybody towards this end. Those responsible for unrest and conflict have to bear the blame for the continuing state of emergency. In the mean time, the state of emergency is inhibiting only those who use chaos and disorder as political instruments.

Otherwise the rules of the game under the state of emergency are the same for everybody.

Against this background the Government is convinced that the decisions I have announced are justified from the security point of view. However, these decisions are justified from a political point of view as well.

Our country and all its people have been embroiled in conflict, tension and violent struggle for decades. It is time for us to break out of the cycle of violence and break through to peace and reconciliation. The silent majority is yearning for this. The youth deserve it.

With the steps the Government has taken, it has proven its good faith and the table is laid for sensible leaders to begin talking about a new dispensation, to reach an understanding by the way of dialogue and discussion.

The agenda is open and the overall aims to which we are aspiring should be acceptable to all reasonable South Africans.

Among other things, those aims include a new, democratic constitution; universal franchise; no domination; equality before an independent judiciary; the protection of minorities as well as of individual rights; freedom of religion; a sound economy based on proven economic principles and private enterprise; dynamic programmes directed at better education, health services, housing and social conditions for all.

In this connection Mr Nelson Mandela could play an important part. The Government has noted that he has declared himself to be willing to make a constructive contribution to the peaceful political process in South Africa.

I wish to put it plainly that the Government has taken a firm decision to release Mr Mandela unconditionally. I am serious about bringing this matter to finality without delay. The Government will take a decision soon on the date of his release. Unfortunately, a further short passage of time is unavoidable.

Normally, there is a certain passage of time between the decision to release and the actual release because of logistical and administrative requirements. In the case of Mr Mandela there are factors in the way of his immediate release, of which his personal circumstances and safety are not the least. He has not been an ordinary prisoner for quite some time. Because of that, his case requires particular circumspection.

Today's announcements, in particular, go to the heart of what Black leaders—also Mr Mandela—have been advancing over the years as their reason for having resorted to violence. The allegation has been that the Government did not wish to talk to them and that they were deprived of their right to normal political activity by the prohibition of their organisations.

Without conceding that violence has ever been justified, I wish to say today to those who argued in this manner:

- The Government wishes to talk to all leaders who seek peace.
- The unconditional lifting of the prohibition on the said organisations places everybody in a position to pursue politics freely.
- The justification for violence which was always advanced, no longer exists.

These facts place everybody in South Africa before a fait accompli. On the basis of numerous previous statements there is no longer any reasonable excuse for the continuation of violence. The time for talking has arrived and whoever still makes excuses does not really wish to talk.

Therefore, I repeat my invitation with greater conviction than ever:—

Walk through the open door, take your place at the negotiating table together with the Government and other leaders who have important power bases inside and outside of Parliament.

Henceforth, everybody's political points of view will be tested against their realism, their workability and their fairness. The time for negotiation has arrived.

To those political leaders who have always resisted violence I say thank you for your principled stand. These include all the leaders of parliamentary parties, leaders of important organisations and movements, such as Chief Minister Buthelezi, all of the other Chief Ministers and urban community leaders.

Through their participation and discussion they have made an important contribution to this moment in which the process of free political participation is able to be restored. Their places in the negotiating process are assured.

Conclusion

In my inaugural address I said the following:

"All reasonable people in this country—by far the majority— anxiously await a message of hope. It is our responsibility as leaders in all spheres to provide that message realistically with courage and conviction. If we fail in that, the ensuing chaos, the demise of stability and progress, will forever be held against us.

"History has thrust upon the leadership of this country the tremendous responsibility to turn our country away from its present direction of conflict and confrontation. Only we, the leaders of our peoples, can do it.

"The eyes of responsible governments across the world are focused on us. The hopes of millions of South Africans are centred around us. The future of Southern Africa depends on us. We dare not falter or fail."

This is where we stand:

- Deeply under the impression of our responsibility.
- Humble in the face of the tremendous challenges ahead.
- Determined to move forward in faith and with conviction.

I ask Parliament to assist me on the road ahead. There is much to be done.

I call on the international community to re-evaluate its position and to adopt a positive attitude towards the dynamic evolution which is taking place in South Africa.

I pray that the Almighty Lord will guide and sustain us on our course through uncharted waters and will bless your labours and deliberations.

Mr Speaker, Members of Parliament, I now declare this Second Session of the Ninth Parliament of the Republic of South Africa to be duly opened.

Source: South African Consulate General, New York, N.Y., February 1990.

APPENDIX B

Public Safety Act, 1953
Security Emergency Regulations

PROCLAMATION
by the
State President of the Republic of South Africa

No. R. 86, 1989

PUBLIC SAFETY ACT, 1953

SECURITY EMERGENCY REGULATIONS

Under the powers vested in me by section 3 of the Public Safety Act, 1953 (Act No. 3 of 1953), I hereby make the regulations contained in the Schedule with effect from 9 June 1989.

Given under my Hand and the Seal of the Republic of South Africa at Cape Town this Eighth day of June, One thousand Nine hundred and Eighty-nine.

P. W. BOTHA,
State President.
By Order of the State President-in-Cabinet:
A. J. Vlok,
Minister of the Cabinet.

SCHEDULE

Definitions

1. (1) In these regulations, unless the context otherwise indicated—
"Act" means the Public Safety Act, 1953 (Act No. 3 of 1953);
"Commissioner" means the Commissioner of the South African Police, and for the purposes of the application of a provision of these regulations in or in respect of—
(a) a division as defined in section 1 of the Police Act, 1958 (Act No. 7 of 1958), the said Commissioner or the Divisional Commissioner designated under that Act for that division; or
(b) a self-governing territory, the said Commissioner or the Commissioner or other officer in charge of the police force of the Government of that self-governing territory;
"gathering" means any gathering, concourse or procession of any number of persons;
(3) If a member of a security force is of the opinion that it is necessary for the safety of the public, the maintenance of public order or the termination of the state of emergency, he may summarily order a person present in a particular area and who is not normally resident therein, to leave that area immediately, and if that person fails to leave the area in question immediately, that member may arrest the person concerned or cause him to be arrested and may remove him from such area or cause him to be so removed.

Arrest and detention of persons

3. (1) A Member of a security force may, without warrant of arrest, arrest or cause to be arrested any person whose detention is, in the opinion of such member, necessary for the safety of the public or the maintenance of public order or for the termination of the state of emergency, and may, under a written order signed by any member of a security force, detain or cause to be detained any such person in custody in a prison.

Note: The numbering in this appendix was reproduced as it appeared in the Government Gazette Staatskoerant, No. 4373.

(2) No person shall be detained in terms of subregulation (1) for a period exceeding 30 days from the date of his arrest, unless that period is extended by the Minister under subregulation (3).

(3) The Minister may, without notice to any person and without hearing any person, by notice signed by him and addressed to the head of a prison, order that a person arrested and detained in terms of subregulation (1), be further detained, and in that prison, for the period specified in the notice or for as long as these regulations remain in force.

(4) A written, printed, telegraphic or similar communication purporting to be from the Minister or an officer acting under his authority, stating that a notice has been issued under subregulation (3) in respect of a particular person, shall have the effect of the said notice: Provided that if such a written, printed, telegraphic or similar communication is used in lieu of the notice in question, the Minister or the said officer shall as soon as possible forward the notice to the head of the prison referred to in subregulation (3) where the person to whom the notice applies is to be detained under such notice.

(5) A person detained in a prison in terms of this regulation may, if the Minister or a commissioned officer, as defined in section 1 of the Police Act, 1958 (Act No. 7 of 1958), or the head of that prison, in writing so directs, be removed in custody from that prison for detention in any other prison, or for any other purposes mentioned in such direction.

(6) A member of a security force may, with a view to the safety of the public or the maintenance of public order or the termination of the state of emergency, interrogate any person arrested or who is detained in terms of this regulation.

(7) No person, other than the Minister or a person acting by virtue of his office in the service of the State or of the Government of a self-governing territory—

(a) shall have access to a person detained in terms of this regulation except with the consent of and subject to such conditions as may be determined by the Minister or a person authorized thereto by him; or

(b) shall be entitled to any official information relating to such person, or to any other information of whatever nature obtained from or in respect of such person.

(8) (a) The Minister may, subject to paragraph (B), at any time by notice signed by him, order that a person who is detained in terms of this regulation be released from detention.

(b) The Minister may, if he is of the opinion that it is necessary for the safety of the public, the maintenance of public order or the termination of the state of emergency, and without prior notice to any person and without hearing any person—

(i) subject the release under paragraph (a) of a person to such conditions as may be specified in a notice signed by him and addressed to that person;

(ii) at any time after the release of such a person, by further notice signed by him and addressed to such person, revoke or amend any condition imposed under subparagraph (i) or impose any new condition as may be specified in such notice.

(c) A condition imposed under paragraph (b) shall be of force for such period as may be specified in the relevant notice or, if no period has been so specified, for as long as these regulations remain in force.

(d) A condition imposed in respect of a person under paragraph (b) of regulation 3(8) of the Security Emergency Regulations, 1988, and which, by virtue of the express terms of the notice through which the condition was imposed or the operation of the provisions of paragraph (c) of the said regulations 3(8), was still in force on the day preceding the commencement of these regulations, shall be deemed to have been imposed at such commencement in respect of the said person under paragraph (b) of this subregulation and shall, notwithstanding the express terms of the said notice or the operation of the said provisions or the fact that the Security Emergency Regulations, 1988, have lapsed, but subject to paragraph (b)(ii) of this subregulation, continue in force for as long as these regulations remain in force.

Threats of harm, hurt or loss

4. No person shall—

(a) by word or conduct threaten to inflict upon any other person, or upon any of such person's relatives or dependents, any harm, hurt or loss, whether to his or their person or property or in any other way; or

(b) prepare, compile, print, publish, transmit, possess or disseminate, or assist in the preparation, compilation, printing, publication, transmission or dissemination of any writing which threatens the infliction upon any other person, or upon any of such person's relatives or dependents, of any harm, hurt or loss, whether to his or their person or property or in any other way.

(d) by distributing the order in a written form among members of the public and by affixing it on public buildings or at prominent public places in the area concerned;

(e) where the order is directed to a particular person, by handing or tendering it or causing it to be handed or tendered in a written form to that person; or

(f) by oral announcement to any particular person, or to members of the public in general, in the area concerned in a manner deemed fit by the Commissioner whenever, due to the urgency thereof or for any other reason whatsoever, it can, in the opinion of the Commissioner, not be published, made known, distributed or announced in accordance with the provisions of paragraph (a), (b), (c), (d) or (e).

Offences

12. Any person who—

(a) contravenes or fails to comply with any order, direction or request under a provision of these regulations;

(b) contravenes or fails to comply with any condition imposed in respect of him under regulation 3(8), 7(4)(e), 8(3), 9(3) or 10(3);

(c) contravenes a provision of regulation 4 or 7(3);

(d) hinders any other person in the carrying out of any duty or the exercise of any power or the performance of any function imposed or conferred by, under or pursuant to any provision of these regulations; or

(e) destroys, defaces or falsifies any notice or other writing issued or purporting to have been issued under these regulations, shall be guilty of an offence.

Penalties

13. Any person convicted of an offence under these regulations shall be liable to a fine not exceeding R20,000 or to imprisonment for a period not exceeding ten years or to such imprisonment without the option of a fine, and the court convicting him may declare any goods, property or instrument by means of which or in

connection with which the offence was committed, to be forfeited to the State.

Direction of Attorney-General required for prosecution

14. No prosecution for an offence under these regulations shall be instituted except by the express direction of the Attorney-General having jurisdiction in respect of that prosecution.

Limitation of liability

15. (1) No civil or criminal proceedings shall be instituted or continued in any court of law against—
    (a) the State or the Government of a self-governing territory;
    (b) the State President;
    (c) any member of the Cabinet or a Ministers' Council or the Cabinet of a self-governing territory;
    (d) any member of a security force;
    (e) any person in the service of the State or of the Government of a self-governing territory; or
    (f) any person acting by direction or with the approval of any member or person referred to in the preceding paragraphs of this subregulation, by reason of any act in good faith advised, commanded, ordered, directed or performed by any person in the carrying out of his duties or the exercise of his powers or the performance of his functions in terms of these regulations or any other regulations made under the Act, with intent to ensure the safety of the public, the maintenance of public order or the termination of the state of emergency or in order to deal with circumstances which have arisen or are likely to arise as a result of the said state of emergency.

(2) (a) Whenever the court in which any proceedings have been instituted is of the opinion that by virtue of subregulation (1) the proceedings may not be continued, the court shall make a finding to that effect.
    (b) Whenever the court has made such a finding, such proceedings shall lapse and be deemed to be void.

(3) No interdict or other process shall issue for the staying or

setting aside of any order, rule or notice made or issued under these regulations or any other regulations made under the Act or any condition determined thereunder, and no such order, rule, notice or condition shall be stayed on the grounds of an appeal against a conviction under these or such other regulations.

(4) If in any proceedings instituted against any member or person referred to in subregulation (1), or the State, or the Government of a self-governing territory, the question arises whether any act advised, commanded, ordered, directed or performed by any person was advised, commanded, ordered, directed or performed by him in good faith, it shall be presumed, until the contrary is proved, that such act was advised, commanded, ordered, directed or performed by him in good faith.

(5) The provisions of this regulation shall apply also in respect of any default by any person or member referred to in subregulation (1) in complying with any provision of any law in connection with advising, commanding, ordering, directing or performing any such act aforesaid.

Short title

16. These regulations shall be called the Security Emergency Regulations, 1989.

Source: Government Gazette Staatskoerant, No. 4373, *vol. 288, Pretoria, 9 June 1989, No. 11946.*

APPENDIX C
Freedom Charter, June 26, 1955

FREEDOM CHARTER
OF THE CONGRESS OF THE PEOPLE

We, the people of South Africa, declare for all our country and the world to know:

that South Africa belongs to all who live in it, black and white, and that no Government can justly claim authority unless it is based on the will of all the people;

that our people have been robbed of their birthright to land, liberty and peace by a form of Government founded on injustice and inequality;

that our country will never be prosperous or free until all our people live in brotherhood, enjoying equal rights and opportunities;

that only a democratic state, based on the will of all the people, can secure to all their birthright without distinction of colour, race, sex or belief;

And therefore, we the people of South Africa, black and white together—equal, countrymen and brothers—adopt this Freedom Charter. And we pledge ourselves to strive together, sparing nothing of our strength and courage, until the democratic changes here set out have been won.

The people shall govern

Every man and woman shall have the right to vote for and to stand as a candidate for all bodies which make laws.

All people shall be entitled to take part in the administration of the country.

The rights of the people shall be the same, regardless of race, colour or sex.

All bodies of minority rule, advisory boards, councils and authorities shall be replaced by democratic organs of self-government.

All national groups shall have equal rights

There shall be equal status in the bodies of state, in the Courts and in the schools for all national groups and races.

All people shall have equal right to use their own languages, and to develop their own folk culture and customs.

All national groups shall be protected by law against insults to their race and national pride.

The preaching and practice of national, race or colour discrimination and contempt shall be a punishable crime.

All apartheid laws and practices shall be set aside.

The people shall share the country's wealth

The national wealth of our country, the heritage of all South Africans, shall be restored to the people.

The mineral wealth beneath the soil, the Banks and monopoly industry shall be transferred to the ownership of the people as a whole.

All other industry and trade shall be controlled to assist the well-being of the people.

All people shall have equal rights to trade where they choose, to manufacture and to enter all trades, crafts and professions.

The land shall be shared among those who work it

Restriction of land ownership on a racial basis shall be ended, and all the land redivided amongst those who work it, to banish famine and land hunger.

The state shall help the peasants with implements, seed, tractors and dams to save the soil and assist the tillers.

Freedom of movement shall be guaranteed to all who work on the land.

All shall have the right to occupy land wherever they choose.

People shall not be robbed of their cattle, and forced labour and farm prisons shall be abolished.

All shall be equal before the law

No one shall be imprisoned, deported or restricted without a fair trial.

No one shall be condemned by the order of any Government official.

The courts shall be representative of all the people.

Imprisonment shall be only for serious crimes against the people, and shall aim at re-education, not vengeance.

The police force and army shall be open to all on an equal basis and shall be the helpers and protectors of the people.

All laws which discriminate on grounds of race, colour or belief shall be repealed.

All shall enjoy equal human rights

The law shall guarantee to all their right to speak, to organize, to meet together, to publish, to preach, to worship and to educate their children.

The privacy of the house from police raids shall be protected by law.

All shall be free to travel without restriction from countryside to town, from province to province, and from South Africa abroad.

Pass Laws, permits and all other laws restricting these freedoms shall be abolished.

There shall be work and security

All who work shall be free to form trade unions, to elect their officers and to make wage agreements with their employers.

The state shall recognize the right and duty of all to work, and to draw full unemployment benefits.

Men and women of all races shall receive equal pay for equal work.

There shall be a forty-hour working week, a national minimum wage, paid annual leave, and sick leave for all workers, and maternity leave on full pay for all working mothers.

Miners, domestic workers, farm workers and civil servants shall have the same rights as all others who work.

Child labour, compound labour, the tot system and contract labour shall be abolished.

The doors of learning and of culture shall be opened

The Government shall discover, develop and encourage national talent for the enhancement of our cultural life.

All the cultural treasures of mankind shall be open to all, by free exchange of books, ideas and contact with other lands.

The aim of education shall be to teach the youth to love their people and their culture, to honour human brotherhood, liberty and peace.

Education shall be free, compulsory, universal and equal for all children.

Higher education and technical training shall be opened to all by means of state allowances and scholarships awarded on the basis of merit.

Adult illiteracy shall be ended by a mass state education plan.

Teachers shall have all the rights of other citizens.

The colour bar in cultural life, in sport and in education shall be abolished.

There shall be houses, security and comfort

All people shall have the right to live where they choose, to be decently housed, and to bring up their families in comfort and security.

Unused housing space is to be made available to the people.

Rent and prices shall be lowered, food plentiful and no one shall go hungry.

A preventive health scheme shall be run by the state. Free medical care and hospitalization shall be provided for all, with special care for mothers and young children.

Slums shall be demolished and new suburbs built where all have transport, roads, lighting, playing fields, creches and social centres.

The aged, the orphans, the disabled and the sick shall be cared for by the state.

Rest, leisure and recreation shall be the right of all.

Fenced locations and ghettoes shall be abolished, and all laws which break up families shall be repealed.

There shall be peace and friendship

South Africa shall be a fully independent state which respects the rights and sovereignty of all nations.

South Africa shall strive to maintain world peace and the settlement of all international disputes by negotiation—not war.

Peace and friendship amongst all our people shall be secured by upholding the equal rights, opportunities and status of all.

The people of the Protectorates—Basutoland, Bechuanaland and Swaziland—shall be free to decide for themselves their own future.

The right of all the peoples of Africa to independence and self-government shall be recognized, and shall be the basis of close co-operation.

Let all who love their people and their country now say, as we say here: "These freedoms we will fight for, side by side, throughout our lives, until we have won our liberty."

Source: Indian Opinion, *July 8, 1955, as quoted by Gwendolen M. Carter in* The Politics of Inequality: South Africa Since 1948 *(revised edition, New York: Frederick A. Praeger, 1958), 486–88.*

APPENDIX D
ANC Constitutional Guidelines for a
Democratic South Africa, 1988

CONSTITUTIONAL GUIDELINES FOR A
DEMOCRATIC SOUTH AFRICA

The Freedom Charter, adopted in 1955 by the Congress of the People at Kliptown near Johannesburg, was the first systematic statement in the history of our country of the political and constitutional vision of a free, democratic and non-racial South Africa.

The Freedom Charter remains today unique as the only South African document of its kind that adheres firmly to democratic principles as accepted throughout the world. Amongst South Africans it has become by far the most widely accepted programme for a post-apartheid country. The stage is now approaching where the Freedom Charter must be converted from a vision for the future into a constitutional reality.

We in the African National Congress submit to the people of South Africa, and to all those throughout the world who wish to see an end to apartheid, our basic guidelines for the foundations of government in a post-apartheid South Africa. Extensive and democratic debate on these guidelines will mobilise the widest sections of our population to achieve agreement on how to put an end to the tyranny and oppression under which our people live, thus enabling them to lead normal and decent lives as free citizens in a free country.

The immediate aim is to create a just and democratic society that will sweep away the centuries-old legacy of colonial conquest and white domination, and abolish all laws imposing racial oppression and discrimination. The removal of discriminatory laws and eradication of all vestiges of the illegitimate regime are, however, not enough; the structures and the institutions of apartheid must be dismantled and be replaced by democratic ones. Steps must be taken to ensure that apartheid ideas and practices are not permitted to appear in old forms or new.

In addition, the effects of centuries of racial domination and inequality must be overcome by constitutional provisions for corrective action which guarantees a rapid and irreversible redistribution of wealth and opening up of facilities to all. The Constitution must also be such as to promote the habits of non-racial and non-sexist thinking, the practice of anti-racist behaviour and the acquisition of genuinely shared patriotic consciousness.

The Constitution must give firm protection to the fundamental human rights of all citizens. There shall be equal rights for all individuals, irrespective of race, colour, sex or creed. In addition, it requires the entrenching of equal cultural, linguistic and religious rights for all.

Under the conditions of contemporary South Africa 87% of the land and 95% of the instruments of production of the country are in the hands of the ruling class, which is solely drawn from the white community. It follows, therefore, that constitutional protection for group rights would perpetuate the status quo and would mean that the mass of the people would continue to be constitutionally trapped in poverty and remain as outsiders in the land of their birth.

Finally, success of the constitution will be, to a large extent, determined by the degree to which it promotes conditions for the active involvement of all sectors of the population at all levels in government and in the economic and cultural life. Bearing these fundamental objectives in mind, we declare that the elimination of apartheid and the creation of a truly just and democratic South Africa requires a constitution based on the following principles:

The State:

a. South Africa shall be an independent, unitary, democratic and non-racial state.
b. i) Sovereignty shall belong to the people as a whole and shall be exercised through one central legislature, executive and administration.

ii) Provision shall be made for the delegation of the powers of the central authority to subordinate administrative units for purposes of more efficient administration and democratic participation.

c. The institution of hereditary rulers and chiefs shall be transformed to serve the interests of the people as a whole in conformity with the democratic principles embodied in the constitution.

d. All organs of government including justice, security and armed forces shall be representative of the people as a whole, democratic in their structure and functioning, and dedicated to defending the principles of the constitution.

Franchise

e. In the exercise of their sovereignty, the people shall have the right to vote under a system of universal suffrage based on the principle of one person, one vote.

f. Every voter shall have the right to stand for election and be elected to all legislative bodies.

National Identity

g. It shall be state policy to promote the growth of a single national identity and loyalty binding on all South Africans. At the same time, the state shall recognise the linguistic and cultural diversity of the people and provide facilities for free linguistic and cultural development.

A Bill of Rights and Affirmative Action

h. The constitution shall include a Bill of Rights based on the Freedom Charter. Such a Bill of Rights shall guarantee the fundamental human rights of all citizens irrespective of race, colour, sex or creed, and shall provide appropriate mechanisms for their enforcement.

i. The state and all social institutions shall be under a constitutional duty to eradicate race discrimination in all its forms.

j. The state and all social institutions shall be under a constitutional duty to take active steps to eradicate, speedily, the economic and social inequalities produced by racial discrimination.

k. The advocacy or practice of racism, fascism, or nazism or the incitement of ethnic or regional exclusiveness or hatred shall be outlawed.

l. Subject to clauses (i) and (k) above, the democratic state shall guarantee the basic rights and freedoms, such as freedom of association, expression, thought, worship and the press. Furthermore, the state shall have the duty to protect the right to work, and guarantee education and social security.

m. All parties which conform to the provisions of paragraphs (i) to (k) shall have the legal right to exist and to take part in the political life of the country.

Economy

n. The state shall ensure that the entire economy serves the interests and well-being of all sections of the population.

o. The state shall have the right to determine the general context in which economic life takes place and define and limit the rights and obligations attaching to the ownership and use of productive capacity.

p. The private sector of the economy shall be obliged to co-operate with the state in realising the objectives of the Freedom Charter in promoting social well-being.

q. The economy shall be a mixed one, with a public sector, a private sector, a co-operative sector and a small-scale family sector.

r. Co-operative forms of economic enterprise, village industries and small-scale family activities shall be supported by the state.

s. The state shall promote the acquisition of managerial, technical and scientific skills among all sections of the population, especially the blacks.

t. Property for personal use and consumption shall be constitutionally protected.

Land

u. The state shall devise and implement a Land Reform Programme that will include and address the following issues:
    i) Abolition of all racial restrictions on ownership and use of land.
    ii) Implementation of land reforms in conformity with the principle of Affirmative Action, taking into account the status of victims of forced removals.

Workers

v. A charter protecting workers' trade union rights, especially the right to strike and collective bargaining, shall be incorporated into the constitution.

Women

w. Women shall have equal rights in all spheres of public and private life and the state shall take affirmative action to eliminate inequalities and discrimination between the sexes.

The Family

x. The family, parenthood and children's rights shall be protected.

International

y. South Africa shall be a non-aligned state committed to the principles of the Charter of the Organisation of African Unity and the Charter of the United Nations and to the achievement of national liberation, world peace and disarmament.

APPENDIX E
Summary of State President F. W. de Klerk's Address,
February 1, 1991

SUMMARY OF PRESIDENT F. W. DE KLERK'S ADDRESS
AT THE OPENING OF PARLIAMENT
1 FEBRUARY 1991

Repeal of All Statutory Discrimination

Opening the 1991 Session of Parliament, State President F. W. de Klerk again exceeded expectations in the scope and extent of political change which he announced. As was anticipated, he gave notice of the repeal of the Land Acts of 1913 and 1936, the Group Areas Act of 1966 and Development of Black Communities Act of 1984 during the current Parliamentary Session. The inclusion of the repeal of the Population Registration Act of 1950 was unexpected. As a result, ". . . the South African statute book will be devoid, within months, of the remnants of racially discriminatory legislation which have become known as the cornerstones of apartheid," the President said.

Nation Building

Recognizing that South Africa lacks the natural cohesion of a single culture and language on which nationhood is built, President de Klerk said that South Africa would have to rely heavily on common values and ideals to provide the necessary bonding. These basic ideals and values were outlined in a Manifesto released by the Government on February 1. The Manifesto will be associated with a Bill of Rights, to which the Government is already committed.

The Multi-Party Conference

There is growing consensus that the time for a multi-party conference has arrived. The Government was especially pleased to note that the ANC in its 8 January Anniversary Message, accepted the principle of holding such a conference. Major political groupings are now ready to attend multi-party exploratory talks which, hopefully, soon will commence.

The Government is opposed to the idea of an elected constituent assembly. The new constitution should be the responsibility of representatives of all political parties which enjoy proven support and are committed to a peaceful and negotiated solution. However, the Government is prepared to consider certain transitional arrangements to give the leaders of the negotiating parties a voice in the formulation of important policy decisions.

Local Government

Without wishing to anticipate the national negotiation process, interim steps will be initiated to accommodate the dynamics of co-operation which have already developed in many communities. These include the joint provision of services, the establishment of single administrations, one tax base and joint decision making.

Community Life

The removal of discrimination and coercion will not alter the reality of the variety of existing communities, which is not unique to South Africa. As elsewhere, there is a deep-rooted desire to exist in communities and the Government therefore remains committed to ensuring community rights without coercion, discrimination, or apartheid, based on freedom of association.

Legal Reform

The Government wishes to bring its aims regarding community life into line with the concept of a just state, in which the rule of law prevails.

The South African legal system has to be subjected to continuous scrutiny to ensure that it meets the needs of the ever-changing demands of our society. In this regard the recognition of indigenous law, alongside common law, remains important.

The independence of the judiciary is essential. Legal procedures are to be simplified to make the legal process more accessible and involve the community to a greater extent.

Education

The Government, conscious of the serious problems in education, intends changing the present system. Education should be devoid of discrimination, allow equality of opportunity, and enjoy the acceptance and support of the people.

The Economy

Economic restructuring is essential to ensure the high growth necessary to meet the reasonable aspirations of the people. This cannot be accomplished overnight, but everything will be done to promote the elimination of existing economic disparities, creation of employment opportunities and the generation of income to meet the needs of the rapidly growing population.

The Government recognizes that economic growth and constitutional reform are inter-dependent. Unless the pressing problem of impoverishment is alleviated, constitutional models alone will be of little avail.

Restructuring the economy and re-allocating available resources will be necessary to ensure a peaceful transition to the new society all South Africans wish to see.

Various state-sponsored organizations such as the Independent Development Trust and the Private Sector Initiative, operating under the aegis of the Urban Foundation, are ready to make major contributions towards addressing endemic problems in housing, health, education as well as home and land ownership of the less privileged.

Foreign Affairs

South Africa's fundamental change of course, primarily motivated by national interest, has created new opportunities internationally. South Africa's diplomatic isolation is ending.

Regional development is of decisive importance to the eleven states of Southern Africa which have a combined population of more than 100 million. The region is endowed with natural resources and has enormous potential. However, the nations in the region, divided for so long by colonialism, wars, conflicts and racial strife, will have to join forces, work and plan together.

Southern Africa should be able to realize the common aim of a better future. Working together, it will succeed in obtaining the active involvement of Europe, the U.S.A. and other developed countries.

Security

The Government is concerned about the high level of lawlessness and crime and has already launched a special crime prevention campaign to combat crime more effectively. Regrettably, mass actions which should be part of the normal democratic process, degenerate all too often and infringe on the safety and rights of others. A distinction should also be drawn between peaceful mass actions and those actions which have revolutionary aims. Political and community leaders have to accept responsibility together with the authorities to settle disputes, control supporters and create a climate for negotiation.

Conclusion

"There is neither time nor room for turning back."

"There is only one road—ahead."

Source: South African Briefing Paper, *compiled and produced by the South African Consulate General, New York, N.Y., February 1991.*

APPENDIX F
ANC Constitutional Proposals, April 1991

CONSTITUTIONAL PRINCIPLES
FOR
A DEMOCRATIC SOUTH AFRICA

Part 1

The African National Congress envisages a united, democratic, non-racial and non-sexist South Africa, a unitary State where a Bill of Rights guarantees fundamental rights and freedoms for all on an equal basis, where our people live in an open and tolerant society, where the organs of government are representative, competent and fair in their functioning, and where opportunities are progressively and rapidly expanded to ensure that all may live under conditions of dignity and equality.

A United South Africa

When we speak of a united South Africa, we have in mind in the first place the territorial unity and constitutional integrity of our country. South Africa must be seen, as recognised by the international community, as a single, non-fragmented entity including Transkei, Bophuthatswana, Venda and Ciskei.

Secondly, we envisage a single citizenship, nation and a common loyalty. We speak many languages, have different origins and varied beliefs, but we are all South Africans.

Thirdly, all apartheid structures must be dismantled and re-placed by institutions of government—central, regional and local—which are truly non-racial and democratic. They must form an integrated and coherent whole, be drawn from all the people and be accountable to the whole community.

Fourthly, there must be a single system of fundamental rights guaranteed on an equal basis for all through the length and breadth of the country. Every South African, irrespective of race, colour, language, gender, status, sexual orientation or creed should know that his or her basic rights and freedoms are guaranteed by the constitution and enforceable by recourse to law.

Fifthly, the flag, names, public holidays and symbols of our country should encourage a sense of shared South Africanness.

A unified South Africa requires a strong and effective Parliament capable of dealing with the great tasks of reconstruction, of overcoming the legacy of apartheid and of nation-building.

We believe that there is a need for strong and effective central government to handle national tasks, strong and effective regional government to deal with the tasks of the region, and strong and effective local government to ensure active local involvement in handling local issues.

All such governmental structures and institutions shall be based on democratic principles, popular participation, accountability and accessibility. A unified South Africa shall not be an over-centralised, impersonal and over-bureaucratised country. The precise relationship between central, regional and local governments can be worked out on the basis of acknowledging the overall integrity of South Africa and the existence of fundamental rights for all citizens throughout the land.

The regions should not be devised as a means of perpetuating privilege, ethnic or racial divisions along territorial zones but should be based upon the distribution of population, availability of economic resources, communications and urban/rural balance.

National tasks would include external links and representation, defence and ensuring the basic security of the country, general economic, fiscal and tax policy, the creation of national policy framework and the furnishing of resources for eradicating racism and racial practices and for the tackling of the vast problems of education, health, housing, nutrition, employment and social welfare.

Regional tasks would include development and the carrying out of the basic tasks of the government at a regional level, bearing in mind regional particularities and resources.

Without detracting from basic constitutional rights and freedoms, provision could be made for special recognition of languages in the different regions.

Local tasks cover all the day-to-day aspects of living which most directly and intimately affect the citizen in an integrated and non-racial local authority area. The active local involvement of all sections of the population will be necessary in the fulfillment of these tasks.

The central government has the responsibility for ensuring that there is a common framework of principles and practices applicable to the whole country and for seeing to it that all areas of the country have equitable access to national resources. However, it is not the function of central government to involve itself in each and every decision that has to be taken at the regional or local levels. Such functions should clearly be delegated to these authorities and performed by them.

Similarly, when we speak of a united South Africa we do not envisage the elimination of cultural, linguistic, religious and political differences. On the contrary, we regard the multiplicity of opinions, beliefs, faiths, tastes, cultures and preferences as contributing towards the richness and texture of South African life. What the new constitution should avoid at all costs is vesting political rights in different linguistic, cultural, ethnic or religious groups.

A free South Africa must therefore ensure that those differences do not become the source of division or conflict or the means of perpetuating and promoting domination or privilege.

The new constitution must consistently and clearly affirm the fundamental principle of equal and undifferentiated citizenship so that the differences of culture, interest and personality can then express themselves in a constructive, free and non-conflictual way.

Democratic

The government must be democratic in the universally accepted meaning of the term. It must be the government of the people, by the people, for the people. It must be chosen by the people in free, fair and regular elections. It must be removable if it loses the confidence of the voters. Elections must be based on the principle of universal and equal suffrage on a common voters' roll without distinction as to race, language, creed, class, social position, birth or gender. Illiterate voters should not be disadvantaged. The precise method of voting and the electoral system can be negotiated within the framework of these universal principles. The African National

Congress favours the system of proportional representation, with regional and national lists.

Secondly, the legislature should be representative of the people as a whole, reflecting such differences of political views and interests as may be present in the community at any particular time.

Thirdly, the institutions of government should not be restricted to any language, religious, racial, ethnic or cultural grouping. The central, regional and local government structures, including the law enforcement agencies and the administration of justice, should reflect the composition of South Africa as a whole and draw on the talents and life experiences of all. Similarly, they should act in a fair and objective manner towards all, without fear, favour or prejudice.

Fourthly, government must be open. Apartheid South Africa has been a highly authoritarian society, characterised by arbitrary decision-making by officials and by excessive secrecy. All South Africans have the right to be informed about the issues and to know what the basis of governmental decisions is. There is far too much fear of the government. We must secure constitutional barriers to detention without trial, to spying on citizens, secret files, dirty tricks departments, disinformation and the use of government money to promote party political objectives.

Fifthly, government should be based on the principle of active involvement of the people. The existence of civic associations, religious bodies, ratepayers' organisations, trade unions and other independent bodies should be encouraged. Similarly, government should collaborate with non-governmental organisations, without interfering with their autonomy.

Finally, government should reflect the will of the majority, be effective but not all-powerful. It should operate within the framework of the constitution, acknowledging a separation of powers and the existence of fundamental rights and freedoms as guaranteed in a Bill of Rights.

Non-Racial

A non-racial South Africa means a South Africa in which all the artificial barriers and assumptions which kept people apart and maintained domination are removed. In its negative sense, non-racial means the elimination of all colour bars. In positive terms it means the affirmation of equal rights for all. It presupposes a South Africa in which every individual has an equal chance, irrespective of his or her birth or colour. It recognises the worth of each individual.

A non-racial constitution can be adopted rapidly but a nonracial South Africa would take many years to evolve. Yet, although the massive discrepancies in education, health and living conditions imposed by decades of racial discrimination cannot be eliminated by constitutional declaration, the constitution must provide the positive means to reduce progressively the imbalances and inequalities and to ensure that everybody has an equal chance in life.

Non-Sexist

The new constitution must reflect a commitment to full, free and equal participation in the new South Africa. Law and practice keep South African women out of their rightful place in helping to build democracy and enable a new nation to evolve, and deprive them of their human rights as individuals.

The new constitution must therefore:

- *guarantee equal rights for women and men in all spheres of public and private life;*
- *create mechanisms whereby the discrimination, disabilities and disadvantages to which women have been subjected are rapidly removed;*
- *give appropriate recognition to reproductive and birth rights;*
- *guarantee constitutional protection against sexual violence, abuse, harassment or defamation;*
- *ensure that women are heard in all issues and participate actively in all levels of society.*

Bill of Rights

A bill of rights based on universally recognised principles of human rights should form an integral part of the new constitution. In particular, it should guarantee all South Africans against the violations of human rights associated with apartheid and stress the principle of the equal dignity and worth of all South Africans.

The bill of rights should in clear and unambiguous language guarantee the rights of personal freedom and political expression. It should also protect and enhance rights of the individual to practise her or his religion and culture and speak her or his language. It should acknowledge the importance of securing minimum conditions of decent and dignified living for all Africans.

It should create mechanisms for enforcing these rights. In particular, the courts should have a primary role in ensuring that the bill of rights is operative. A Constitutional Court that enjoys the respect of all South Africans, that draws on the experience and talents of the whole population, that is independent and that functions in a manifestly fair and objective fashion, accountable only to the principles of the constitution, should be created.

Similarly, a human rights commission should be established to ensure that violations of human rights are investigated and appropriate remedies found, examine patterns of discrimination and make proposals for their elimination.

Finally, the post of Ombud should be created to deal with questions of abusive, arbitrary, capricious, discourteous and corrupt exercise of office by any official.

Open Society

The constitution should guarantee the free articulation of differences within the framework of equal rights and tolerance.

An open society requires guarantees for the free functioning of non-governmental organisations, such as religious bodies, trade unions, sporting and cultural associations, subject only to respect for fundamental human rights as set out in the constitution.

Non-governmental organisations should be encouraged to collaborate with the Government in furthering the aims of the constitution, without thereby compromising their identity or independence.

All men and women shall be entitled to all necessary information to enable them to make effective use of their rights as citizens, workers and consumers and to impart such information.

There should be freedom of the press, and the media should be open, accessible and respond to all the views, opinions and interests of the community.

The Civil, the Defence, Police and Prison Services

The three principal qualities of the civil service, the defence, police and prison service shall be:

representativity, competence and impartiality.

Representativity. All organs of government shall draw on the life experience and talents of all sectors of the community in such a manner as to instill a common South African perspective of public service. The present barriers based on race shall be eliminated and special steps shall be taken to redress patterns of discrimination attributable to apartheid.

Competency. It is in the interest of the population of a free South Africa that the standard and quality of service of the public service shall be as high as possible. To attain this goal, and consistent with the principle of representativity, special programmes of training, retraining and advancement shall be undertaken to enable the best South Africans to give the best possible service to all their fellow citizens.

Impartiality. The organs of government shall be accountable to Parliament and to the whole community. It is not their function to serve the interests of any party or sectional grouping. Impartiality presupposes a balanced composition of the bodies concerned and a sensitivity to the needs and aspirations of all sections of the community.

There should be adequate control and supervision over the civil service, defence, police and prison service, an effective machinery to investigate complaints against these services and the provision of redress.

Administration of justice. Without interfering with its independence, and with a view to ensuring that justice is manifestly seen to be done in a non-racial way and that the wisdom, experience and judicial skills of all South Africans are represented on the bench, the judiciary shall be transformed in such a way as to consist of men and women drawn from all sectors of South African society.

In a free South Africa, the legal system shall be transformed to be consistent with the new constitution.

The courts shall be accessible to all and shall guarantee to all equal rights before the law.

Guarantees of Opportunities for a Dignified Life for All

A new South Africa can never evolve if the white part of the population lives in relative luxury while the great majority of black South Africans live in conditions of want, squalor and deprivation.

Appropriate constitutional expression must therefore be found to guarantee basic human rights in relation to nutrition, shelter, education, health, employment and welfare. Government should be under a constitutional duty to work towards the establishment of a guaranteed and expanding floor of social, economic and educational rights for everybody.

It is particularly important that the constitution facilitate access to education, employment and land, so that people have real and effective opportunities for improving their situation and pursuing happiness.

THE STRUCTURE OF A CONSTITUTION FOR A DEMOCRATIC SOUTH AFRICA

Part 2

1. South Africa shall be reconstituted as a non-racial, non-sexist, democratic and unitary republic.

2. South Africa shall consist of the whole territory recognised by the international community as South Africa and shall include the Transkei, Ciskei, Venda and Bophuthatswana.

3.1 Provision will be made for the three branches of government: the executive, legislature and the judiciary.

3.2 The head of the executive will be an elected President who will also be the Head of State. The question that arises is whether the president should be elected directly by the public and vested with greater executive powers, or whether s/he should be elected by and answerable to Parliament. This is a matter on which there must be greater public debate.

3.3 The President will act in consultation with a Cabinet of Ministers headed by a Prime Minister. The President will appoint a Prime Minister and other members of the Cabinet.

3.4 The President may only hold office for a maximum of two terms of five years each. He or she will be subject to removal only by a resolution passed for good cause by a two thirds majority of the National Assembly.

3.5 The legislative branch of government will consist of two houses of Parliament. The first house of Parliament will be the National Assembly which will be elected on the basis of proportional representation by universal suffrage in which all persons will have an equal vote without regard to race, gender, ethnic origin, language or creed.

3.6 The power of enacting legislation will primarily be vested in the National Assembly.

3.7 The second house of Parliament will be the Senate, which will also be elected according to universal suffrage without regard to race, gender, colour, ethnic origin, language or creed. The Senate will neither be a corporatist chamber made up of interest groups (youth, labour, women or business, or other groups) nor will it represent ethnic or so-called "community" interests. The electoral system will, however, be different to that adopted for the election of the National Assembly, and will make provision for representation on a regional but not on an ethnic basis.

3.7 The Senate will be the guardian of the Constitution, with power to refer any dispute concerning the interpretation or application of the constitution to the appropriate court for its decision and the power to review. Where appropriate the Senate may delay the passage of legislation passed by the National Assembly, but it will not have the power to veto legislation.

3.8 Elections for the Presidency, National Assembly and the Senate will be held by secret ballot at periodic intervals of not more than five years and procedures will be enacted to ensure that the elections are genuine and are conducted in accordance with the principles and procedures consistent with those obtaining in a democracy.

3.9 All South Africans shall be entitled to stand for election as President, to Parliament and to other elected offices. Elections will be supervised by an independent Electoral Commission, and conducted in accordance with the standards designed to ensure that the elections are fair and free.

4.1 The National Assembly will be elected on the basis of proportional representation. The rationale behind proportional representation lies in the following factors:

a) It encourages participation by groups which have significant followings. This is more satisfactory than forcing political or subversive activity outside Parliament. Fringe parties would be excluded by imposing a threshold of 5% of the vote.

b) Votes in excess of fifty percent would count and hence be an inducement to vote in areas where one party is dominant. Similarly "losing" parties' votes in those areas would also contribute to their overall performance.

c) It leads to a more exact political reflection of the popularity of parties.

d) It avoids the time, expense and accusations of bias in the process of delimiting constituencies. This process can take months or years.

4.2 Proportional representation on the basis of a national party list system may present problems. Under such a system there is no way of ensuring adequate regional or local representation. Party bureaucracies benefit at the expense of local party structures or local sentiment. There is little direct accountability to constituencies.

4.3 Accordingly the ANC favours incorporating elements of a national list and regional accountability into the electoral system. This could be done most simply by combining a national list with a regional list. For example: regions could be allocated say half of the total seats, to be divided between the different regions in proportion to the registered voters in each region. The remaining half of the seats could be allocated on a national basis. Voters would vote for a party within their region and the regional seats will be allocated between the parties according to the percentages obtained by each party in each region. The second stage would be for regional votes to be aggregated so as to determine the national percentage of the total vote of each party. Each party would then be entitled to nominate from its national list the additional members needed to make up its total entitlement of seats.

4.4 The end result will be the representation of each party in the assembly in proportion to its total votes, but reflecting a regional choice of members as well. The system requires the electorate to cast one vote only. It will be easy to administer and easy for voters to follow.

4.5 It is recommended that proportional representation, based on the list system, be the preferred system of voting for Senate, regional and other elections.

5. It is important that there be a guarantee of free and fair elections and that procedures be enacted to see to this. It is therefore recommended that the conduct and supervision of all elections be vested in an independent electoral commission to oversee every aspect of elections from the printing of ballot papers to the adoption of regulations for access by parties to the public media and fairness to all political parties by the public media.

6. There will be an independent judiciary responsible for the interpretation of the Constitution and the application of the law of the land. The judicial power will include the power to review and set aside legislation and actions which are unconstitutional. A Constitu-

tional Court, appointed by the President on the recommendation of a judicial service commission, or by other methods acceptable in a democracy, comprised of judges, practitioners and academics would be set up.

7. Provision will be made for elected local and regional government on the basis of universal franchise without regard to race, gender, ethnic origin, language or creed. Local and regional government will exercise delegated powers but will have wide discretions in regard to the priorities to be pursued at these levels, provided always that such policies do not conflict with national policies. Functions presently vested in the provincial administrations will be vested in the regional government. The boundaries of local and regional districts will be determined with due regard to economic and development considerations and without regard to race, colour, ethnic origin, language or creed.

8. Provision shall be made for one common and equal citizenship acquired by birth, descent and naturalisation in accordance with conventional standards. Provision will also be made for the restoration of South African citizenship to persons who have lost their citizenship as a result of the denationalisation process through the homelands policy, or as a result of having gone into exile for political reasons, and provision will also be made for the acquisition of South African citizenship by the spouses and children of such persons.

9.1 All languages of South Africa will have equal status. They will be set up in a Schedule to the Constitution and will include in alphabetical order the following: Afrikaans, English, Sipedi, Sesotho, Seswati, Tsonga, Tswana, Venda, Xhosa, Zulu.

9.2 The State shall take all reasonable and necessary steps to protect, promote and enhance the language rights of all the people of South Africa in relation to education and culture and in the functioning of the State at local, regional and national levels.

9.3 The language policy of the State shall be directed towards promoting and encouraging multilingualism and preventing the use of any language or languages for the purposes of domination or division.

9.4 The State shall, however, be empowered to make reasonable provision by law for the use of one or more of the languages in different regions of the country, or for specific purposes.

9.5 The question may, of course be asked whether there should be one official language for the country. But if this choice is made it would mean the demotion of some languages or the promotion of a single one. Also, it would mean that the official language would be one which most of the people either do not speak or do not speak fluently.

9.6 It would seem therefore that the most appropriate thing to do is to give equal status to all languages subject to the right of the government to give primacy to one or more languages in any region or throughout the State as the language of administrative communication or judicial record, or for other purposes either throughout the State or in any area, but everyone should be entitled to use her or his language for purposes of communicating with the public service.

10.1 There will be a justiciable Bill of Rights leaving the way open for legitimate State action but affirming and protecting internationally recognised rights and freedoms including equality before the law; freedom from detention without trial; protection against arbitrary arrest and detentions; protection against arbitrary search and seizure; the prohibition of forced labour; the right to fair trial; the prohibition of cruel and unusual punishment; protection of life including the abolition of the death sentence; protection of women's rights; protection of children; freedom from discrimination; the right to privacy; freedom of expression including a free press; the right to information; freedom of religion and conscience; freedom of assembly; freedom of association; freedom of movement including the right of citizens to leave and return to South Africa; trade union rights including the right to work and the right to strike; the right to form political parties; the right to education, welfare and health care consistent with the needs of the people and the resources of the State; environmental rights; family and cultural rights, and providing for just compensation to be paid for property taken by the state.

10.2 We do not propose to discuss here the formulation of each right and the enforcement of rights as this has already been done in a detailed fashion in a discussion paper *The Draft Bill of Rights,* published in November 1990 by the African National Congress.

11. Provision will be made for discrimination to be eliminated in substance as well as in form. At all levels of government the State will

be empowered to pursue policies of affirmative action for the advancement of persons who have been socially, economically or educationally disadvantaged by past discriminatory laws and practices and in order to redress social, economic and educational imbalances in South Africa resulting from such discrimination, with special regard to the maldistribution of land and the need for housing. Special provision will also be made to redress the added discrimination which has been suffered by women and the victims of forced removals.

12. All discriminatory legislation and all other legislation inconsistent with the bill of rights will be invalidated by the bill of rights. All other legislation will remain in force unless repealed by Parliament or set aside by a court under its power of judicial review.

13. There will be a public service commission charged with the responsibility of overseeing the recruitment, promotion and dismissal to and from posts in the civil service. Such a commission will also be required to implement an affirmative action programme in regard to appointments to senior positions in order to redress existing race and gender disparities. Provision will be made for a representative structuring of the public service, the police service and the defence services and to ensure that the public service will be accountable for its actions.

14. There will be an independent Ombud with powers to investigate complaints against members of the public service including the police and other holders of public and private power and to investigate allegations of corruption.

15. The Constitution will also make provision for a state of emergency to be declared when the life of the nation is threatened. Such a power will be subject to strict controls by Parliament and the judiciary. The Constitution will provide for the recognition and protection as far as possible of fundamental rights during the period of emergency.

16. The Constitution will be subject to amendment only if a majority of two thirds of the National Assembly approve of the amendment or if approved by two thirds of the votes cast at a national referendum.

2 April 1991.

Source: Monitor, *Port Elizabeth, June 1991.*

APPENDIX G

Constitutional Rule in a Participatory Democracy,
September 4, 1991

CONSTITUTIONAL RULE IN A
PARTICIPATORY DEMOCRACY

In his opening address to the Federal Congress of the National Party held on September 4, 1991, the leader of the National Party, Mr. F. W. de Klerk, introduced the National Party's constitutional proposals for a new democratic dispensation for South Africa. Hereunder follow excerpts from this opening address by way of an introduction to the constitutional framework that has been proposed:

After two years of hard work, we are on the threshold of negotiations for a new constitution for the Republic of South Africa.

What is before you today is the result of many hours of research, dialogue, debate, formulation and reformulation.

It is not a blueprint, but a framework.

It is not rigid, but aims at laying a clear foundation for the negotiations for a realistic constitution.

It is no magic formula, but does offer a plan for a workable constitution which can guarantee democratic values.

It is not a government plan, but it does bear the stamp of the National Party.

Two years ago we stated the following point of departure in our Action Plan:

"South Africa is one undivided state with one citizenship for all. Every South African has the right to participate in political decision making on all levels of government which affects his interests, subject to the principle of no domination."

This is precisely what the document before you can and intends to bring about.

It offers full participation to all South Africans at all levels of government and does so on a universally acceptable basis. It is in line with successful democratic systems all over the free world.

As in other systems, it also offers effective protection against domination and abuse of power at all levels of government.

It is totally stripped of any racial basis and of discrimination and gives full expression to the principle of free association.

It will be able to preclude that a majority, however composed, could be able to misuse its power to suppress minorities, communities or individual rights.

And yet nobody can assert that it does not offer every South African full political rights on an equitable basis.

It will ensure that the new constitution and manifesto of fundamental rights cannot be manipulated or undermined.

It offers a place in the sun for the cultural diversities of our country, and the possibility of reasonable self-determination by communities in matters of intimate concern.

Briefly, this is what the National Party stands for:

A reasonable, just, new system which must strike a balance between protection of existing, established rights and the extension of rights to all South Africans;

A new dispensation which will do away with all forms of racial discrimination, while taking into account the needs of the diversity of our population;

A new dispensation which will be in line with the highest values which have proved themselves in successful democracies all over the world.

Of necessity, such a just, democratic dispensation has to be brought about by orderly, peaceful negotiations. It will not simply happen out of the blue. Every party which has significant and proven support will have to be able to put its points of view at the negotiating table. There we will have to toil, sweat and wrestle with the issues. There is no other way; and the National Party is ready for it.

That is what you support, when you support the National Party— balance, realism and a proven and civilised value system.

In our defence of these values, we shall not waver. The National Party has the capacity to prevent the adoption of a constitution which will militate against these values. We will not hesitate to use that ability.

The National Party will continue to work towards peaceful negotiation, with full recognition of the rights of all parties to take part in it. We will walk the road of negotiation, but we will not succumb to blustering and pressure from any source.

I am convinced that we are near a breakthrough to real negotiations. A great deal of progress has recently been made in co-operation among parties regarding violence and intimidation. It is as if the time is visibly becoming ripe.

Humanly spoken, the next two years, like the past two, will determine our country's course for the next five years. If ever there was a time for the supporters of our Party to be steadfast, then it is now. If ever there was a need for dedication and hard work, it has never been greater than now.

The National Party has taken a calculated leap. We have shed what was unjustifiable in our policy. We have taken the bull by the horns. Today we are a Party prepared for the future. We know what we want. We believe in our cause. We are carrying the banner of justice and nothing will stop us from playing a decisive role in the New South Africa.

Herewith follow the constitutional proposals as submitted at the Federal Congress:

BASIC POINTS OF DEPARTURE

The National Party has repeatedly committed itself to the creation of a new constitutional dispensation through negotiation. Such a new dispensation must be based on certain fixed points of departure. A system must be sought which, inter alia:

- ensures that universally accepted values and norms in South Africa are maintained
- is based on universal franchise in a democratic structure of government
- is free from apartheid and discrimination in any form
- is free from domination
- establishes an ordered and orderly society
- makes good government possible
- ensures justice for all
- promotes a market-orientated economy coupled with private initiative and social responsibility
- accommodates the cultural differences in South Africa
- enables all South Africans to share in peace, progress and prosperity.

There are considerable differences of opinion as to the specific constitutional model in which these basic points of departure may best be realized. In order to achieve the best possible result the National Party is striving for:

- negotiation at national level in order to reach agreement on the broad structure of government and to establish the position of central, regional and local authorities within that structure
- negotiation at regional level so that the needs, aspirations and problems of the residents of such a region may be properly accommodated and
- negotiation at local level in order to accomplish co-operation and harmony at grassroots level.

STRUCTURAL PRINCIPLES

A Three-Tier Government

The National Party proposes a three-tier government in which full legislative and executive functions and authority are conferred on central government and regional and local authorities. Regional and local authorities are therefore not merely administrative extensions of the central government; they are not merely the consequence of decentralized administration; on the contrary, every tier is "government" in its own right, with its own:

- elected authority that is responsible to the voters
- legislative and executive power
- tax base.

A three-tier system of government takes account of:

- the rich diversity of the population of South Africa, the needs of the communities in regional and local context, and the consequent need for self-determination in regional and local context
- the need to bring government as close to the people as possible, so that decisions can be taken at a level where the citizen's position is best understood
- the need for a rationalized and effective state administration.

The question is how the boundaries of regions are to be determined for regional government purposes. It is essential in any event for the present multiplicity of second-tier governments, consisting of four provinces, six self-governing territories and three own affairs administrations, to be simplified and included in a single system of regional government. It is suggested that the present nine development regions may present a good starting point for negotiation about new regional boundaries. Naturally adjustments to these will have to be considered. The present development regions which may be used as a starting point currently comprise **Region A** (Western Cape), **Region B** (Northern Cape), **Region C** (Orange Free State and Qwaqwa), **Region D** (Eastern Cape), **Region E** (Natal and KwaZulu), **Region F** (Eastern Transvaal and KaNgwane, **Region G** (Northern Transvaal, Lebowa and Gazankulu), **Region H** (Pretoria, Witwatersrand and Vereeniging area and KwaNdebele) and **Region J** (Western Transvaal).
(Please refer to the map of South Africa)
Although the present development regions include the four independent national states (Transkei, Bophuthatswana, Venda and Ciskei) in terms of agreements for purposes of co-operation regard-

ing regional development, their relationship with the new South Africa will have to be negotiated with each state individually.

As far as local authorities are concerned, municipal boundaries will have to be delimited on an appropriate geographical basis so as to replace current boundaries based on race. A delimitation authority could handle this task. A question which requires attention is whether the concepts "municipality" or "city council" should possibly be extended to include the whole of a district (that is, a town together with its rural district).

The Separation of Powers

A clear separation of the legislative, executive and judicial powers is a characteristic of modern democracies. Such separation is accepted as an essential feature of a new dispensation in South Africa.

The separation of powers prevents an over-concentration of power being vested in a specific part of government and contributes to achieving checks and balances. Consequently the constitution must contain arrangements that:

- prevent the executive authority from dominating the legislative authority, and vice versa
- confer on Parliament the authority to call the executive to account
- confer on the judicial authority jurisdiction, based on the constitution and the Charter of Fundamental Rights, to test and set aside Acts of Parliament and actions of the executive.

PARTICIPATORY DEMOCRACY:

Two Pillars

For the framework sketched above to really satisfy the unique needs of the South African situation, and to conform to our basic points of departure, it is necessary to frame the constitution in such a way that:

- a constitutional state is established
- a system is designed which will ensure the realization of a participatory democracy.

The First Pillar:
A Constitutional State

The term rule of law is used in constitutional debates to express the pursuit of justice and a limit on the power of the state. The National Party accepts the rule of law as the foundation on which such endeavors must be based. However, this term was developed within the distinctive milieu of the Westminster system and an unwritten constitution. The term constitutional state is therefore used to indicate that we are striving for a system that may rightfully be described as "constitutional government": a system in which the constitution and the law are the source of justice, and at the same time serve to curtail the powers of government.

The concept "constitutional state" expresses the view that the constitution of a country should regulate the power of government in such a way that freedom, justice and legal certainty are guaranteed for all.

Thus we are concerned with a constitutionally entrenched legal dispensation involving seven principles:

- The constitution must be the all-embracing criterion and guideline for the state and the citizen. Consequently it will enjoy a higher status than all other law; it may only be amended if special procedures are followed and compliance with its prescriptions will be enforceable by the courts.
- A Charter of Fundamental Rights must be constitutionally protected and legally enforceable. This will equip the citizen to protect himself against unlawful action by government. Effective protection of the fundamental rights of the individual will at the same time offer important protection of the interests of groups and communities.
- An independent judiciary is a cornerstone of the constitutional state. An independent court structure must have the jurisdiction to declare Acts of Parliament and actions of the government null and void if they do not comply in all respects with the criteria of the Constitution and the Charter of Fundamental Rights. The individual must have free access to the courts.
- Organizations and institutions that function in non-political spheres must enjoy the highest possible measure of self-determination in respect of their own fields of

interest in the community. Full recognition must be given to their autonomy in this regard.

- Mechanisms must be built in to prevent the abuse of government power and state structures. The office of an independent and objective Ombudsman must be instituted. The Auditor-General, the Public Service Commission and the Reserve Bank must be vested with greater autonomy, and a procedure for the appointment of judges must ensure the objectivity, professionalism and independence of the Bench.
- The integrity of the constitution must be ensured. The constitution must be protected against infringements. A system must be developed that ensures effective and balanced control over the security forces as the instrument for maintaining the constitution at all times.
- An impartial and professional civil service with career security for employees must be ensured and the Commission for Administration must be vested with sufficient authority.

Building these seven principles into the constitution effectively will ensure that:

- the interests of the citizens, as entrenched in the constitution, are respected by government
- the fundamental rights of the individual, including rights exercised in group and community context, are protected against infringement
- the government remains subject to the law, and cannot take arbitrary decisions
- the government will not interfere in fields where there is no legal authorization for doing so
- the abuse of power and maladministration are prevented
- the constitution is maintained.

The Second Pillar: Participatory Democracy

By "participatory democracy" is meant that a system of government is developed in which a number of political parties effectively participate and in which power-sharing therefore takes place. This is in contrast to the Westminster system in which one party exclusively enjoys power.

Participatory democracy takes into account the diversity of South African society and the reality of the existence of a multiplicity of socio-economic and cultural interest groups. Such groups do not exist in the community because they have been created or recognized in terms of legislation, but by virtue of the fact that people naturally and voluntarily associate with one another because they have some kind of interest in common. In its Five Year Action Plan of 1989 the National Party undertook to seek, through negotiation between leaders, a more just and meaningful basis than race and color on which groups may be defined for purposes of political participation. In the constitutional sphere the political party is the most effective means of furthering the interests of such groups. In other spheres interest groups define themselves in terms of other criteria. The National Party's conviction is that a new constitution should offer the opportunity for every viable political party to play an effective role at local, regional and central government [levels].

This concept may be put into effect in two ways:

- First, political power may be divided among various authorities. Most important here is the distribution of power among the different tiers of government. This is normally referred to as the principle of devolution of power.

Functions must be distributed among the different tiers of government in such a way that the constitution confers autonomous authority on every tier. (That is, original and entrenched authority with which the other tiers of government may not interfere.) The constitution must therefore stipulate which powers and duties are to be vested in the central government, regional government and municipal or local government. In each case it must be determined which tier of government can perform a particular function in the most appropriate and effective manner. While some functions may as a whole be allocated to one of the three tiers, it will be appropriate to spread other functions among all three tiers so as to allocate to each tier that aspect of a function which can be handled there most effectively in the interest of the community.

- Secondly, an effective say and participation in state power for a number of parties may be brought about.

These principles are elucidated below by outlining the framework of a model.

A Political Model

Introduction

This exposition presents the framework of a model embodying the above principles. The National Party has already received a mandate from the voters to negotiate a new constitution based on these principles. This particular model is not necessarily a final proposal which cannot be amended. It may be revised as a result of further reflection in the NP and by negotiations and also in the light of the expected reports of the South African Law Commission on fundamental rights on constitutional models that may be appropriate for the South African situation.

Central Government

Parliament

It is proposed that Parliament should consist of two Houses. Both Houses must adopt legislation.

The First House

The First House is elected proportionally, so that each political party receives a number of seats in accordance with the share of the political support which that party enjoys nationally on the strength of a general election. The electoral system may further be so organized that voters are also given the opportunity to express their preference for specific candidates in particular electoral districts, without the requirement of proportionality being sacrificed.

Legislation will be passed by a simple majority, but will be subject to a weighted majority (e.g. two-thirds) in respect of those issues entrenched in the constitution.

The Second House

A Second House, which is smaller than the First House, is proposed. An equal number of seats in the Second House will be allocated to each region. Each political party which has gained a specific amount of support in the election in the region's legislative body will be allocated an equal number of seats for that region in the Second House. Thus every democratic party which enjoys a significant amount of support in the region will be represented in the Second House. This will result in equal representation of both the regions and those political parties with significant support.

The functions of the Second House are to:

- deliberate on the bills which are approved by the First House and for which increased majorities are not required, and pass them by a simple majority
- deliberate on a pass by a weighted majority legislation which:
  - amends the constitution
  - relates to the interests of minorities
  - relates to the interests of regions
  - is entrenched in the constitution
- initiate legislation relating to circumscribed matters and which affects the specific interests of minorities and regions.

Executive Authority

The core of the National Party's proposals is that the executive should not be constituted from one party alone, but from members of a number of the major parties.

Thus a multiparty government (of which Western European coalition-style-government is an example) is preferred to a system where the majority party alone forms the executive of government. (The Westminster system usually results in this situation).

The present constitution excessively concentrates functions and authority in a single person, the State President. Instead, it is proposed that the office of head of state and government should be vested in a collective body known as the Presidency. The Presidency will consist of the leaders of the three largest parties in the First House. In the event that the three largest parties do not together represent the majority of the voters, the Presidency will be supplemented by as many additional leaders, in order of the size of their party, as may be required to represent a joint majority. A party that qualifies in these terms may however, if it so wishes, abstain from participating.

The chairmanship may rotate among the members on an annual basis. Decisions are taken by consensus. Likewise, a State President may be elected on a rotating basis from the ranks of the Presidency. The two Houses of Parliament may pass a motion of no confidence in the Presidency collectively (but not in individual members), in the Cabinet and in individual Ministers.

Source: South African Briefing Paper, *compiled and produced by the South African Consulate General, New York, N.Y., September 1991. Appendix is not complete paper; it omits three major sections at end: regional government, local government, freedom and justice.*

Notes

Chapter I: THE LAW OF APARTHEID (John Dugard)

1. *Debates of Parliament* [*Hansard*], 2 February 1990, col. 2.

2. In the 1950s South Africa's highest court, the Appellate Division of the Supreme Court, succeeded for several years in blocking a legislative scheme to remove Coloured voters in the Cape Province from the common voters' roll. This action was, however, the final attempt on the part of the courts to curb the excesses of the legislature. See John Dugard, *Human Rights and the South African Legal Order* (Princeton, N.J.: Princeton University Press, 1978), 28–34.

3. Union of South Africa Constitution Act 32 of 1961.

4. Ibid., Section 59.

5. Republic of South Africa Constitution Act 110 of 1983.

6. Ibid., Section 14(1).

7. Internal Security Amendment Act 66 of 1986, discussed in *South African Journal on Human Rights* 2 (1986): 258.

8. Republic of South Africa Constitution Act 110 of 1983, Sections 18(2) and 34(3).

9. Provincial Government Act 69 of 1986.

10. This figure does not include the populations of the so-called independent homelands of Transkei, Bophuthatswana, Venda, and Ciskei, which number a further six million.

11. Population Registration Act 30 of 1950, as amended by the Identification Act 72 of 1986.

12. Ibid., Sections 1 and 5(5).

13. Republic of South Africa Constitution Act 110 of 1983, Sections 52 and 100.

14. By the Population Registration Repeal Act 114 of 1991.

15. *Nationality* is a term of international law used to describe the relationship

between a state and its subject. *Citizenship*, on the other hand, is a term of constitutional law used to describe the status, and the entitlement to civil and political rights, of subjects within their state. South African law, however, does not maintain a clear distinction between these two concepts.

16. By the promotion of the Bantu Self-Government Act 46 of 1959. Subsequent important legislative measures furthering this policy were the Bantu Homelands Citizenship Act 26 of 1970 and the Homelands Constitution Act 21 of 1971.

17. *House of Assembly Debates*, vol. 72, 7 February 1978, col. 579.

18. *Citizen* (Johannesburg), 1 May 1987.

19. Development Trust and Land Act 18 of 1936.

20. Borders of Particular States Extension Act 2 of 1980.

21. Mathebe v. Government of the Republic of South Africa, 1988 (3) SA 667 (A).

22. State President v. Lefuo, 1990 (2) SA 679 (A).

23. Abolition of Racially Based Land Measures Act 108 of 1991; preface by the state president to the government's White Paper on Land Reform of 1991.

24. *Who Owns South Africa? Can the Repeal of the Land Acts Deracialise Land Ownership in South Africa?* Centre for Legal Applied Studies, Occasional Paper II, February 1991.

25. Abolition of Influx Control Act 68 of 1986.

26. See John Dugard, "The Denationalization of Black South Africans in Pursuance of Apartheid: A Question for the International Court of Justice?" *International Commission of Jurists Review*, No. 33 (1984): 49.

27. Restoration of South African Citizenship Act 73 of 1986.

28. *House of Assembly Debates*, vol. 11, 23 June 1986, col. 9375. See, too, *Race Relations Survey 1986*, Part 1 (Johannesburg: South African Institute of Race Relations, 1985), 94–95, 344.

29. Prevention of Illegal Squatting Act 52 of 1951; Slums Act 76 of 1976; and Trespass Act 66 of 1959.

30. *Statute Book of the Orange Free State*, ch. 33; Asiatics in the Northern Districts of Natal Act 33 of 1927; matters concerning Admission to and Residence in the Republic Amendment Act 53 of 1986.

31. Group Areas Act 36 of 1966, replacing the earlier Group Areas Act 41 of 1950.

32. Minister of the Interior v. Lockhat, 1961 (2) SA 587 (A), confirmed by the Appellate Division in S. v. Adams; S. v. Werner, 1981 (1) SA 187 (A).

33. S. v. Govender, 1986 (3) SA 969 (T).

34. Free Settlement Areas Act 102 of 1988.

35. Abolition of Racially Based Land Measures Act 108 of 1991.

36. Ibid., Section 98.

37. Prohibition of Mixed Marriages Act 55 of 1949 and Immorality Act 23 of 1957; Group Areas Act 36 of 1966, replacing the earlier Group Areas Act 41 of 1950; Bantu (Abolition of Passes and Coordination of Documents) Act 67 of 1952 and Bantu (Urban Areas) Consolidation Act 25 of 1945; Extension of University Education Act 45 of 1959 and Bantu Education Act 47 of 1953; and Reservation of Separate Amenities Act 49 of 1953.

38. Immorality and Prohibition of Mixed Marriages Amendment Act 72 of 1985.

39. Abolition of Influx Control Act 68 of 1986.

40. Industrial Conciliation Amendment Act 94 of 1979 and Labor Relations Amendment Act 57 of 1981.

41. Universities Amendment Act 83 of 1983.

42. Black Communities Development Amendment Act 74 of 1986.

43. Free Settlement Areas Act 102 of 1988.

44. Waks v. Jacobs, 1990 (1) SA 913 (T).

45. Reservation of Separate Amenities Act 49 of 1953.

46. Discriminatory Legislation Regarding Public Amenities Act 100 of 1990.

47. As a result of the Universities Amendment Act 83 of 1983.

48. Jane Hofmeyr, "Liberals and the Education Crisis," in *Democratic Liberalism in South Africa: Its History and Prospects*, ed. J. Butler, R. Elphick, and D. Welsh (Middletown, Conn.: Wesleyan University Press, 1987), 300 and 303.

49. Brown v. Board of Education of Topeka, 347 US 483 (1954) at 494–95.

50. United Nations Security Council Resolution 418 (4 November 1977). See, too, Resolution 417 (31 October 1977).

51. Suppression of Communism Act 44 of 1950. This law was renamed the Internal Security Act in 1976 to make it clear that it was not aimed only at communist activity, but at any activity that endangered the security of the state.

52. In R. v. Sisulu, 1953 (3) SA 276 (A), the leaders of the ANC were convicted of furthering the objects of "communism" by organizing a civil disobedience campaign aimed at the abolition of apartheid.

53. By the Criminal Law Amendment Act 8 of 1953; Public Safety Act 3 of 1953.

54. In terms of Section 14 of the General Law Amendment Act 37 of 1963 and Section 22 of the General Law Further Amendment Act 93 of 1963.

55. Section 17 of the General Law Amendment Act 37 of 1963; Section 215 *bis* of the Criminal Procedure Act 56 of 1955, inserted by Section 7 of Criminal Procedure Amendment Act 96 of 1965; and Terrorism Act 83 of 1967, Section 6.

56. Internal Security Act 74 of 1982.

57. Ibid., Sections 1 and 4; Section 5; Section 46; Sections 18–25.

58. Ibid., Section 31.

59. Ibid., Section 50A.

60. Ibid., Section 28.

61. Ibid., Section 29.

62. Ibid., Section 54(1). Like treason, this crime is punishable by death or life imprisonment; Section 54(2), punishable by a maximum of twenty years imprisonment; Section 54(3), punishable by a maximum of twenty years imprisonment; Section 55, punishable by imprisonment for a period not exceeding ten years; and Sections 58–59, provisions reenact the Criminal Law Amendment Act 8 of 1953.

63. Anthony S. Mathews, *Freedom, State Security and the Rule of Law* (Cape Town: Juta & Co., 1986): 37–38.

64. *Report on Police Conduct During Township Protests, August–November 1984* (Johannesburg: Southern African Catholic Bishops' Conference, 1984), 1–38.

65. Proc. R186, *Government Gazette* 12802 of 18 October 1990.

66. The text of this Minute appears in *South African Journal on Human Rights* 6 (1990): 318.

67. Internal Security and Intimidation Amendment Act 138 of 1991.

68. Internal Security Act 74 of 1982, Section 29.

69. *Star*, 20 June 1991.

70. Sections 18(2) and 34(3) of the South African Constitution.

71. The common law of South Africa is a blend of Roman-Dutch common law, which was inherited from the Netherlands during the days of Dutch rule from 1652–1806, and English common law.

72. Minister of the Interior v. Lockhat, 1961 (2) SA 587 (A); S. v. Adams; S. v. Werner, 1981 (1) SA 187 (A).

73. Anthony S. Mathews and R. C. Albino, "The Permanence of the Temporary," *South African Law Journal* 83 (1966): 16; John Dugard, "The Judicial Process, Positivism and Civil Liberty," *South African Law Journal* 88 (1971): 181.

74. *In re* Duma, 1983 (4) SA 469 (N).

75. Oos Randse Administrasieraad v. Rikhoto, 1983 (3) SA 595 (A); Black Affairs Administration Board, Western Cape v. Mthiya, 1985 (4) SA 744 (A).

76. Government of Republic of South Africa v. Government of KwaZulu, 1983 (1) SA 164 (A).

77. More v. Minister of Cooperation and Development, 1986 (1) SA 102 (A).

78. S. v. Govender, 1986 (3) SA 969 (T).

79. Mathebe v. Government of the Republic of South Africa, 1988 (3) SA 667 (A); State President v. Lefuo, 1990 (2) SA 679 (A).

80. S. v. Ramgobin, 1985 (3) SA 587 (N) at 588.

81. Nkondo v. Minister of Law and Order, 1986 (2) SA 756 (A).

82. Minister of Law and Order v. Hurley, 1986 (3) SA 568 (A).

83. C. Forsyth, "The Sleep of Reason: Security Cases Before the Appellate Division," *South African Law Journal* 105 (1988): 679.

84. Minister of Law and Order v. Dempsey, 1988 (3) SA 19 (A).

85. During N.O. v. Boesak, 1990 (3) SA 661 (A), particularly at 663 and 679–80.

86. S. v. Ebrahim, 1991 (2) 553 (A).

87. John Dugard, "No Jurisdiction Over Abducted Persons in Roman Dutch Law: Male Captus, Male Detentus," *South African Journal on Human Rights* 7 (1991): 199.

Chapter II: CIVIL LIBERTIES UNDER EMERGENCY RULE (Gilbert Marcus)

1. *States of Emergency: Their Impact on Human Rights* (Geneva: International Commission of Jurists, 1983), i.

2. Public Safety Act 3 of 1953, Section 2.

3. Ibid., Section 3(1)(a).

4. Ibid., Section 3(4) and 3(4) *bis*.

5. Section 1 *bis* inserted by the War Measures Act 32 of 1940.

6. *House of Assembly Debates*, vol. 81, 11 February 1953, col. 969.

7. Tom Lodge, *Black Politics in South Africa Since 1945* (Johannesburg: Ravan Press, 1983), 43.

8. *House of Assembly Debates*, vol. 81, 19 February 1953, col. 1544.

9. Ibid.

10. Criminal Law Amendment Act 8 of 1953.

11. Ibid., Section 2(b).

12. Albert Lutuli, *Let My People Go* (London: Fontana Books, 1962).

13. Proc. R90, *Government Gazette* 6403 of 30 March 1960.

14. *House of Assembly Debates*, 3 February 1961, cols. 699–700.

15. For a discussion of the regulations, see Anthony S. Mathews, *Law, Order and Liberty in South Africa* (Cape Town: Juta & Co., 1971), 221–30.

16. Unlawful Organizations Act 32 of 1960.

17. Procs. R91–94, *Government Gazette Extraordinary* 49 of 10 May 1963, and Procs. R183–85, *Government Gazette Extraordinary* 556 of 12 July 1963.

18. *House of Assembly Debates*, 2 February 1990, cols. 1–18. The following day special *Government Gazettes* were published giving effect to the state president's speech. The banning of all unlawful organizations was lifted by Government Notice 229, *Government Gazette* 12287 of 3 February 1990.

19. Cited in T. Karis and G. Gerhart, *From Protest to Challenge: Documents of African Politics in South Africa, 1882–1964*, vol. 3 (Stanford, Calif.: Hoover Institution Press, Stanford University, 1977), 777.

20. General Law Amendment Act 37 of 1963, Section 17(2).

21. Loza v. Police Station Commander, 1964 (2) SA 545 (A).

22. Mbele v. Minister of Justice, 1963 (4) SA 606 (D) at 608.

23. Loza v. Police Station Commander, 1964 (2) SA 545 (A) at 550.

24. Rossouw v. Sachs, 1964 (2) SA 551 (A).

25. Ibid., 564–65.

26. Schermbrucker v. Klindt N.O., 1965 (4) SA 606 (A).

27. Ibid., 619.

28. C. Forsyth, *In Danger For Their Talents* (Cape Town: Juta & Co., 1985), 144.

29. Section 215 *bis* of the Criminal Procedure Act 56 of 1955 inserted by Section 7 of the Criminal Procedure Amendment Act 96 of 1955.

30. Ibid.

31. Terrorism Act 83 of 1967, Section 6(6).

32. Ibid., Section 6(7).

33. Mathews, *Law, Order and Liberty in South Africa*, 151.

34. Riotous Assemblies Amendment Act 30 of 1974.

35. Government Notice 1125, *Government Gazette* 5189 of 18 June 1976.

36. Internal Security Amendment Act 79 of 1976, which inserted Section 10(1)(a) *bis* and Section 10(1)(a) *sex* into the Suppression of Communism Act 44 of 1950 and changed the title of the latter act to the Internal Security Act.

37. Report of the Commission of Inquiry into Security Legislation, no. R.P. 90/1981.

38. Internal Security Act 74 of 1982, Section 29; Sections 28 and 50; Section 31; Section 46; Section 4; Section 5; and Sections 18, 19, 20, 22, and 23, respectively.

39. Protection of Information Act 84 of 1982; Demonstrations In or Near Court Buildings Prohibition Act 71 of 1982; and Intimidation Act 72 of 1982, respectively.

40. Publications Act 42 of 1974, Section 47(2)(e).

41. Police Act 7 of 1958, Section 27B; Prisons Act 8 of 1959, Section 44 (1)(f); Defense Act 44 of 1957, Section 118; and Protection of Information Act 84 of 1982, respectively.

42. Detainees' Parents Support Committee, *Review of 1984*, 31 January 1985, 2.

43. *House of Assembly Debates*, 27 March 1985, col. 2827.

44. The term "raw recruit" was used by Judge Kannemeyer in Nkwinti v. Commissioner of Police, 1986 (2) SA 421 (E) at 438.

45. Public Safety Act 3 of 1953, Section 3(4).

46. *House of Assembly Debates*, 30 April 1986, col. 4520.

47. *House of Assembly Debates* (Questions and Replies), vol. 14, cols. 70–77.

48. Detainees' Parents Support Committee, *The DPSC Review of Detentions in 1986*, 31 January 1987, 3.

49. *Star*, 5 February 1987.

50. Affidavit of Major-General Francois Michael Alexander Steenkamp filed in the matter of Release Mandela Campaign v. State President, DCLD Case No. 2401/87, 28 April 1987, unreported, at 450 of the Record.

51. The Minister of Law and Order reported to Parliament on 9 June 1987 that he had ordered a "special and urgent high-level investigation into every individual case" and that all emergency detainees under sixteen years, with the exception of eleven, had been released. The eleven remaining detainees comprised one thirteen-year-old, two fourteen-year-olds, and eight fifteen-year-olds. See *House of Assembly Debates* (Questions and Replies), vol. 17, 9 June 1987, cols. 85–89.

52. Indicator Project of South Africa, *Political Conflict in South Africa: Data Trends 1984–1988* (December 1988).

53. *Star*, 19 February 1987.

54. See, generally, *The War Against Children: South Africa's Youngest Victims*, based on research by Helena Cook (New York: The Lawyers Committee for Human Rights, 1986); Lawyers Committee for Human Rights and Abantwana Bazabalaza, *A Memorandum on Children Under Oppression in South Africa* (Johannesburg: Detainees' Parents Support Committee, 1986).

55. Gilbert Marcus, "Judicial Attitudes to the Detention of Children," *South African Journal on Human Rights* 3 (1987): 234.

56. Statement issued by hunger strikers, reproduced in *South African Journal on Human Rights* 5 (1989): 98–99.

57. *Star*, 26 January 1989.

58. *Weekly Mail*, 10 February 1989.

59. Proc. R123, *Government Gazette* 10880 of 28 August 1987.

60. International Commission of Jurists, *States of Emergency: Their Impact on Human Rights*, 419.

61. Internal Security Amendment Act 66 of 1986; Public Safety Amendment Act 67 of 1986.

62. See Gilbert Marcus, "The Empire Strikes Back," *South African Journal on Human Rights* 2 (1986): 338.

63. Release Mandela Campaign v. State President, 1988 (1) SA 201 (N).

64. Sir Henry de Villiers C. J. in *In re* Willem Kok and Nathaniel Bailie, 1879 Buch. 45 at 66.

65. *Erosion of the Rule of Law in South Africa* (Geneva: International Commission of Jurists, 1968), iv.

66. Geoffrey Bindman, ed., *South Africa and the Rule of Law* (London: International Commission of Jurists, 1988), 113–14.

67. Per Acting Chief Justice Stratford in Sachs v. Minister of Justice, 1934 AD 11 at 37.

68. Per Judge Milne in R. v. Maphumulo, 1960 (3) SA 793 (N) at 798–99.

69. See, for example, Metal and Allied Workers' Union v. State President, 1986 (4) SA 358 (D), and Natal Newspapers (Pty) Limited v. State President, 1986 (4) SA 1109 (N).

70. See, for example, Dempsey v. Minister of Law and Order, 1986 (4) SA 530 (C); Jaffer v. Minister of Law and Order, 1986 (4) SA 1027 (C); and Radebe v. Minister of Law and Order, 1987 (1) SA 586 (W).

71. Nkwinti v. Commissioner of Police, 1986 (2) SA 421 (E).

72. DCLD Case No. 4988/86, 8 August 1986, unreported.

73. Kerchhoff v. Minister of Law and Order, NPD Case No. 1912/86, 14 August 1986, unreported.

74. Tsenoli v. State President, 1986 (4) SA 1150 (A) at 1178.

75. Rossouw v. Sachs, 1964 (2) SA 551 (A).

76. Nkwinti v. Commissioner of Police, 1986 (2) SA 421 (E); Metal and Allied Workers' Union v. State President, 1986 (4) SA 358 (D); Bloem v. State President, 1986 (4) SA 1064 (0); Release Mandela Campaign v. State President, 1988 (1) SA 201 (N); and Mokwena v. State President, 1988 (2) SA 91 (T).

77. Omar v. Minister of Law and Order, 1987 (3) SA 859 (A). The judgment is a composite one involving three cases: Omar, Fani v. Minister of Law and Order, and State President v. Bill.

78. Lawrence Baxter, "A Judicial Declaration of Martial Law," *South African Journal on Human Rights* 3 (1987): 318.

79. Minister of Law and Order v. Dempsey, 1988 (3) SA 19 (A).

80. Ngqumba v. Staatspresident, 1988 (4) SA 224 (A).

81. The "ouster clause" is contained in s5B of the Public Safety Act and provides that "no interdict or other process shall issue for the staying or setting aside of any proclamation issued by the state president and no court shall be competent to enquire into or give judgment on the validity of any such proclamation . . . ." Traditional construction of such clauses had previously never precluded judicial review on the grounds of

vagueness and uncertainty. See, generally, *1988 Annual Survey of South African Law* at 62–64.

82. Internal Security and Intimidation Amendment Bill 118B, 91 (GA).

83. Section 29(1) of the Internal Security Act as amended by Section 13 of the Internal Security and Intimidation Amendment Act 138 of 1991.

84. Section 4 of the Internal Security Act as amended by Section 5 of the Internal Security and Intimidation Amendment Act 138 of 1991.

85. G. Budlender, "Law and Lawlessness in South Africa," *South African Journal on Human Rights* 4 (1988): 152.

Chapter III: THE TOTAL STRATEGY: THE SOUTH AFRICAN SECURITY FORCES AND THE SUPPRESSION OF CIVIL LIBERTIES (Nicholas Haysom)

1. See Robert S. Jaster, Moeletsi Mbeki, Morley Nkosi, and Michael Clough, *Changing Fortunes: War, Diplomacy, and Economics in Southern Africa* (New York: Ford Foundation and Foreign Policy Association, 1992).

2. J. Seiler, *The South African State Security System*, U.S. Army John F. Kennedy Special Warfare Center and School (1983).

3. 1977 White Paper on Defense and Armaments Supply, Department of Defense, 1977, 4.

4. André Beaufre, *An Introduction to Strategy* (London: Faber & Faber, 1963); P. Frankel, *Pretoria's Praetorians: Civil-Military Relations in South Africa* (Cambridge: Cambridge University Press, 1984), 46; W. Ebersohn, "How South Africa Fights the Total Onslaught," *Star*, 10 November 1988.

5. S. Miles, "The Real War: Low Intensity Conflict in Central America," *Report on the Americas* 20, no. 2 (1986): 45.

6. Frankel, *Pretoria's Praetorians*, 11.

7. J. Fullerton, "South Africa: Day of the Generals," *Now!* (London), 5 October 1979; *Observer*, 13 January 1981.

8. R. Leonard, *South Africa at War* (Westport, Conn.: Lawrence Hill & Company, 1983), 23–28; G. Cawthra, *Brutal Force* (London: International Defence and Aid Fund for Southern Africa, 1986), 38–40; Kenneth W. Grundy, *The Rise of the South African Security Establishment: An Essay on the Changing Locus of State Power* (Johannesburg: South African Institute of International Affairs, 1983), 13.

9. P. Frankel, "Race and Counter-Revolution: South Africa's Total Strategy," *Journal of Commonwealth and Comparative Studies* 18, no. 3 (1980): 277.

10. *Sunday Times* (Johannesburg), 11 July 1982. See also M. Phillips and M.

Swilling, "State Power in the 1980s," in J. Cock and L. Nathan, *War and Society* (Cape Town: David Philip, 1989).

11. Grundy, *The Rise of the South African Security Establishment.*

12. *Weekly Mail,* 3 October 1986; *Star,* 10 November 1988; *Weekly Mail,* 3 October 1986.

13. *Weekly Mail,* 3 October 1986. See also Cawthra, *Brutal Force,* 123.

14. *The Argus,* 9 December 1986.

15. *Weekly Mail,* 3 October 1986. There were twelve Joint Management Centres and sixty sub-Joint Management Centres, each chaired by a military or police officer.

16. Ibid.

17. In 1986 the SADF "leaked" a high-level "confidential" memorandum complaining of police practices in the townships. N. Haysom et al., "Human Rights Index, 1 July 1986–30 September 1986," *South African Journal on Human Rights* 2 (1986): 390. In private, SADF officers suggested that one of the reasons the SADF was called into the townships was to supervise police behavior.

18. Leonard, *South Africa at War,* 100. The SADF denied that it had supported the Mozambican Resistance Movement (RENAMO) since 1984.

19. Captain Dirk J. Coetzee, "Urban Terror and Counter Measures," unpublished conference paper, 1983, 13, cited in Cawthra, *Brutal Force,* 221.

20. *A Rigid Constitution, the Decentralization of Government, and the Administration of Justice. A Report Prepared for the Progressive Party of South Africa by a Commission of Experts,* vol. 2 (Cape Town, 1962), 29.

21. Police Act 7 of 1958, Section 5.

22. T. Weaver, "Caught in the Crossfire: The War in Namibia," *Work in Progress,* No. 29 (1983): 5; Cawthra, *Brutal Force,* 123; N. Haysom et al., "Human Rights Index, November 1985–February 1986," *South African Journal on Human Rights* 2 (1986): 133; N. Haysom and D. Smuts, "Human Rights Index, July 1985–October 1985," *South African Journal on Human Rights* 1 (1985): 319.

23. P. Frankel, "South Africa: The Politics of Police Control," *Comparative Politics* 12 (1980): 486.

24. *Official Yearbook of the Republic of South Africa Bureau for Information* (Pretoria, 1986), 296.

25. Ibid.

26. Ibid.

27. *Debates of Parliament* (Questions and Replies), vol. 17, 21 March 1990, col. 614. See also *Financial Mail,* 26 January 1990, which gives the 1988 figure for the SAP as 60,878.

28. *Financial Mail,* 26 January 1990; *Business Day,* 15 May 1991.

29. Seiler, *The South African State Security System.*

30. *House of Assembly Debates*, vol. 63, 22 June 1976, col. 10103.

31. *Servamus* (South African Police), November 1984.

32. *Debates of Parliament* (Questions and Replies), vol. 17, 21 March 1990, col. 614. See also *Financial Mail*, 26 January 1990, which gives the 1988 figure for the SAP as 60,878.

33. Annual Report of the Commissioner of the South African Police for the period 1 July 1985 to 30 June 1986, no. R.P. 91/1987.

34. *Now Everyone Is Afraid: The Changing Face of Policing in South Africa* (London: Catholic Institute for International Relations, 1989). See also *Natal Witness*, 8 September 1990.

35. *Servamus*, June 1983.

36. Cawthra, *Brutal Force*, 259. Figures based on official sources, specifically the "Estimate of Expenditure to be Defrayed from the State Revenue Account" (Pretoria, various years).

37. "South Africa (Republic) Estimate of the Expenditure to be Defrayed from the State Revenue Account During Financial Year Ending 31 March 1990," no. R.P. 2/1989, 2.6.1.

38. *Business Day*, 18 June 1990.

39. B. van Niekerk, "The Police in Apartheid Society," in *Law, Justice and Society: Report of the Spro-Cas Legal Commission* (Johannesburg: Spro-Cas, 1972), 56; Frankel, "South Africa: The Politics of Police Control," 486; *Cape Times*, 16 August 1985, cited in D. Foster and C. Luyt, "The Blue Man's Burden: Policing the Police in South Africa," *South African Journal on Human Rights* 2 (1986): 310.

40. *Business Day*, 21 May 1991.

41. *Cape Times*, 16 August 1985, cited in Foster and Luyt, "The Blue Man's Burden," 305.

42. Ibid.

43. *Star*, 19 April 1969, cited in van Niekerk, "The Police in Apartheid Society," 60.

44. *Report on Police Conduct During Township Protests August–November 1984*, Southern African Catholic Bishops' Conference, Johannesburg, 1984, 2–18.

45. *Star*, 19 April 1969, cited in van Niekerk, "The Police in Apartheid Society," 43.

46. Frankel, "South Africa: The Politics of Police Control," 492.

47. Ibid.

48. Lawyers Committee for Civil Rights Under Law, *Deaths in Detention and South Africa's Security Laws*, Washington, D.C., 1983, 30.

49. Ibid., 65.

50. Ibid.

51. Ibid.

52. Internal Security Act 74 of 1982; Government Notice 877, *Government Gazette* 8467, 3 December 1982.

53. According to the *New York Times*, 2 December 1990, the Human Rights Commission identified seventy-three deaths in detention between 1963 and 1990.

54. Detainees' Parents Support Committee Memorandum on Security Police Abuses of Political Detainees, Johannesburg, 1983.

55. D. Foster, D. Davis, and D. Sandler, *Detention and Torture in South Africa: Psychological, Legal and Historical Studies* (Cape Town: David Philip, 1987).

56. N. Haysom, "Closed Circuit Television for Detainees," *Lawyers for Human Rights Bulletin*, No. 4 (1984): 100.

57. *Human Rights in the Homelands: South Africa's Delegation of Repression* (New York: Fund for Free Expression, 1984).

58. National States Constitution Act 21 of 1971.

59. *Human Rights in the Homelands.*

60. N. Haysom, *Ruling with the Whip: A Report on the Violation of Human Rights in the Ciskei*, Occasional Paper No. 5, Centre for Applied Legal Studies, University of the Witwatersrand, 1983.

61. Inquest into the Death of Peter Nchabaleng, Seshego Magistrates Court Inquest No. 1/1987, 17 August 1987; *Star*, 18 August 1987.

62. Inquest into the Death of Lucky Kutumela, Mokopane Magistrates Court Inquest No. 1/1986, 4 March 1987; *The Argus*, 9 June 1987.

63. N. Haysom et al., "Human Rights Index, March 1986–July 1986," *South African Journal on Human Rights* 2 (1986): 265.

64. Ibid.; *South African Journal on Human Rights* 3 (1987): 4.

65. Haysom et al., "Human Rights Index, November 1985–February 1986," 126.

66. Ibid., 126–27, 266–67; Haysom, *Ruling with the Whip*; *Human Rights in the Homelands*. The government of KwaNdebele changed in 1988 and the many abuses of the Skosana regime were the subject of the Parsons Commission of Inquiry. See *Sowetan*, 26 September 1989.

67. Defense Act 44 of 1957, Section 3(2).

68. *Kommando*, May 1960, 5–6, cited in Cawthra, *Brutal Force*, 14.

69. Defense Amendment Act 35 of 1977.

70. Lieutenant-General J. R. Dutton, "The Military Aspects of National Security," in *National Security: A Modern Approach*, ed. Michael H. H. Louw (Pretoria: Institute for Strategic Studies, University of Pretoria, 1978), 107.

71. Cawthra, *Brutal Force*, 225.

72. Defense Amendment Act 87 of 1984. See also *Race Relations Survey 1984*, 738.

73. British Broadcasting Corporation, 11 October 1984. See also *Race Relations Survey 1984*, 751.

74. Leonard, *South Africa at War*, 100; Cawthra, *Brutal Force*, 116.

75. Leonard, *South Africa at War*, 99.

76. Estimates by Cawthra, *Brutal Force*, 260, on the basis of figures supplied in the 1984 Defense White Paper. The minister of defense now refuses to disclose figures of SADF membership. *House of Assembly Debates* (Questions and Replies), vol. 20, 7 August 1987, cols. 507–8.

77. Cawthra, *Brutal Force*, 264.

78. Ibid.

79. Defense Amendment Act 34 of 1983.

80. *Race Relations Survey 1984*, 750–51.

81. N. Haysom et al., "Human Rights Index, 1 February 1987–16 June 1987," *South African Journal on Human Rights* 3 (1987): 275.

82. End Conscription Campaign v. Minister of Defense, 1989 (2) SA 180 (C).

83. See Professor Tjaart van der Walt's "Report on the Investigation into Education for Blacks in the Vaal Triangle Following Upon the Occurrences of 3 September 1984 and Thereafter," R.P. 88/1985.

84. During the twelve months of the 1986–87 emergency, fifty-four orders were issued by commissioners of police in the Republic alone (excluding homelands). They are summarized in L. Levin, "State of Emergency, 12 June 1986–11 June 1987," *South African Journal on Human Rights* 3 (1987): 424–28.

85. Regulation 16 of Proc. R109, *Government Gazette* 10280 of 12 June 1986 and regulation 12 of Proc. R96, *Government Gazette* 10771 of 11 June 1987; regulation 15 of Proc. R97, *Government Gazette* 11340 of 10 June 1988; regulation 15 of Proc. R86, *Government Gazette* 11946 of 9 June 1989.

86. Regulation 3(10) of Proc. R109, *Government Gazette* 10280 of 12 June 1986; regulation 3(8) of Proc. R96, *Government Gazette* 10771 of 11 June 1987; regulation 3(7) of Proc. R97, *Government Gazette* 11340 of 10 June 1988; regulation 3(7) of Proc. R86, *Government Gazette* 11946 of 9 June 1989.

87. Proc. R109, *Government Gazette* 10280 of 12 June 1986; Proc. R224, *Government Gazette* 10541 of 11 December 1986; Proc. R97, *Government Gazette* of 11 June 1987.

88. Zwelakhe Sisulu, editor of the newspaper *New Nation*, was detained in October 1986 and released only in 1989. Alan Cowell of the *New York Times*, Peter Sharp (Independent Television News), Michael Buerk (BBC), and Steve Mufson (freelance journalist) were compelled to leave the country in 1987. N. Haysom et al., "Human Rights Index, October 1986–January 1987," *South African Journal on Human Rights* 3 (1987): 132; id., "Human Rights Index, 1 February 1987–16 June 1987," 271.

89. *House of Assembly Debates*, vol. 14, 23 February 1987, col. 1302.

90. *Report on Police Conduct During Township Protests*, Southern African Catholic Bishops' Conference, August–November 1984.

91. See N. Haysom et al., "Human Rights Index, March 1986–July 1986," 255.

92. "Apartheid's Violence Against Children," General Working Paper A1, International Conference on Children, Repression and the Law in South Africa, Harare, 1987. This figure excludes children killed by homeland agencies, municipal police, or vigilantes.

93. See N. Haysom et al., "Human Rights Index, March 1986–July 1986," 255.

94. Report of the Commission Appointed to Inquire into the Incident Which Occurred on 21 March 1985 at Uitenhage (Chairperson: Justice Kannemeyer), no. R.P. 74/1985.

95. See N. Haysom, "Licence to Kill: The South African Police and the Use of Deadly Force," *South African Journal on Human Rights* 3 (1987): 3.

96. See N. Haysom and D. Smuts, "Human Rights Index, July 1985–October 1985," 298; Hans Pienaar and Hein Willemse, *Die Trojaanse Perd: Onderhoude Oor Die Noodtoestand in Die Kaap—1985* (Johannesburg: Taurus, 1986).

97. *The War Against Children: South Africa's Youngest Victims* (New York: Lawyers Committee for Human Rights, 1986), 48–49.

98. See *DPSC Sixth Special Report on State of Emergency*, Johannesburg, 30 April 1987; Haysom, "Licence to Kill," 216.

99. See N. Haysom et al., "Human Rights Index, November 1985–February 1986," 112–13.

100. *Business Day*, 8 July 1987.

101. *Servamus*, September 1985, 31.

102. Ibid. See also *Business Day*, 8 July 1987.

103. For the period of the 1986/87 emergency, the Detainees' Parents Support Committee estimates that 25,000 people were detained (*DPSC Sixth Special Report on State of Emergency*). During June 1987, an estimated further 3,000 people were detained. However, it is thought that of the 3,000 half may have been redetentions, resulting in a final estimated figure of 26,500 (*DPSC Seventh Special Report on State of Emergency*, Johannesburg, 30 June 1987).

104. *Anatomy of Repression* (Johannesburg: Human Rights Commission, December 1989), 2.

105. *DPSC Sixth Special Report on State of Emergency*.

106. Lawyers Committee for Human Rights and Abantwana Bazabalaza, *A Memorandum on Children Under Oppression* (Johannesburg: Detainees' Parents Support Committee, 1986), 6.

107. Miles, "The Real War," 21–23.

108. Ibid.

109. Ibid., 19.

110. M. Phillips and M. Swilling, "The Politics of State Power in the 1980s," Centre for Policy Studies, University of the Witwatersrand, July 1988; G. Evans and M. Phillips, "Intensifying Civil War: The Role of the South African Defense Force," in *State Resistance and Change in South Africa*, ed. P. Frankel, N. Pines, and M. Swilling (Johannesburg: Southern Book, 1989).

111. D. Webster and M. Friedman, *Suppressing Apartheid's Opponents* (Johannesburg: Detainees' Parents Support Committee, 1989), 3.

112. Phillips and Swilling, "The Politics of State Power in the 1980s," 22–23.

113. For the linkage of repression and reform, see Coetzee, "Urban Terror and Counter Measures," 13, cited in Cawthra, *Brutal Force*, 221.

114. N. Haysom, "Mabangalala: The Rise of Rightwing Vigilantes," in Occasional Paper No. 10, Centre for Applied Legal Studies, University of the Witwatersrand, 1986.

115. Ibid.

116. Ibid.

117. Ibid.

118. Ibid. These events are now the subject of the Parsons Commission of Inquiry into Unrest and Mismanagement in KwaNdebele. *Sowetan*, 26 September 1989.

119. These vigilantes were referred to as *witdoeke*, meaning "white scarves," because many of them wore a scarf tied around their heads. See Josette Cole, *Crossroads: The Politics of Reform and Repression 1976–1986* (Johannesburg: Ravan Press, 1987), 131–57.

120. See N. Haysom et al., "Human Rights Index, March 1986–July 1986," 256–57; Mzamke v. Minister of Law and Order, CPD Case No. 13082/86.

121. *Report on Imbali Stage I: Role of the Police in Vigilante Violence in the Pietermaritzburg Area* (Pietermaritzburg: Congress of South African Trade Unions, 29 March 1989).

122. "Unrest Chronology," *Indicator SA* 5, no. 3 (1988): 50.

123. *Report on Imbali Stage I.*

124. M. S. Dontzin, "Crisis in the Administration of Justice in South Africa: A Case Study of Vigilante Violence, Police Partiality and Prosecutorial Incompetence in Pietermaritzburg, Natal," Report to the New York Bar Association, 15 March 1989.

125. *Weekly Mail*, 15 June 1989.

126. *Report on Imbali Stage I*, 1; "Unrest Chronology," 50.

127. *ANC/Inkatha Responsibility for Reef Violence: Some Statistics* (Johannesburg: Community Agency for Social Enquiry, May 1991), 2–6.

128. These regulations are to be found in Proc. R121, *Government Gazette* 9877 of 21 July 1985; Proc. R109, *Government Gazette* 10280 of 12 June 1986; Proc. R96, *Government Gazette* 10771 of 11 June 1987; Proc. R97, *Government Gazette* 11340 of 10 June 1988; Proc. R86, *Government Gazette* 11946 of 9 June 1989.

129. *Weekly Mail*, 20 October 1989.

130. S. v. Yengeni, Cape Provincial Division, 11 May 1989 unreported; *Cape Times*, 12 May 1989.

131. *Business Day*, 30 March 1990.

132. Ibid.

133. L. Levin, ed., "Human Rights Index, 1 October 1989–28 February 1990," *South African Journal on Human Rights* 6 (1990): 127; id., "Human Rights Index, 1 March 1990–30 June 1990," *South African Journal on Human Rights* 6 (1990): 330; *Monthly Report of the Independent Board of Inquiry into Informal Repression*, Johannesburg, June–July 1990.

134. *IBIIR Response to the Harms Commission Report* (Johannesburg: Independent Board of Inquiry into Informal Repression, November 1990).

135. *Report of the Commission of Inquiry into Certain Alleged Murders*, Justice Harms, no. R.P. 109/1990.

136. *Monthly Report of the Independent Board of Inquiry into Informal Repression*, June 1990, 11.

137. Ibid., 9.

138. General Lothar Paul Neethling v. Max du Preez, WLD, 18 March 1991, Case No. 24659/89 unreported.

139. Helmoed-Romer Heitman, "Some Possibilities in Counter-Insurgency Operations," *Militaire* (1977), cited in *Weekly Mail*, 24 November 1989.

140. M. S. Diokno, *Self-Styled Guardians of Democracy: Vigilantes in the Philippines* (Catholic Institute for International Relations, 1988); "Death Squads and Vigilantes," paper prepared for the Catholic Institute for International Relations (CIIR) conference, London, 18–19 May 1988.

141. Interview with Lt. Gregory Rockman, SAP press release, 6 September 1989.

142. *Weekly Mail*, 29 September 1989.

143. *Weekly Mail*, 13 October 1989.

144. *Business Day*, 12 September 1989.

145. *Star*, 22 October 1989; *Cape Times*, 2 November 1989.

146. *Star*, 22 October 1989.

147. L. Levin, "Human Rights Index," *South African Journal on Human Rights* 6 (1990): 132.

148. *SA Barometer* (Johannesburg) 4, no. 5 (30 March 1990).

149. *Report of the Commission of Inquiry into Certain Alleged Murders* (Chairper-

son: Justice L.T.C. Harms), *Government Gazette* 12286 of 2 February 1990; *Commission of Inquiry into the Death in Detention of Clayton Sithole* (Chairman: Justice R. J. Goldstone), *Government Gazette* 12286 of 2 February 1990.

150. *South African Journal on Human Rights* 6 (1990): 322.

151. *Star,* 4 April 1990.

152. *Sunday Times,* 28 January 1990.

153. *Financial Mail,* 26 January 1990.

154. *Business Day,* 10 July 1990.

155. *Weekly Mail,* 5 April 1990.

Chapter IV: BLACKS AND THE ADMINISTRATION OF JUSTICE (John Dugard)

1. *Race Relations Survey 1988/89,* 521–22.

2. Section 10 of the Supreme Court Act 59 of 1959 provides for the appointment of "fit and proper" persons as judges. In South African judicial history, only one woman has been appointed to the bench.

3. See D. D. Mokgatle, "The Exclusion of Blacks from the South African Judicial System," *South African Journal on Human Rights* 3 (1987): 44.

4. *Race Relations Survey 1987/88,* 550.

5. *Race Relations Survey 1988/89,* 530–31. Cf. Amon M. Dlamini, "Apartheid and the Black Judge," *South African Journal on Human Rights* 5 (1989): 246.

6. Section 92 of the Magistrates Courts Act 32 of 1944.

7. *Debates of Parliament [Hansard]* (Questions and Replies), vol. 1, 27 March 1990, cols. 723–24.

8. In the TBVC states there were twenty regional magistrates, of whom nine were African. Of the fifty-three district magistrates, forty-eight were African.

9. *Debates of Parliament [Hansard],* vol. 1, 27 March 1990, col. 722. This figure takes no account of the prosecutors in the TBVC states and self-governing homelands.

10. S. A. Strauss, "The Jury in South Africa," *University of Western Australia Review* 11 (1973): 133; John Dugard, "Introduction to Criminal Procedure," *South African Criminal Law and Procedure* 4 (Cape Town: Juta & Co., 1977), 42–43.

11. P. R. Spiller, "Race and the Courts in the Colonial and Modern Eras," in *Race and the Law in South Africa* (Cape Town: Juta & Co., 1987), 58–59.

12. Abolition of Juries Act 34 of 1969; *House of Assembly Debates,* vol. 25, 27 February 1969, col. 1537.

13. Criminal Procedure Act 51 of 1977, Section 145.

14. Ibid., Section 145(1)(b).

15. Mokgatle, "The Exclusion of Blacks from the South African Judicial System," 47–48.

16. Louis Fischer, *The Life of Mahatma Gandhi*, Part One (London: Jonathan Cape, 1951).

17. A. Sachs, *Justice in South Africa* (Berkeley: University of California Press, 1973), 205.

18. Ibid., 213–14.

19. For many years, Ismail Mahomed, who became South Africa's first black Supreme Court judge, was obliged to work from the bar library on account of the prohibition on occupying chambers. See Nelson Mandela's statement on this subject when he appeared in court in 1962, charged with inciting African workers to strike and leaving the country illegally. Nelson Mandela, *No Easy Walk to Freedom* (London: Heineman Educational Books, 1965), 148–49.

20. R. v. Pitje, 1960 (4) SA 709 (A).

21. Mandela, *No Easy Walk to Freedom*, 149–50.

22. This figure was made up of twenty-six Indians, thirteen Africans, and five Coloured persons. Sachs, *Justice in South Africa*, 211.

23. D. D. Mokgatle, "Choosing Law as a Career," *African Law Review* 1, no. 1 (January 1987): 11–13; "How Many Black Lawyers in South Africa," *African Law Review* 1, no. 2 (May 1987): 16–18.

24. In 1990, 278 (37 percent) of the 749 law students in the Faculty of Law at the University of the Witwatersrand were black.

25. Mokgatle, "The Exclusion of Blacks from the South African Judicial System," 47.

26. C. Dlamini, "The Influence of Race on the Administration of Justice in South Africa," *South African Journal on Human Rights* 4 (1988), 38–39.

27. Karis and Gerhart, *From Protest to Challenge*.

28. Ibid., 726–30; Mandela, *No Easy Walk to Freedom*, 126–29.

29. Karis and Gerhart, *From Protest to Challenge*, 728; Mandela, *No Easy Walk to Freedom*, 127–28.

30. See Sachs, *Justice in South Africa*, 203–5.

31. *Race Relations Survey 1988/89*, 529.

32. R. v. Tusini, 1953 (4) SA 406 (A); R. v. A, 1952 (3) SA 212 (A); S. v. M, 1965 (4) SA 577 (N); S. v. Sihlani, 1966 (3) SA 148 (E); Mcunu v. R., 1938 NPD 229; S. v. Magwaza, 1985 (3) SA 29 (A); Dlamini, "The Influence of Race on the Administration of Justice in South Africa," 37.

33. See the remarks of Rumpff C.J. in S. v. Holder, 1979 (2) SA 70 (A) at 76.

34. According to Amnesty International's *When the State Kills . . . The Death Penalty v. Human Rights* (1989), South Africa (with 537 executions) was second only to Iran (with 743 executions)—and possibly Iraq—in the

number of executions carried out between 1985 and mid-1988 (page 263). Many studies have been conducted on the death penalty in South Africa. See, for example, B. van Niekerk, ". . . Hanged by the Neck Until You Are Dead," *South African Law Journal* 86 (1969): 457; *South African Law Journal* 87 (1970): 60; E. Kahn, "The Death Penalty in South Africa," *Tydskrif vir Hedendaagse Romeins-Hollandse Reg* 33 (1970): 108; "Focus on Capital Punishment," *South African Journal of Criminal Justice* 2 (1989): 135–270.

35. *The Death Penalty in South Africa*, Fact Paper No. 5 (Johannesburg: Human Rights Commission, October 1989), 1–12. Of the 2,740 persons executed before 1970, less than 100, it is estimated, were white; see Kahn, "The Death Penalty in South Africa," 119–21; *South African Law Journal* 87 (1970): 72. Between 1980 and 1988, 97 percent of the 1,070 persons hanged were black; see *Inside South Africa's Death Factory*, pamphlet (Johannesburg: Black Sash, 1989), 5. In 1989, fifty-three persons were executed, of whom two were white; see *Debates of Parliament [Hansard]* (Questions and Replies), 2 March 1990, col. 273. Whites comprise about 14 percent of the South African population.

36. "Mentioning the Unmentionable: Race as a Factor in Sentencing," *South African Journal of Criminal Law and Criminology* 3 (1979): 155. See, too, Sachs, *Justice in South Africa*, 154–55.

37. In 1989 Barend Strydom, a member of a racist organization known as the "White Wolves," was sentenced to death for killing eight blacks. This sentence was later commuted to life imprisonment.

38. F. McClead and F. Kaganas, comp., "Statement on Sentencing," *South African Journal on Human Rights* 1 (1985): 106.

39. *Race Relations Survey 1988/89*, 531.

40. Minister of the Interior vs. Lockhat, 1961 (2) SA 587 (A) at 602. See, further, John Dugard, *Human Rights and the South African Legal Order* (Princeton, N.J.: Princeton University Press, 1978), 319.

41. R. v. Pitje, 1960 (4) SA 709 (A); Dugard, *Human Rights and the South African Legal Order*, 321.

42. Dugard, *Human Rights and the South African Legal Order*, 303–65.

43. The Zimbabwean experience provides an excellent example of how blacks may be appointed to the bench in a previously white-dominated society. See, on this, John Redgment, *"Plus ca change. . .* Fifty Years of Judges in Southern Rhodesia, Rhodesia, and Zimbabwe," *South African Law Journal* 102 (1985): 537. Today the Zimbabwean bench enjoys great respect for its competence and independence.

44. Dlamini, "The Influence of Race on the Administration of Justice in South Africa," 53–54. See, too, Mokgatle, "The Exclusion of Blacks from the South African Judicial System," 51; Cf. Dlamini, "Apartheid and the Black Judge," 246.

Chapter V: *LOOKING AHEAD* (John Dugard)

1. *Debates of Parliament [Hansard]*, 2 February 1990, col. 2 at 15–16.

2. The text of the Groote Schuur Minute appears in *South African Journal on Human Rights* 6 (1990): 318.

3. Ibid., 322.

4. Ibid., 319.

5. *Debates of Parliament [Hansard]*, 1 February 1991, cols. 6–7.

6. *House of Assembly Debates*, vol. 7, 7 February 1986, col. 428.

7. *Star*, 20 February 1990.

8. L. M. Thompson, *The Unification of South Africa 1902–1910* (Oxford: Clarendon Press, 1960), 97–109.

9. In 1962 the Progressive Party approved a report prepared by a commission of experts under the chairmanship of Donald Molteno, Q.C., advocating a federal solution; see *A Rigid Constitution, the Decentralization of Government, and the Administration of Justice*. This report is known as the "Molteno Report."

10. This policy was advocated by the United Party, the official white opposition party in Parliament in the 1960s and 1970s. It finds its intellectual stimulation in Carl Friedrich's idea of "corporate federalism," which contemplates a federation based on ethnic groupings rather than territorial divisions; see Carl Friedrich, *Trends of Federalism in Theory and Practice* (London: Pall Mall, 1968).

11. Nathaniel H. Masemola, "Rights and a Future South African Constitution: The Controversial and the Non-Controversial," *Columbia Human Rights Law Review* 21 (1989): 45, 49.

12. Leon Louw and Frances Kendall, *South Africa: The Solution* (Bisho, Ciskei: Amagi Publications, 1986).

13. See John Dugard, "The Quest for a Liberal Democracy in South Africa," in *Acta Juridica* (1987): 236.

14. See Murray Forsyth, *Federalism and the Future of South Africa*, Bradlow Series No. 2 (Johannesburg: South African Institute of International Affairs, 1984), 8.

15. Donald L. Horowitz, *A Democratic South Africa? Constitutional Engineering in a Divided Society* (Cape Town: Oxford University Press, 1991); *Power Sharing in South Africa*, Policy Papers in International Affairs No. 24, Institute of International Studies, 1985, 23–24; "Federal, Confederal and Consociational Options for the South African Plural Society," *Conflict and Compromise in South Africa*, ed. R. Rotberg and J. Barratt (Cape Town: David Philip, 1980), 51–75.

16. Namibian Constitution of 1990, Article 102(2).

17. Ibid., Article 49 and schedule 2.

18. Clauses 3.6 and 3.7 of the Structure of a Constitution for a Democratic South Africa, contained in the *Discussion Document*.

19. A. Sachs, "Towards a Bill of Rights in a Democratic South Africa," *South African Journal on Human Rights* 6 (1990): 1, 10.

20. See *A Rigid Constitution*.

21. Second Report of the Constitutional Committee of the President's Council, P.C. 4/1982, para. 9.10.

22. See A. Leon, "New Hope for Natal: An Examination of the KwaZulu Natal Indaba Bill of Rights," *Reality* 19 (1987): 7; Proc. R101, *Government Gazette* 9790 of 17 June 1985, and Proc. R157, *Government Gazette* 10418 of 8 September 1986.

23. *House of Assembly Debates* [*Hansard*], vol. 8, 23 April 1986, cols. 4014–15.

24. A. Sachs, "Towards the Constitutional Reconstruction of South Africa," *Lesotho Law Journal* 2 (1986): 205.

25. See A. Sachs, "A Bill of Rights for South Africa: Areas of Agreement and Disagreement," *Columbia Human Rights Law Review* 21 (1989): 3; Masemola, "Rights and a Future South African Constitution," 45; Penuell M. Maduna, "Judicial Review and Protection of Human Rights Under a New Constitutional Order in South Africa," *Columbia Human Rights Law Review* 21 (1989): 73.

26. See Sachs, "A Bill of Rights for South Africa," 19–20. See, further, A. Sachs, *Protecting Human Rights in a New South Africa* (Cape Town: Oxford University Press, 1990).

27. Masemola, "Rights and a Future South African Constitution," 51.

28. See John Dugard, "The Judiciary and Constitutional Change," in *Political Alternatives for South Africa*, ed. D. J. van Vuuren and D. J. Kriek (Johannesburg: Macmillan, 1983), 332.

29. *Discussion Document on Structures and Principles of a Constitution for a Democratic South Africa*, Part 1 (Johannesburg: ANC Constitutional Committee, April 1990).

30. Ibid., Part 2, clause 6.

31. Ibid., Part 2, clause 9.2.

32. *House of Assembly Debates* [*Hansard*], 2 February 1990, col. 6.

33. For a justification of this restriction on free speech, see Sachs, *Protecting Human Rights*, 50–52; Raymond Suttner, "Freedom of Speech," *South African Journal on Human Rights* 6 (1990): 372. These views are criticized by Denise Meyerson in "No Platform for Racists? What Should the View of Those on the Left Be?" *South African Journal on Human Rights* 6 (1990): 394.

34. "Practical Workings of a Bill of Rights," in *A Bill of Rights for South Africa*, ed. J. van der Westhuizen and H. Viljoen (Durban: Butterworths, 1988), 58.

35. African Charter on Human and Peoples' Rights, Articles 15–24.

36. Namibian Constitution of 1990, Articles 95–101.

37. On this subject, see further Zola Skweyiya, "Towards a Solution of the Land Question in a Post-Apartheid South Africa: Problems and Models," *Columbia Human Rights Law Review* 21 (1989): 211; Michael Robertson, "Land Reforms: South African Options," *Columbia Human Rights Law Review* 21 (1989): 193; G. Budlender et al., "Debating the Land Issue," *South African Journal on Human Rights* 6 (1990): 155–227.

38. A guarantee of property rights is not an essential feature of a human rights convention or a bill of rights. While the Universal Declaration of Human Rights of 1948 recognizes the right to own property and declares that "no one shall be arbitrarily deprived of his property" (Article 17), the International Covenant on Civil and Political Rights of 1966 is silent on this subject. The European Convention on Human Rights of 1950 provides no guarantee for property rights, but leaves it to a protocol to affirm this right. The Canadian Charter of Rights and Freedoms of 1982 makes no mention of property rights.

39. Namibian Constitution of 1990, Article 16.

40. See ANC's Constitutional Committee's *Working Document on a Bill of Rights for a New South Africa*, booklet (Bellville: Centre for Development Studies, 1990), Article 11.

41. Lochner v. New York, 198 US 45, 75 (1905).

42. South African Law Commission Draft Bill of Rights, Article 14. The *Working Paper on Group & Human Rights*, No. 25 (1989) contains a draft bill of rights and a discussion of the various methods.

43. The Namibian Constitution adopts a similar approach. It provides that "the economic order of Namibia shall be based on the principles of a mixed economy, with the objective of securing economic growth, prosperity and a life of human dignity for all Namibians" (Article 98).

44. United Steelworkers v. Weber, 443 US 193 (1979); Fullilove v. Klutznick, 448 US 448 (1980).

45. The experience of the School of Law of the University of the Witwatersrand provides some indication of the extent of this voluntary affirmative action. In 1980 the student body in the School of Law was 84.55 percent white, 3.5 percent African, 1.3 percent Coloured, and 10.7 percent Asian. By 1991 the student body in the School of Law was 59 percent white, 32 percent African, 2 percent Coloured, and 7 percent Asian.

46. South African Law Commission, Working Paper No. 25 (1989), 437.

47. South African Law Commission Draft Bill of Rights, Article 2.

48. Ibid., Article 1(4), Article 15(2), and Sections 15(4) and 16(4).

49. Sachs, *Protecting Human Rights*, 19.

50. Ibid., 30.

51. ANC Constitutional Guidelines, clauses (j) and (u).

52. *Working Document on a Bill of Rights for a New South Africa*, Article 13.

53. Ibid., Articles 14(5) and (6).

54. Ibid., Article 11(5).

55. See *State Crimes, Punishment or Pardon* (Wye Center, Queenstown, Maryland: Aspen Institute, 1988); Naomi Roht-Arriaza, "State Responsibility to Investigate and Prosecute Grave Human Rights Violations in International Law," *California Law Review* 78 (1990): 451.

56. See, in this connection, H. L. A. Hart, "Positivism and the Separation of Law and Morals," *Harvard Law Review* 71 (1958): 593; Lon L. Fuller, "Positivism and Fidelity to the Law—A Reply to Professor Hart," *Harvard Law Review* 71 (1958): 630.

Selected Bibliography:
Civil Liberties in South Africa

CORDER, H. *Judges at Work: The Role and Attitude of the South African Appellate Judiciary 1910–1950.* Cape Town: Juta & Co., 1984.

———, ed. *Democracy and the Judiciary.* Cape Town: Institute for a Democratic Alternative for South Africa, 1989.

DLAMINI, C. R. M. "The Influence of Race on the Administration of Justice in South Africa." *South African Journal on Human Rights* 4 (1988): 37–54.

DUGARD, J. *Human Rights and the South African Legal Order.* Princeton: Princeton University Press, 1978.

———. "The Quest for a Liberal Democracy in South Africa." *Acta Juridica* (1987): 236–58.

———. "A Bill of Rights for South Africa?" *Cornell International Law Journal* 23 (1990): 441–66.

———. "Towards a Democratic Legal Order for South Africa." *African Journal of International and Comparative Law* 2 (1990): 361–83.

FORSYTH, C. *In Danger for Their Talents: A Study of the Appellate Division of the Supreme Court of South Africa from 1950–1980.* Cape Town: Juta & Co., 1985.

HAYSOM, N. "Licence to Kill: The South African Police and the Use of Deadly Force." *South African Journal on Human Rights* 3 (1987): 3–27, 202–22.

———. *Mabangalala: The Rise of Right-Wing Vigilantes in South Africa.* Johannesburg: Centre for Applied Legal Studies, University of the Witwatersrand, 1987.

———. "Policing the Police: A Comparative Survey of Police Control Mechanisms in the United States, South Africa and the United Kingdom." *Acta Juridica* (1990).

HAYSOM, N., and MANGAN, L., eds. *Emergency Law.* Johannesburg: Centre for Applied Legal Studies, University of the Witwatersrand, 1987.

HAYSOM, N., and PLASKET, C. "The War Against Law: Judicial Activism and the Appellate Division." *South African Journal on Human Rights* 4 (1988): 303–23.

————, eds. *Developments in Emergency Law*. Johannesburg: Centre for Applied Legal Studies, University of the Witwatersrand, 1989.

Human Rights and Labour Law Yearbook 1990. Cape Town: Oxford University Press, 1990.

"Human Rights in the Post-Apartheid South Africa Constitution." *Columbia Human Rights Law Review* 21 (1989): 1–251.

MATHEWS, A. S. *Law, Order and Liberty in South Africa*. Cape Town: Juta & Co., 1971.

————. *Freedom, State Security and the Rule of Law*. Cape Town: Juta & Co., 1986.

MOKGATLE, D. D. "The Exclusion of Blacks from the South African Judicial System." *South African Journal on Human Rights* 3 (1987): 44–51.

ROBERTSON, M., ed. *Human Rights for South Africans*. Cape Town: Oxford University Press, 1991.

RYCROFT, A., ed. *Race and Law in South Africa*. Cape Town: Juta & Co., 1987.

SACHS, A. *Justice in South Africa*. Berkeley: University of California Press, 1973.

————. *Protecting Human Rights in a New South Africa*. Cape Town: Oxford University Press, 1990.

————. "Towards a Bill of Rights in a Democratic South Africa." *South African Journal on Human Rights* 6 (1990): 1–24.

SOUTH AFRICAN LAW COMMISSION. Working Paper 25. Project 58: Group and Human Rights. Pretoria: South Africa Law Commission, 1989.

STUART, K. *The Newspaperman's Guide to the Law*. 5th ed. Rev. by W. Lane, D. Hoffe, D. Dison, and L. Jacobsen. Durban: Butterworths, 1990.

VAN BLERK, A. *Judge and Be Judged*. Cape Town: Juta & Co., 1988.

VAN DER WESTHUIZEN, J., and VILJOEN, H., eds. *A Bill of Rights for South Africa*. Durban: Butterworths, 1988.

VAN VUUREN, D. J., and KRIEK, D. J., eds. *Political Alternatives for South Africa*. Durban: Butterworths, 1983.

Selected Annotated Bibliography: South Africa

The books below, most of which were written for a general audience, provide an introduction to South African history, politics, and society. Most have been published in the last decade and are available in libraries and college bookstores in the United States, except for the annual surveys of the South African Institute of Race Relations. Books issued by South African publishers have been omitted, although they are an essential resource for readers who intend to study South Africa in depth.

ADAM, Heribert, and GILIOMEE, Hermann. *Ethnic Power Mobilized: Can South Africa Change?* New Haven: Yale University Press, 1979.
    A collection of essays about Afrikaner history and politics through the Vorster era.

BAKER, Pauline. *The United States and South Africa: The Reagan Years.* New York: Ford Foundation and Foreign Policy Association, 1989.
    A concise analysis of the forces that produced the rise and fall of constructive engagement.

BARBER, James, and BARRATT, John. *South Africa's Foreign Policy: The Search for Status and Security 1945–1988.* New York: Cambridge University Press, 1990.
    This useful and highly readable account of South Africa's diplomacy stops a year short of the De Klerk era. The authors chart four distinct phases, each resulting in the progressive isolation of Pretoria in Africa and the world. They show how persistent opposition from blacks and their allies eventually doomed the efforts of the Western powers to separate economic from political relations with South Africa.

BENSON, Mary. *Nelson Mandela: The Man and the Movement.* New York: W. W. Norton and Company, 1986.
    A sympathetic biography of the African National Congress leader imprisoned from 1962 to 1990, describing his early life and political career, his nationalist beliefs, and his central role within the ANC.

BERGER, Peter L., and GODSELL, Bobby, eds. *A Future South Africa: Visions, Strategies and Realities.* Boulder, Colo.: Westview Press, 1988.
    Eight chapters by liberal analysts survey the contemporary array of political protagonists in South Africa. A conclusion by the editors

predicts a slow, painful evolutionary transition to a post-apartheid society.

BIKO, Steve. *I Write What I Like*. San Francisco: Harper & Row, 1986. (First edition: London: Bowerdean Press, 1978.)
The collected writings of the martyred founder of the black consciousness movement, who was South Africa's most influential black leader in the post-Sharpeville era.

BRINK, André. *A Dry White Season*. New York: Morrow, 1980.
A powerful story by South Africa's leading Afrikaner novelist about an apolitical Afrikaner teacher drawn by the death of a black friend into a web of state repression and social isolation.

BUNDY, Colin, and SAUNDERS, Christopher, principal consultants. *Illustrated History of South Africa: The Real Story*. Pleasantville, N.Y., and Montreal: The Reader's Digest Association, 1989.
Excellent general history directed at nonspecialist readers, extensively illustrated and incorporating the most recent scholarship.

BUTLER, Jeffrey; ELPHICK, Richard; and WELSH, David, eds. *Democratic Liberalism in South Africa: Its History and Prospect*. Middletown, Conn.: Wesleyan University Press, 1987.
This book brings together twenty-four essays by white liberals who critically review the principles, policies, history, and historiography of liberalism in South Africa and argue for the continuing relevance of liberal beliefs.

DAVIS, Stephen M. *Apartheid's Rebels: Inside South Africa's Hidden War*. New Haven: Yale University Press, 1987.
Focusing on the African National Congress in its exile years, this book offers the fullest portrait to date of the ANC's guerrilla campaign.

DUGARD, John. *Human Rights and the South African Legal Order*. Princeton: Princeton University Press, 1978.
An introduction to what the author, a prominent South African jurist, calls "the pursuit of justice within an unjust legal order." Covers the laws involving civil rights and liberties, state security laws, judicial procedures in political trials, and the South African judiciary.

FINNEGAN, William. *Crossing the Line: A Year in the Land of Apartheid*. New York: Harper & Row, 1986.
An appealing memoir by a young American writer who discovers South Africa through teaching at a Coloured high school in Cape Town.

FREDRICKSON, George M. *White Supremacy: A Comparative Study in American and South African History*. New York: Oxford University Press, 1981.
An interpretive work by an American historian on the causes, character, and consequences of white supremacist ideology and practice.

GERHART, Gail M. *Black Power in South Africa: The Evolution of an Ideology.* Berkeley: University of California Press, 1978.
Explores the historical strain of African nationalism, still popular today, which eschews white participation in black liberation movements.

GORDIMER, Nadine. *Burger's Daughter.* New York: Viking Press, 1979.
This, the most political of Gordimer's novels, is loosely based on the life and legacy of Abram Fischer, a distinguished Afrikaner lawyer sentenced to life imprisonment for his role in South Africa's underground Communist Party.

GRUNDY, Kenneth W. *The Militarization of South African Politics.* Bloomington: Indiana University Press, 1986.
An examination of the influence of the military establishment in fashioning both foreign and domestic security policy under the Botha government.

HANLON, Joseph. *Beggar Your Neighbours: Apartheid Power in South Africa.* Bloomington: Indiana University Press, 1986.
A comprehensive assessment of political, military, and economic relationships between South Africa and the Frontline States by a journalist critical of South Africa's policies.

HANLON, Joseph, and OMOND, Roger. *The Sanctions Handbook.* New York: Viking Penguin, 1987.
A summary of the evidence, the arguments, and the politics surrounding the sanctions debate in the United States and Britain.

HARRISON, David. *The White Tribe of Africa: South Africa in Perspective.* Berkeley and Los Angeles: University of California Press, 1981.
Engaging and informative sketches of personalities and episodes in Afrikaner history.

JOUBERT, Elsa. *Poppie.* London: Hodder and Stoughton, 1980.
A novel that movingly portrays the needless human suffering caused by the apartheid system and the forbearance of its victims.

KANE-BERMAN, John. *South Africa: A Method in the Madness.* London: Pluto Press, 1979. [Published in South Africa under the title: *Soweto—Black Revolt, White Reaction.* Johannesburg: Ravan Press, 1978.]
An informative account of the causes and circumstances surrounding the Soweto revolt of 1976–77, written by a journalist who later became director of the South African Institute of Race Relations.

KARIS, Thomas, and CARTER, Gwendolen, eds. *From Protest to Challenge: A Documentary History of African Politics in South Africa 1882–1964* (four volumes). Stanford: Hoover Institution Press, 1972–77.
A comprehensive survey of the history of extraparliamentary black and allied opposition groups. Volumes 1–3 contain primary source documents explained in their historical context, and Volume 4 presents biographical profiles of over three hundred political leaders.

LELYVELD, Joseph. *Move Your Shadow: South Africa, Black and White.* New York: Times Books, 1985.
A Pulitzer Prize–winning book by a *New York Times* correspondent. Sensitively chronicles the tragedy and absurdity of apartheid.

LEWIS, Stephen R., Jr. *The Economics of Apartheid.* New York: Council on Foreign Relations Press, 1990.
A nontechnical overview of South Africa's economy, focusing on historical evolution, pressures for fundamental policy change, and alternative strategies for future development.

LIPTON, Merle. *Capitalism and Apartheid: South Africa, 1910–1984.* Totowa, N.J.: Rowman and Allanheld, 1985.
A lucid contribution to the debate about the historic and possible future role of capitalism in fostering racial inequality. The author, a South African–born economist, comes down on the side of nonracial capitalism.

LODGE, Tom. *Black Politics in South Africa Since 1945.* New York: Longman, 1983.
A well-documented interpretation of key events, issues, and personalities in the African nationalist struggle.

MACSHANE, Denis; PLAUT, Martin; and WARD, David. *Power! Black Workers, Their Unions and the Struggle for Freedom in South Africa.* Boston: South End Press, 1984.
An introduction to the South African trade union movement; less authoritative than Steven Friedman's *Building Tomorrow Today: African Workers in Trade Unions 1970–1984,* published in South Africa by the Ravan Press in 1987.

MATHABANE, Mark. *Kaffir Boy: The True Story of a Black Youth's Coming of Age in Apartheid South Africa.* New York: Macmillan, 1986.
An autobiographical account of life in Alexandra, long one of South Africa's poorest and most neglected black townships. The author describes his struggle to obtain an education and to escape the straitjacket of apartheid.

MERMELSTEIN, David, ed. *The Anti-Apartheid Reader: South Africa and the Struggle Against White Racist Rule.* New York: Grove Press, 1987.
A wide-ranging anthology of eighty pieces excerpted from the writings of scholars, journalists, and activists. Provides a thought-provoking excursion through the complexities of the current South African scene.

MINTER, William. *King Solomon's Mines Revisited: Western Interests and the Burdened History of South Africa.* New York: Basic Books, 1986.
One of America's leading anti-apartheid activists reviews the history of U.S. and British involvement in the economic exploitation of southern Africa and makes the case for sanctions.

MUFSON, Steven. *Fighting Years: Black Resistance and the Struggle for a New South Africa.* Boston: Beacon Press, 1990.

Focusing entirely on the underreported black resistance, this lively and intelligent contribution to the history of South Africa's transformation in the 1980s is written by a former correspondent of the *Wall Street Journal.* Enough of the larger national scene is sketched in to add context to the mass of detail.

MUTLOATSE, Mothobi, ed. *Africa South: Contemporary Writings.* Exeter, N.H.: Heinemann Educational Books, 1981.

An anthology of short stories and other pieces by South Africa's current generation of black writers.

OMOND, Roger. *The Apartheid Handbook: A Guide to South Africa's Everyday Racial Policies.* New York: Viking Penguin, 1985.

Arranged in simple question-and-answer form, this is a detailed factual guide to the racial laws and practices of South Africa in the mid-1980s.

RUSSELL, Diana E. H. *Lives of Courage: Women for a New South Africa.* New York: Basic Books, 1989.

Interviews with twenty-four South African women active in opposition politics, on topics ranging from experiences in prison and exile to sexism in the African National Congress and the labor movement.

SAMPSON, Anthony. *Black and Gold: Tycoons, Revolutionaries and Apartheid.* New York: Pantheon Books, 1987.

A highly readable analysis of the relationship between international business and black nationalism in the modern era, by a British writer and journalist with long South African experience.

SAUL, John, and GELB, Stephen. *The Crisis in South Africa,* revised edition. New York: Monthly Review Press, 1986.

An influential Marxist analysis of what the authors perceive as an "organic crisis" in the South African system that will lead to its ultimate demise.

SECRETARY OF STATE'S ADVISORY COMMITTEE ON SOUTH AFRICA. *A U.S. Policy Toward South Africa.* Washington, D.C.: U.S. Department of State, January 1987.

A post–U.S. sanctions assessment of the situation in South Africa and an incisive critique of the Reagan administration's policy of constructive engagement.

SMITH, David M., ed. *Living Under Apartheid: Aspects of Urbanization and Social Change in South Africa.* Boston: George Allen & Unwin, 1982.

A collection of twelve essays on housing, land use, migration, unemployment, and other contemporary social issues.

SOUTH AFRICAN INSTITUTE OF RACE RELATIONS. *Race Relations Survey.* Johannesburg. Annual publication.

This yearly compendium of facts, events, and statistics, published in South Africa, is an invaluable resource for research on social and political developments.

SPARKS, Allister. *The Mind of South Africa.* New York: Alfred A. Knopf, 1990.

An engaging and perceptive interpretation of South African history and society by a former editor of the defunct *Rand Daily Mail.*

STUDY COMMISSION ON U.S. POLICY TOWARD SOUTHERN AFRICA. *South Africa: Time Running Out.* Berkeley: University of California Press and Foreign Policy Study Foundation, 1981.

One of the most comprehensive introductions to South Africa and to U.S. interests and policy options; a useful reference work.

THOMPSON, Leonard. *A History of South Africa.* New Haven: Yale University Press, 1990.

Covers South African history from precolonial times to the present; written for the general reader but synthesizes the best of modern scholarship.

VILLA-VICENCIO, Charles, and DE GRUCHY, John W., eds. *Resistance and Hope: South African Essays in Honour of Beyers Naudé.* Grand Rapids: Wm. B. Eerdmans Publishing Co., 1985.

Tutu, Boesak, Chikane, Tlhagale, and other prominent church leaders have contributed chapters to this collection of essays on religion in contemporary South Africa.

WILSON, Francis, and RAMPHELE, Mamphela. *Uprooting Poverty: The South African Challenge. Report for the Second Carnegie Inquiry into Poverty and Development in Southern Africa.* New York: W. W. Norton and Company, 1989.

A vivid and extensively documented landmark study of socioeconomic conditions affecting South Africa's impoverished majority. The authors draw on the work of dozens of researchers in the fields of health, employment, literacy, and housing and present recommendations for transforming South African society.

This bibliography was prepared by Gail M. Gerhart, Ph.D., currently at the City University of New York.

Key Events in South African History

B.C.–1902

B.C.: San ("Bushmen") and Khoikhoi ("Hottentots") reside in area now known as South Africa. **A.D. 200–300**: Bantu-speaking African farmers cross Limpopo River and move southward into the eastern part of present-day South Africa. **1488**: Portuguese explorers circumnavigate Cape of Good Hope. **1500–1600**: Africans settle in Transvaal, Orange Free State, Natal, and Eastern Cape. **1652–1795**: Dutch East India Company establishes a station in Cape Peninsula. Dutch, German, and French Huguenot immigrants settle in the Cape and merge to become "Afrikaners" (called "Boers" by the British); slaves are imported from East Indies, Madagascar, and other parts of Africa; indigenous San and Khoikhoi die off or are assimilated. **1760**: First "pass laws" introduced; all slaves in the Cape required to carry documents designed to control movement of population.

1795–1806: British capture Cape Colony from Dutch in 1795; conquest legalized by treaty in 1806. **1811–78**: Xhosa and British fight frontier wars in Eastern Cape; Xhosa defeated. **1816–28**: Zulu kingdom rises under Shaka. **1820**: Several thousand English immigrants arrive; most settle in Eastern Cape. **1834**: Britain abolishes slavery throughout empire.

1836–40: Afrikaner farmers, rejecting British rule, make "Great Trek" into interior. **1838**: Afrikaners defeat Zulus at battle of Blood River in Natal; event celebrated by Afrikaners annually on December 16 as "Day of the Covenant." **1841**: Lovedale Missionary Institution established in Eastern Cape, first African secondary school. **1843**: Britain annexes Natal. **1852–54**: Britain recognizes South African Republic (Transvaal) and Orange Free State as independent Afrikaner states. **1853**: Nonracial, qualified franchise established in Cape Colony through British influence. In later decades, Cape legislature redefines property qualifications to curb the expansion of the African electorate; but African voters, around 1900, hold balance of power in a handful of districts. **1860–1911**: Indentured laborers brought from India by British to work on Natal sugar plantations; most settle permanently.

1867: Diamonds discovered north of Cape Colony, near Kimberley. **1877**: Britain annexes Transvaal. **1879**: Zulus defeat British at Isandhlwana;

British crush Zulu military power at Ulundi and later annex Zululand. **1880–81:** First Anglo-Boer War; Transvaal Afrikaners regain their independence. **1884:** First African-edited newspaper started. **1886:** Gold discovered on the Witwatersrand. **1894:** Natal Indian Congress (NIC) formed under Mohandas K. Gandhi, who lived in South Africa from 1893 until 1914. **1898:** Afrikaners defeat Venda, the last independent African kingdom. **1899–1902:** Second Anglo-Boer War ends with Afrikaner defeat; Transvaal and Orange Free State become self-governing crown colonies.

1902

Cape Coloureds form African Political Organization.

1906

Rebellion led by Chief Bambatha against imposition of poll tax in Natal; thirty whites and three thousand Zulus killed.

1909

Africans hold South African Native Convention to protest racial segregation in proposed constitution.

1910

Union of South Africa formed as self-governing British dominion; Parliament limited to whites; General Louis Botha, leader of Afrikaner-English coalition and supported by General Jan C. Smuts, becomes first prime minister.

1912

South African Native National Congress, first national African political movement, founded to overcome ethnic divisions and oppose racial segregation; renamed African National Congress (ANC) in 1923.

1913

Native Land Act limits land purchases by Africans, 70 percent of population, to reserves, which equal 7 percent of the land. African reserves form basis of today's tribal homelands.

1914

Afrikaners form National Party under General J. B. M. Hertzog to oppose Botha and Smuts. South African armed forces fight in World War I on side of Britain; Afrikaner nationalists oppose decision.

1915

South Africa conquers German colony of South-West Africa (Namibia).

1916

South African Native College opens at Fort Hare, Eastern Cape.

1919

Smuts becomes prime minister. South African Native National Congress campaigns against pass laws; hundreds arrested.

1920

Industrial and Commercial Workers' Union formed, the first nationwide mass movement for Africans. League of Nations grants South Africa trusteeship to govern South-West Africa.

1921

South African Communist Party (SACP) formed.

1924

General Hertzog, leader of National Party, becomes prime minister in coalition with English-speaking Labor Party.

1925

Afrikaans recognized as second official language after English.

1930

White women enfranchised.

1931

All property and literacy tests removed for white voters. Britain recognizes South Africa's legal sovereignty within the Commonwealth.

1934

Hertzog and Smuts, during worldwide depression, join forces to form the United Party under Hertzog's leadership. Afrikaner nationalists, under Dr. Daniel F. Malan, break away to establish "purified" National Party.

1936

Native Land and Trust Act provides for eventual increase of African reserves from 7 percent to 13.7 percent of all land; companion legislation removes Africans from common voters' roll in Cape Province, places them on separate roll to elect seven whites to Parliament, and creates national advisory Natives' Representative Council; in protest, All-African Convention held.

1939

Parliament by a small margin votes to enter World War II. Smuts succeeds Hertzog and becomes prominent Allied leader. South African volunteer forces, including Africans as labor auxiliaries, join Allies; some Afrikaner leaders advocate neutrality or support for Nazi Germany.

1940s

During World War II, pass laws suspended in all major towns.

1943

ANC adopts "African Claims," based on 1941 Atlantic Charter, and bill of rights calling for nonracial franchise; authorizes formation of Youth League, later led by Nelson Mandela and Oliver Tambo. Non-European Unity Movement formed, primarily in Western Cape, and advocates non-collaboration with all segregated bodies.

1946

NIC and Transvaal Indian Congress (TIC) begin two-year passive resistance campaign, the first since Gandhi, to protest policies on land and representation. About seventy thousand African mine workers stop work; strike broken by government forces. Natives' Representative Council adjourns indefinitely.

1947

Declaration of Cooperation by leaders of ANC, NIC, and TIC.

1948

National Party, led by Malan, wins narrow surprise victory; introduces "apartheid," which codifies and expands racial segregation.

1949

Prohibition of marriage between Africans and whites extended to Coloureds and whites. ANC adopts Program of Action calling for boycotts, strikes, and (for the first time) nonviolent civil disobedience. Legislation abolishes remaining Indian and Coloured voting rights in Natal province.

1950

Population Registration Act requires racial classification of all South Africans. Group Areas Act requires segregated residential and business areas for whites, Coloureds, and Asians. Prohibition of sexual relations between whites and Africans extended to whites and Coloureds. SACP dissolves before enactment of Suppression of Communism Act, later used against all forms of dissent. **June 26:** National stay-at-home; date becomes ANC commemorative day.

1951

Bantu Authorities Act abolishes Natives' Representative Council and establishes basis for ethnic government in African reserves or "homelands." Bill to remove Coloureds from common voters' roll by simple legislative majority provokes five-year constitutional crisis. ANC and South African Indian Congress form Joint Planning Council.

1952

June 26: ANC and allied groups begin nonviolent Defiance Campaign against discriminatory laws that lasts all year; about eighty-five hundred protesters are jailed. **December:** Albert Lutuli, deposed as chief by government, is elected ANC president.

1953

Public Safety Act empowers government to declare stringent states of emergency. Companion legislation authorizes severe penalties for protesters, virtually eliminating passive resistance as a tactic. In opposition to mission-run schools, Bantu Education Act imposes government control over African schools. Government legislation enacted designed to undermine African unions. Reservation of Separate Amenities Act overturns judicial precedent of "separate but equal." **May 9:** United Party dissidents form Liberal Party, favoring nonracial but qualified franchise for blacks. **October 10:** Leftwing whites form Congress of Democrats in sympathy with ANC.

1954

December: J. G. Strijdom succeeds Malan as prime minister.

1955

ANC defies Bantu Education Act, keeping thousands of children out of school. Government packs Senate and the highest court in order to remove Coloureds from common voters' roll. **March 5–6:** Formation of South African Congress of Trade Unions links African and multiracial trade unions to ANC. **June 25–26:** ANC, in alliance with Indian, Coloured, and white organizations, endorses Freedom Charter at Congress of the People; adopts it officially in 1956.

1956

Coloureds removed from common voters' roll and placed on separate roll to elect four whites to represent them in Parliament. Government systematically begins to issue passes to African women. Twenty thousand women of all races, organized by the Federation of South African Women, march in

Pretoria to protest issuance of passes to African women. Albert Lutuli, Nelson Mandela, and 154 others arrested on charges of treason; those not yet discharged found not guilty in March 1961. Legislation prohibits formation of racially mixed unions and requires existing mixed unions to split into segregated unions or form segregated branches under an all-white executive. Enactment of Riotous Assemblies Act provides for control of public meetings of twelve or more persons.

1957

January: Africans in Johannesburg wage bus boycott against fare increase; ends successfully after three months. **May:** Parliament approves bill to bar blacks from white church services. Thousands demonstrate in Cape Town.

1958

September: Dr. Hendrik Verwoerd, theoretician of apartheid, becomes prime minister. **November:** "Africanists," who oppose inclusion of non-Africans, break away from ANC.

1959

Promotion of Bantu Self-Government Act provides for an end to African representation by whites in Parliament and envisages that all Africans will belong to one of eight ethnic "national units" that will eventually become independent. Apartheid and increased government control extended to higher education. Africanists form Pan Africanist Congress of Azania (PAC) under the leadership of Robert Sobukwe. Ovamboland People's Organization is formed to oppose South African rule in South-West Africa (Namibia); becomes the South West Africa People's Organization (SWAPO) in 1966. Former United Party members form Progressive Party (later the Progressive Federal Party) favoring high but nonracial qualifications for the franchise.

1960

March 21: In Sharpeville, police kill 69 unarmed Africans and wound 186 during demonstration against pass laws organized by PAC. Lutuli burns his pass and urges Africans to follow his example. Government declares state of emergency (ends August 31), detains nearly two thousand activists of all races, and outlaws ANC and PAC. **October 5:** Majority of whites vote yes in whites-only referendum on South Africa becoming a republic within the Commonwealth.

1961

May 31: South Africa leaves Commonwealth. ANC abandons policy of nonviolence. **October 23:** Lutuli awarded Nobel Peace Prize. **December 16:** *Umkhonto we Sizwe* (Spear of the Nation), armed wing of ANC, launches sabotage campaign.

1962

Sabotage Act provides for prolonged detention without trial. **November 7:**

Mandela sentenced to five years in prison for inciting workers and leaving country without passport. **November 21–22:** *Poqo* (Africans Alone), armed offshoot of PAC, attacks whites.

1963

"90-Day Act" virtually abrogates habeas corpus. **July 11:** *Umkhonto* leaders arrested in Rivonia, a white Johannesburg suburb.

1964

June 12: Eight *Umkhonto* leaders, including Nelson Mandela, Walter Sisulu, and Govan Mbeki, sentenced to life imprisonment after admitting sabotage and preparation for guerrilla warfare.

1966

September 6: Prime Minister Verwoerd assassinated; succeeded by B. J. Vorster.

1967

Terrorism Act broadens the definition of terrorism and provides for indefinite detention.

1968

Legislation outlaws multiracial political parties; Liberal Party disbands. Parliamentary representation of Coloureds by whites ended. Coloured Persons' Representative Council and South African Indian Council established. **December:** South African Students' Organization, formed under leadership of Steve Biko, is precursor to various black consciousness organizations.

1969

April: ANC conference in Tanzania invites non-Africans to join while stressing African "national consciousness."

1971

NIC revived.

1972

July: Black People's Convention formed to advance black consciousness outside schools and colleges.

1973

January: Wave of strikes by black workers in Durban leads to growth of independent nonracial (but mainly African) trade union movement. **March:** Steve Biko and seven other leaders of black consciousness movement banned.

1974

April 25: Young army officers in Lisbon overthrow Portuguese government. **November:** UN General Assembly suspends credentials of South African delegation; first time UN member denied participation. UN General Assembly invites ANC and PAC (both recognized by the Organization of African Unity) to participate as observers.

1975

June 25: Mozambique becomes independent. **August:** South African Defense Force invades Angola. **November 11:** Angola becomes independent.

1976

June 16: Soweto students, protesting inferior education and use of Afrikaans as medium of instruction, fired on by police; countrywide protest results in deaths of estimated one thousand protesters during following months. Internal Security Act supersedes Suppression of Communism Act, broadening government's power to crush dissent. **October 26:** Transkei becomes first homeland given "independence" (Bophuthatswana follows in 1977, Venda in 1979, and Ciskei in 1981).

1977

May 19: Winnie Mandela, wife of Nelson Mandela, banished to Brandfort in Orange Free State; one in a series of restrictive and harassing actions. **September 12:** Steve Biko dies after police beatings while in detention. **October 19:** Black consciousness groups, Christian Institute, and the *World*, a major black newspaper, outlawed; black consciousness leaders and others detained. **November 4:** UN Security Council makes 1963 voluntary arms embargo against South Africa mandatory.

1978

September 20: Prime Minister Vorster resigns after "Muldergate affair," a major scandal in the National Party involving misappropriation of public funds; P. W. Botha becomes prime minister. **September 29:** UN Security Council Resolution 435 endorses plan, brokered by Western "Contact Group," for UN–supervised elections leading to Namibian independence in 1979 (finally implemented in 1990).

1979

Industrial Relations Act officially recognizes African trade unions. **April:** Federation of South African Trade Unions (FOSATU) organized. **April 6:**

Solomon Mahlangu is first guerrilla to be executed. ANC school in Tanzania later named after him. **September:** Azanian People's Organization holds inaugural conference. **November:** Azanian Students' Organization (AZASO) formed for college students; Congress of South African Students (COSAS) formed for high school students. Western Cape hit by a wave of stayaways with broad community support and focusing on a wide range of issues.

1980

March: Thousands of black high school and university students begin prolonged boycott of schools. **April 18:** Zimbabwe becomes independent. **June 1:** Resurgence of ANC marked by sabotage attacks on South Africa's oil-from-coal installations at Sasolburg. **June 26:** ANC publicly breaks with Zulu Chief Mangosuthu Gatsha Buthelezi. Countrywide protests erupt over wages, rents, bus fares, and education.

1981

April: National Party wins election with reduced majority. **May:** Widespread opposition to twentieth anniversary of the Republic. Burning of South African flag becomes an offense.

1982

February: Rightwing breaks away from National Party over proposed constitution providing a tricameral Parliament with separate chambers for whites, Coloureds, and Indians, but excluding Africans; forms Conservative Party. **December 19:** ANC sabotages South Africa's nuclear power complex at Koeberg.

1983

January 3: Coloured Labor Party votes to support proposed constitution. **May 20:** ANC car bomb outside military headquarters in Pretoria kills nineteen people. South African planes attack ANC sanctuaries in Mozambique. **June 11–12:** National Forum, organized primarily by black consciousness leaders, attended by representatives of nearly two hundred anti-apartheid organizations. **August 20–21:** United Democratic Front (UDF), a coalition of anti-apartheid organizations sympathetic to the Freedom Charter, launched nationally. **November 2:** Whites-only referendum approves proposed constitution.

1984

March 16: Nkomati Accord, a "nonaggression and good neighborliness" pact, signed by South Africa and Mozambique. **August:** Labor Party wins seventy-six of eighty seats in Coloured chamber of new tricameral Parliament. National People's Party wins in Indian chamber. Less than one-fifth of Coloured and Indian voters participate. **September 3:** New constitution goes into effect. Most widespread and prolonged black uprising since 1976 erupts in Vaal Triangle. **October 16:** Anglican Bishop Desmond Tutu awarded Nobel Peace Prize for nonviolent opposition to apartheid. **October 23:** Some seven thousand soldiers, in unprecedented action, enter Sebokeng township to join police in house-to-house raids. **November 5–6:** Transvaal stayaway, largest yet, organized by COSAS and FOSATU, signals student-worker alliance.

1985

February 19: Thirteen top leaders of UDF arrested; six charged with high treason. **March 21:** On twenty-fifth anniversary of Sharpeville shootings, police in Langa township kill nineteen African funeral mourners. **July 20:** State of emergency imposed in parts of the country following nearly five hundred deaths in township violence since September 1984. **August 15:** President Botha, in the "Rubicon" speech, rejects foreign and domestic calls for fundamental change. **August 28:** COSAS banned. **September 4:** Foreign banks suspend credit following Chase Manhattan's July 31 refusal to roll over loans; action sets off financial crisis. **September 9:** U.S. President Reagan imposes limited sanctions against South Africa to preempt stronger measures by Congress. **September 13:** White South African businessmen and newspaper editors hold talks in Zambia with ANC leaders. **November 2:** Government announces media restrictions in locations covered by emergency decree. **November 30:** Congress of South African Trade Unions (COSATU) formed, creating largest mainly African labor federation.

1986

February 7: Frederick Van Zyl Slabbert resigns as leader of the Progressive Federal Party, rejecting white political structure. **March 7:** Partial state of emergency lifted. **May 1:** Some 1.5 million blacks stage largest stayaway in South Africa's history. Buthelezi's Inkatha launches United Workers' Union of South Africa. **May 19:** South Africa attacks alleged ANC bases in capitals of Botswana, Zambia, and Zimbabwe, all Commonwealth countries. Commonwealth Eminent Persons Group abandons attempt to mediate between Pretoria and its opponents. **June 12:** Nationwide state of emergency imposed. **July 1:** Pass laws repealed; indirect controls on movement remain. **July 7:** Winnie Mandela freed from government restrictions after twenty-four years. **September 7:** Reverend Desmond Tutu becomes first black archbishop of the Anglican Church in southern Africa. **October 2:** U.S. Congress overrides presidential veto to pass Comprehensive Anti-Apartheid Act imposing economic sanctions against South Africa. **December 11:** Almost total censorship imposed on media reports of political protest.

1987

January 28: Oliver Tambo, head of exiled ANC, meets with U.S. Secretary of State George Shultz in Washington, D.C. **May 6:** Conservative Party displaces Progressive Federal Party as official opposition to National Party in Parliament. **June 12:** State of emergency extended for a second year. **July 9:**

Delegation of sixty whites, led by Frederick Van Zyl Slabbert, head of Institute for a Democratic Alternative in South Africa, arrive in Dakar, Senegal, for talks with members of ANC. **August 9:** Estimated two hundred thousand members of black National Union of Mineworkers begin three-week strike — longest legal strike in South African history. **November:** Violence escalates around Pietermaritzburg, Natal, between supporters of Inkatha and supporters of UDF; by end of year, 230 persons killed. **November 3:** Natal province and KwaZulu announce formation of Natal-KwaZulu Joint Executive Authority, first multiracial administrative body. **November 4:** Govan Mbeki released from Robben Island prison. **December 30:** Transkei prime minister ousted in coup led by Major General Bantu Holomisa. South African Youth Congress organized semiclandestinely; claims over one million followers.

1988

February 10: Troops put down attempted coup against Lucas Mangope, president of Bophuthatswana. **February 24:** Activities of seventeen anti-apartheid organizations, including UDF, effectively banned; COSATU prohibited from engaging in political activities. **May 3–4:** Negotiations over Namibia's independence and removal of Cuban troops from Angola begin among Angola, Cuba, and South Africa, with United States as mediator and Soviet Union as observer. **June 8:** Estimated three million black workers end three-day nationwide strike to protest antilabor legislation and government action of February 24. **June 9:** State of emergency extended for third year. **August 8:** ANC issues Constitutional Guidelines for a Democratic South Africa in Lusaka, Zambia. **August 31:** Bombs destroy headquarters of South African Council of Churches and several leading anti-apartheid groups in Johannesburg; twenty-three wounded. **September 2:** Inkatha and UDF/COSATU sign accord to end twenty months of fighting in Natal. Violence continues. **November 18:** Popo Molefe, Patrick Lekota, and others in Delmas treason trial are convicted. Convictions reversed on December 15, 1989. **November 26:** Zephania Mothopeng, PAC president, and Harry Gwala, senior ANC and SACP member, released from prison. **December 2:** Pro–ANC newspaper editor Zwelakhe Sisulu released after nearly two years of detention. **December 22:** Angola, Cuba, and South Africa sign two interlocking accords providing for independence of Namibia and withdrawal of fifty thousand Cuban troops from Angola.

1989

February 2: P. W. Botha, following a stroke, resigns as leader of National Party; retains post of president. Frederik W. de Klerk elected to succeed Botha as National Party leader. **February 9:** Prison hunger strike increases pressure on government to formally charge political detainees. **April:** Progressive Federal Party and two other smaller white-led parties form multiracial Democratic Party. **April 24:** "Alexandra Five," black anti-apartheid activists, acquitted by Supreme Court of charges of subversion and sedition. **April 26:** Soviet Union sends diplomatic mission to South Africa, for first time since countries broke off relations in 1956, to discuss implementation of Namibian peace agreement. **May 18:** Anglican Archbishop Desmond

Tutu, the Reverend Allan Boesak, and the Reverend Beyers Naudé meet with U.S. President George Bush. **June 9:** Nationwide state of emergency extended for fourth year. **June 30:** Albertina Sisulu and other UDF leaders meet with President Bush. **July 5:** Nelson Mandela and President Botha have unprecedented meeting in Cape Town. **August 2:** Black South Africans present themselves at white hospitals and are treated despite apartheid regulations. **August 14:** Botha resigns as president. De Klerk becomes acting president and on September 14 is elected president for five-year term. **August 21:** Organization of African Unity Ad Hoc Committee on Southern Africa issues the Harare Declaration, approving ANC's position for negotiating with South African government. **September 5:** Beginning of two-day strike to protest exclusion of blacks from next day's parliamentary elections; hundreds of thousands boycott work and schools. **September 6:** National Party suffers major setback but retains control; Conservative and Democratic parties gain seats. **September 15:** Anti-apartheid demonstrations in Johannesburg, Pretoria, and Port Elizabeth permitted by government. **October 15:** Walter Sisulu, former ANC secretary-general, and seven others released from long-term imprisonment. **November 16:** All public beaches are desegregated. **November 28:** Pan Africanist Movement, surrogate for PAC, launched.

1990

February 2: President De Klerk announces unbanning of ANC, SACP, and PAC; lifting of restrictions on UDF, COSATU, and thirty-one other organizations; release of political prisoners; and suspension of death penalty. **February 11:** Nelson Mandela released from jail after twenty-seven years of imprisonment. **March 2:** Nelson Mandela named deputy president of ANC, making him effective leader; ANC president Oliver Tambo had been partially disabled by a stroke in 1989. **March 4:** Lennox Sebe, leader of "independent" homeland of Ciskei, overthrown by military. **March 21:** Namibia becomes independent under SWAPO government led by Sam Nujoma, after seventy-five years of colonial rule. **April 5:** Venda government overthrown by military coup. **May 2–4:** First formal talks between ANC and South African government produce progress on release of political prisoners and return of exiles; Groote Schuur Minute signed. **June 7:** South African government lifts nationwide state of emergency in all provinces except Natal. **June 9:** Nelson Mandela begins world tour that includes eleven-day visit to United States, where he meets President George Bush; also addresses joint session of Congress. **June 19:** Repeal of Separate Amenities Act. **July 14:** Inkatha leader Chief Buthelezi announces that his movement, renamed Inkatha Freedom Party, will be open to all races. **July 22:** Fighting between Inkatha and UDF/ANC supporters spreads from Natal to townships around Johannesburg. **July 28:** SACP holds first public rally in forty years. **August 6–7:** Second round of talks between ANC and South African government results in Pretoria Minute; ANC announces cease-fire, ending thirty-year-old armed struggle; government pledges to release political prisoners, beginning September 1, and to allow political exiles to return beginning October 1. **September 23–25:** President De Klerk visits United

States and meets President George Bush and members of Congress. **September 24:** Soweto municipal councillors, Transvaal Provincial Authority, and Soweto People's Delegation sign accord ending four-year rent boycott and laying foundations for unified metropolitan area embracing Johannesburg, Soweto, and other white towns and black townships. **October 18:** Government ends emergency rule in Natal. **October 19:** National Party opens membership to all races. **October 23:** Zephania Mothopeng, president of PAC, dies; Clarence Makwetu succeeds him. **November 7:** Dutch Reformed church joins other churches in condemning apartheid as a sin. **December 3:** Renewed clashes between Inkatha and UDF/ANC supporters around Johannesburg claim more than one hundred lives. **December 13:** ANC president Oliver Tambo returns to South Africa after thirty-one years in exile. **December 16:** Ending its first legal meeting inside South Africa in thirty years, ANC threatens suspension of talks with government if a number of conditions are not met.

1991

January: Fighting between rival political groups continues in many townships. **January 29:** Nelson Mandela and Chief Buthelezi meet, for first time since Mandela's release, in Durban; they agree to end Inkatha–ANC rivalry. **February 1:** President De Klerk announces that government will repeal remaining apartheid laws affecting land, residence, and racial classification in forthcoming parliamentary session. **March 4:** UDF announces that it will disband on August 20, the eighth anniversary of its founding. **April:** ANC and PAC announce intention to form a common front after unity talks in Harare, Zimbabwe. ANC's Constitutional Proposals for a Democratic South Africa published. **April 28:** In Angola MPLA party congress rejects Marxism-Leninism in favor of social democracy and accepts plan for elections. **April 29:** Lesotho military leader Major General Justin Lekhanya ousted by rebel army officers in bloodless coup. **May 1:** Peace accord signed by Angolan government and UNITA in Portugal calls for cease-fire and elections in second half of 1992. President De Klerk announces plans to end preventive detention and other repressive provisions of the Internal Security Act of 1982. **May 4:** Winnie Mandela found guilty of kidnapping and accessory to assault of four Soweto youths; sentenced to six years in prison; appeals sentence. **June 5:** Native Land and Trust Act of 1936 and Group Areas Act repealed. **June 17:** Population Registration Act repealed. **July 5:** ANC holds first legal national conference in South Africa since banning in 1960; elects Nelson Mandela president, Oliver Tambo national chairman, Walter Sisulu deputy president, and Cyril Ramaphosa secretary-general. **July 10:** United States lifts economic sanctions against South Africa. **July 19:** *Weekly Mail* exposes secret government funding of Inkatha and its allied labor movement, the United Workers' Union of South Africa (UWUSA). **July 20–31:** "Inkathagate" scandal becomes major crisis for government, leading to demotion of Minister of Police Adriaan Vlok and Minister of Defense Magnus Malan and review of all legislation affecting secret funds. Nelson Mandela demands establishment of interim government. **August 9:** Three members of a white extremist paramilitary group killed by police during political meeting held by President De Klerk in Ventersdorp, Transvaal. **August 10:** Government appoints first black judge (Ismail Mahomed) to Transvaal Provincial Division of Supreme Court. **August 16:** South African government declares broad amnesty for political exiles, removing major barrier to negotiations and making it possible for UN High Commissioner for Refugees to establish South African office to help with repatriation. **September 4:** De Klerk presents National Party's constitutional proposals that feature proportional representation for a lower house, veto powers for an upper one, and a collective presidency; rejected by ANC and allies. **September 14:** National Peace Accord aimed at ending violence and regulating conduct of political activity signed by government, ANC/SACP, Inkatha, and other smaller groups; radical parties on right and left reject pact.

INDEX

Abolition of Racially Based Land
    Measures Act (1991), 14–15
Administration of justice, blacks and, 95–
    111
    attitudes toward law, 102–11
    absence of black participation in
        lawmaking, 103–4
    discriminatory nature of law, 104
    exclusion of blacks, 104–5
    judicial conduct, 105–6
    police conduct, 105
    sentencing, 106–11
    shortage of legal representation, 105
    participation and, 95–102
    judges, 97–98
    juries and assessors, 98–99
    legal profession, 99–102
    magistrates, 98
    prosecution, 98
Adversary system of criminal justice, 98
Advisory Commission on Land
    Allocation, 15
Affirmative action, 132–34
African Charter on Human and Peoples'
    Rights, 130
African Law Review, 101
African National Congress (ANC), 21,
    24–25, 30, 33, 41, 64, 86–88, 92,
    99, 112–20, 122, 135–36
    banning of, 22, 34–35
    bill of rights and, 123, 125–27, 129–36
    Constitutional Committee of, 115, 122,
        126–27, 129, 132, 134
    Constitutional Guidelines of (1988),
        118–19, 125, 126, 167–71
    Constitutional Proposals of (1991),
        176–88
    total strategy and, 55
    unbanning of, 13, 26, 34, 46, 89, 91,
        112, 114
    vigilantes and, 82–84

Africans. *See also* Blacks (Africans)
    1983 Constitution and, 5, 9
    voting rights of, 5
Afrikaners, 118, 132. *See also* Whites
    bill of rights and, 124–25
    courts and, 28
    Land Acts and, 15
    language and culture of, 20
    1983 Constitution and, 8
    partition and, 116–17
Aggett, Neil, 65
Alexandra, 59
Alternative press, censorship and, 47
Angola, 56, 70, 72
Apartheid, 3–31. *See also specific laws and
    policies*
    conclusion of, 31
    courts and, 27–30
    crumbling of, 3–4, 13, 19, 25–26, 31
    grand, 10, 12, 31, 95–96
    petty, 10–11
    political, territorial, and social
        segregation, 10–21
    denationalization, 11–12, 16–17
    education and health, 20–21
    homelands, 11–13
    land division and population
        removals, 13–16
    movement, 17
    public amenities, 19–20
    racial discrimination, 18–19
    residential zoning, 17–18
    political repression and, 21–26
    racial classification and, 9–10
Appeal Court, 14, 27–28, 30
Argus, The (newspaper), 59
Armscor, 58, 91
Arms embargo, 21
"Art of Counter–Revolutionary Warfare,
    The," 79
Assassinations, 84–89

Australia, 15
Azanian People's Organization (AZAPO),
  45
Banishment, 22, 29
Banning orders, 22, 26
Bantu Education, 21
Bantustans. *See* Homelands
Baxter, Lawrence, 52
Beaufre, Gen. André, 57
Biko, Steve, 64–65
Bill of rights, 123–34
  affirmative action and, 132–34
  economic policy and, 132
  freedom of speech and, 129
  individual or group rights and, 127–29
  judiciary and, 127
  property rights and, 131–32
  social and economic rights and, 129–30
Bill of Rights for a New South Africa, A
  (ANC), 115, 126, 134
Bill of Rights, U.S., 129
Black Land Act (1913), 13–15
Black Lawyers' Association (BLA), 102
Blacks (Africans)
  administration of justice and. *See*
    Administration of justice, blacks
    and
  courts and, 27, 29
  definition of, 9–10
  homelands of, 11–14
  1983 Constitution and, 10, 115–16
  Parliament and, 11–12, 13
  police relationship with, 63–64
  security forces and revolt by, 56, 68–
    69, 73–84, 88–89. *See also* Soweto
    uprising
  assassinations, 84–89
  low-intensity warfare, 80, 83, 88
  maximum force policing, 73–78
  Sharpeville massacre and, 34
  social segregation and, 18–21
  education, 19–21
  in SADF, 71–72
  in SAP, 61–62
  territorial segregation and, 13–18
  land division and population
    removals, 13–16
  orderly urbanization and, 16–17
  voting rights, 11
Blanke Bevrydingsbeweging van Suid Afrika
  (White Liberation Movement of
  South Africa), 45
Board for Religious Objection, 72
Boksburg, 20
Bophuthatswana, 11–12, 16–17, 67–68,
  117–20
  judges in, 98

Borders of Particular States Extension
  Act (1980), 14
Botha, Pieter W., 3, 5, 12–13, 19, 55–56,
  58, 69, 73, 112
  emergency rule, 39
  political repression and, 23, 25
  SADF and, 60
  territorial segregation and, 14
Botshabelo, 14
Boycotts
  education, 25
  political, 24
  school, 45
Brown v. Board of Education of Topeka, 21
Budlender, Geoffrey, 54
Bureau for State Security (BOSS), 57–58
Buthelezi, Chief Mangosuthu Gatsha, 13,
  114

Canadian Charter of Rights and
  Freedom, 133
Cape Corps, 71
Cape of Good Hope (colony), 4, 118
Cape Province, 4–5, 28
Cape Town, District Six in, 18
Cape Town, University of, Institute of
  Criminology at the, 66
Carletonville, 20
Casspir (armored personnel carriers), 92
Censorship, 38, 45–48
Checks and balances, constitutional, 120–
  23
Children, detention of, 41–43, 77–78
Ciskei, 11–12, 16–17, 95, 117, 119–20
  police in, 67–69
Citizen Force, 71
Citizenship, restoration of, 16–17
Civil Cooperation Bureau (CCB), 86–88
Civil disobedience, 24
Claassens, Aninka, 15
Clausewitz, Von, 89
Coetsee, Hendrik J. ("Kobie"), 90, 124
Coetzee, Capt. Dirk, 85–87
Coloured Labor Party, 129
Coloureds, 73. *See also* Indians
  definition of, 9–10
  in justice system, 98
  1983 Constitution and, 5–10, 31, 115–
    16
  residential zoning and, 17–18
  social segregation and, 19
  in SADF, 71–72
  in SAP, 61
  voting rights of, 5, 8–9, 24, 28
Commandos, 71
Commission of Inquiry into Security
  Legislation, 38

Comprehensive Anti–Apartheid Act, 25
Confederation, 117–18
Congress, U.S., 25
Congress Alliance, 123
Congress of South African Trade Unions (COSATU), 82–85, 87
Congress of the People (1955), 123
Conscription, as controversial issue, 72–73
Conservative Party, 15, 20, 116
Consociational engineering, 121
Constitution, Bophuthatswana, 68
Constitution, Namibian (1990), 114, 121–22, 126, 129–31
Constitution, South African
  ANC guidelines for (1988), 167–71
  ANC proposals for (1991), 176–88
  new, 114–16
  1910, 4–5, 8
  1961, 5, 8
  1983, 4–11, 39, 115–16, 124
    apartheid and, 4–9
    approval of, 8
    racial classification and, 10
Constitutional checks and balances, 116, 120–23
Constitutional Rule in a Participatory Democracy (De Klerk), 116, 189–200
Corbett, M. M., 30, 53
Correctional Services Department, South African, 55
Courts, 14. *See also specific courts*
  apartheid and, 27–30
  desegregation and, 20
  racial liberalism of, 29
  security laws and, 29–30, 35, 37, 39, 41–42, 49–53
  structure of, 27–28, 96
Crimes, unsolved, 63–64
Criminal Investigation Department (CID), 61, 63, 92
Criminal Law Amendment Act (1953), 33–34
Criminal Procedure Act, 99
Crocker, Chester, 80
Crossroads squatter camp, 76, 81–82
Curlewis, D., 108

Daily death rate, 75, 78
Dalling, David, 26
Death penalty, 107
Death squads, 85–86, 91
Defense Act (1957), 69–70
Defense, Department of, 70
Defense Force, Bophuthatswana, 67

De Klerk, Frederik W., 10, 13, 15, 19, 31, 56, 59, 89–94, 112, 131
  address by (Feb. 1, 1991), 114, 172–75
  address by (Feb. 2, 1990), 3, 9, 34, 112–13, 128, 139–54
  address by (Sept. 4, 1991), 116, 189–200
  demise of the securocrats and, 89–93
De Kock, Maj. Eugene, 86
Democratic Lawyers Association, 97
Democratic Party, 116, 118, 120
Denationalization, 11–12, 16–17
Department of National Security (DONS), 58
Desegregation, 19–21
Detainees' Parents Support Committee (DPSC), 41, 66, 77–78
Detention, 77–78, 91
  of children, 41–43, 77–78
  courts and, 30
  deaths in, 22, 64–66, 91
  hunger strikes and, 43–44
  introduction of, 35
  90-day, 35–36
  180-day, 36
  security laws and, 35–44
  SAP powers of, 7
  without trial, 22–24
Didcott, J. M., 130
Discrimination, racial. *See* Apartheid; racial discrimination
Discussion Document on Structures and Principles of a Constitution for a Democratic South Africa, A (ANC), 115, 120, 122–23, 129
Dlamini, Charles, 103, 105–6, 110–11
Duncan Village, 59
Du Flou, Joe, 75–76
During N.O. v. Boesak, 53
Dutton, Lt.-Gen. J. R., 70

Economic policy, bill of rights and, 132
Economic rights, 129–30
Education, 19–21, 96
  boycotts and, 25
  school boycotts and, 45
  social segregation and, 20–21
Election of 1984, 8–9, 24
Election of 1989, in Namibia, 121
Emergency rule, 32–54, 124
  declaration of, 9
  judiciary and, 49–53
  lifting of, 9, 113
  origin of, 32–34
  political repression and, 21–22
  security forces and, 39–49
    censorship, 45–48

detention, 40–44
gatherings, 44
restrictions on organizations and
  individuals, 44–45
school boycotts and educational
  matters, 45
Empilisweni Clinic, 76
End Conscription Campaign (ECC), 72

Federation vs. unitary state, 118–20
Forsyth, C., 36
Foster, D., 63
Fouché, J. J., 69
Frankel, Philip, 58, 63–64
Freedom Charter (1955), 24, 123–25,
  162–66
Free Settlement Areas Act (1988), 18
Friedman, David, 29
Funerals, 39, 44
  black revolt and, 75–76

Gandhi, Mohandas, 99–102
Gatherings, control of, 39, 44
Gazankulu, 12, 17, 95–96
General affairs, 7–8
General Law Amendment Act (1966), 37
Goldstone, Richard, 91
Goniwe, Matthew, 84
Government Gazette, 65
Grand apartheid, 10, 12, 31, 95–96
Great Britain
  courts in, 30
  legal system in, 97–98, 100
  Parliament of, 118
  troops in Zimbabwe of, 93
Groote Schuur Minute, 26, 113
Group Areas Act, 15, 17–19, 100, 104,
  110
  courts and, 28–29
  repeal of, 31

Habeas corpus, 24, 26, 68
Harare Declaration, 112, 125
Harker, Neil, 108–9
Harms, Louis, 86–87
Harms Commission, 86–87, 91
Health, social segregation and, 20–21
Heitman, Helmoed-Romer, 77, 88
Hendrickse, Rev. H. J. (Allan), 19
Hermbrucker v. Klindt N.O., 36
Hiemstra, Victor, 88
Holmes, Benito, 108–9, 132
Home Affairs, Department of, 10
Homelands, 11–14, 116–17. See also
  specific homelands
  consolidation of, 14
  vigilantes in, 80–82

Homeland police, 67–69
Horowitz, Donald L., 121
House of Assembly, 6–7
House of Delegates, 6–8
House of Representatives, 6–8
Human Rights Commission, 77, 84–89
Hunger strikes, 43–44

Imbali Stage I, 83
Independent Board of Inquiry into
  Informal Repression (IBIIR), 86–
  87
Indian Constitution (1949), 130, 133
Indians, 73
  in justice system, 97–99
  1983 Constitution and, 5–10, 31, 115–
  16
  racial classification and, 9
  residential zoning and, 17–18
  social segregation and, 19
  in SADF, 71
  in SAP, 61
  voting rights of, 9, 24
Individuals, restrictions on, 44–45
Individual or group rights, 127–29
Inkatha, 82–84, 113–15, 120
Inkatha Freedom Party (IFP), 114, 116,
  129
Inkathagate scandal, 83
Institute of Criminology, University of
  Cape Town, 66
Internal Security Act (1982), 4, 7, 38, 48,
  53, 65, 74, 92
  amendment of, 7, 31
  courts and, 30
  detention allowances of, 23–24
  1991 Constitution and, 26
International Commission of Jurists, 47,
  49
International Convention on the
  Elimination of All Forms of Racial
  Discrimination, 133
International Covenant on Economic,
  Social, and Cultural Rights (1966),
  130

Introduction to Strategy, An (Beaufre), 57
Jane's Defence Weekly (journal), 88
Johannesburg, 113
Johannesburg Bar, 100
Johannesburg City Council, 88, 91
Joint Management Centers (JMCs), 59, 80
Jooste, Stephanus, 107–8
Judges, 27–28, 49, 97–98, 105–6
Judiciary, 8. See also Courts; specific courts
  apartheid and, 27–30
  bill of rights and, 127

emergency rule and, 49–53
Juries and assessors, 98–99
Justice
  administration of. *See* Administration
    of justice, blacks and
Justice Department, 96

KaNgwane, 12, 17, 95–96
Khayelitsha, 59
Kitskonstabels (instant police), 61–62
Kruger, Jimmy T., 62
Kutumela, Lucky, 68
KwaNdebele, 12, 14, 17, 59, 95–96, 113
  police in, 67–69, 87
  vigilantes in, 81
KwaZulu, 12, 17, 29, 59, 67, 95–96
  vigilantes and, 82–84
KwaZulu-Natal Indaba Constitutional
  Proposals (1986), 121

Labor Party, 116
Labor Party (Coloured), 120
Land Acts, 4, 13–15
  repeal of, 31
Land division, territorial segregation and,
  13–16
Langa, 39, 59, 76
Law Society of the Transvaal, 100
Lawyers, 97–102
  emergency rule and, 50
  shortage of, 105
Lawyers Committee for Human Rights,
  76–77
Lebowa, 12, 17, 59, 67–68, 95–96
Lerm, Brig. Hertzog, 87
Lijphart, Arend, 121
Lochner v. New York, 132
Lodge, Tom, 33
Low-intensity conflict, 78–80, 83, 88
Loza v. Police Station Commander, 35
Lubowski, Anton, 85, 86, 91
Lutuli, Albert, 34
Luyt, C., 63

McCuen, Col. John J., 78–79
Magistrates, 98, 105–6
Magistrates courts, 27, 96, 98, 100
Mahomed, Ismail, 97
Malan, Gen. Magnus, 57–60, 69
Mall, Hassan, 97
Mandela, Nelson, 35, 99–100, 103–5, 114
  release of, 13, 91, 113
Mangope, Lucas, 12, 117
Marriage, interracial, 18–19
Masemola, Nathaniel M., 119
Mathews, Anthony S., 37
Media Emergency Regulations, 47

Mellet, Brig. Leon, 92
Mentz, Moolman, 90
Merriman, John X., 118
Military, 8, 25, 70
Military Intelligence, 84, 86, 88
Milne, A. J., 99
Minister of Law and Order v. Dempsey, 30,
  52
Minister of Law and Order v. Hurley, 30
Minister of the Interior v. Lockhat, 110
Ministers councils, 8, 13
Ministry of Law and Order, 60
Minority veto, 121
Mitchell's Plain assault, 89–90
Mokgatle, Dolly, 101–2
Molope, Col. Andrew, 68
Molteno Commission, 60
Mozambique, 70–71, 123
Mulder, Connie P., 11
Muldergate scandal, 58
Mxenge, Griffiths, 84–86
Mxenge, Victoria, 84–85
Myburgh, A. P., 108

Namibia, 31, 56, 61, 71–73, 93, 112, 114,
  121, 124
  constitution of, 114, 121–22, 126, 129–
    31
  election of 1989 in, 121
Natal, 4–5, 12–13, 17, 25, 71, 91, 113,
  117–18, 121, 124
  courts in, 28–30
  vigilantes in, 82–84
National Association of Democratic
  Lawyers (NADEL), 102
National Intelligence Service (NIS), 58
National Party, 3–6, 12, 25, 28, 31, 116,
  120, 122–23, 135–36
  bill of rights and, 124–25, 128–29, 132
  racial discrimination and, 18–19
  split in, 20
National Security Management Systems
  (NSMS), 59, 79, 90
National Statutory Council, 13
Nazism, 12, 135
Nchabaleng, Peter, 68
Ndondo, Bathandwa, 68
Neethling, Gen. Lothar, 87
New Nation (newspaper), 47
New Zealand, 15
Ngqumba v. Staatspresident, 52
Nkondo v. Minister of Law and Order, 30
Nkwinti v. Commissioner of Police, 51
Nofomela, Butane, 85–87, 91
North End Prison, 42
Nuremburg Tribunal, 135

Omar v. Minister of Law and Order, 52
Orange Free State, 4–5, 14, 17, 24–25, 102, 117
Orange River Colony, 4, 118
Orderly urbanization, 16–17
Organizations, restrictions on, 44–45
Orr, Wendy, 42
Own affairs, 6–8

Pan Africanist Congress (PAC), 64, 116, 131
  banning of, 22, 34–35
  unbanning of, 13, 26, 34, 89, 91, 112
Parliament, British, 4–5, 118
Parliament, South African, 4–6, 118, 123
  blacks (Africans) and, 11, 13
  1983 Constitution and, 58
  courts and, 27–29
  De Klerk's address to (Feb. 1, 1991), 114, 172–175
  De Klerk's address to (Feb. 2, 1990), 3, 9, 34, 112–13, 128, 139–54
  emergency rule and, 33, 40–41, 49–50
  tricameral, 5–18
Parsons Commission of Inquiry, 87
Partition, 116–17
Pass laws, 16, 19, 104
Permanent Force, 71
Petty apartheid, 10–11
Phillips, Mark, 79
Pietermaritzburg, townships of, 82
Police. *See* SAP
Police, homeland, 67–69
Police, KwaNdebele, 87
Police Act (1958), 60, 63, 69
Political prisoners, release of, 13, 90–91, 113
Political repression, 21–26. *See also* Internal Security Act (1982)
Political segregation, 10–13
Population Registration Act (1950), 9–10
Population removals, 29
  territorial segregation and, 13–16
President, 1983 Constitution and, 68
President's Council, 7, 46, 48, 124
Pretoria Minute, 113
Prevention of Illegal Squatting Act, 17
Prisons Service, 38, 40
Progressive Party, 60, 118, 124
Progressive Federal Party, 41
Promotion of Constitutional Development Act (1988), 13
Property rights, 131–32
Proportional representation, 121–23
Protecting Human Rights in a New South Africa (Sachs), 133

Public amenities, social segregation and, 19–20
Publications Act, 38
Public Safety Act (1953), 21–22, 25, 32–34, 40, 48, 155–61
  ouster clause in, 52
Public Safety Amendment Act, 48

Qwaqwa, 12, 14, 17, 95–96

Rabie, Pierre J., 23, 30, 51, 53
Racial classification, 9–10, 31
Racial discrimination, 18–19, 104
Representation, proportional, 121–23
Reservation of Separate Amenities Act, 20
Residential zoning, 17–18
Restoration of South African Citizenship Act (1986), 16
Ribiero, Fabian, 85
Riotous Assemblies Act (1974), 38
Riot squads, 62
Rockman, Lt. Gregory, 89–90
Rossouw v. Sachs, 35, 51
R. v. Pitje, 110

S. v. Ramgobin, 29
Sachs, Albie, 123–26, 133
St. Albans Prison, 42–43
School boycotts, 45
Schools. *See* Education
Sebe, Lennox, 81
Sebokeng, 70, 91–92
Security forces. *See also* Prisons Service; SADF; SAP
  emergency rule and, 39–49
  censorship, 45–48
  detention, 40–44
  gatherings, 39, 44
  restrictions on organizations and individuals, 44–45
  school boycotts, 45
  total strategy and, 55–94
South African Journal on Human Rights, 107–8
Security laws. *See also* Internal Security Act (1982)
  courts and, 29–30, 35, 37, 39, 41–42, 49–53
  genesis of, 35–39
  repeal of, 114–15
Securocrats, 58. *See also* security forces
  demise of, 89–93
Segregation. *See* Political segregation; social segregation; territorial segregation
Senate, U.S., 122

Sentencing, 106–11
Separate development, 10
Servamus (SAP journal), 77
"Service in defence of the Republic,"
definition of, 69–70
Sexual relations, interracial, 18–19
Sharpeville massacre, 34
Sisulu, Walter, 90
Slums Act, 17
Smuts, Jan, 28, 118
Sobukwe, Robert, 103
Social segregation, 18–21
education and health and, 20–21
public amenities, 19–20
racial discrimination and, 18–19
South Africa, Union of, 5
racist image of, 12
South African Communist Party (SACP),
21, 41
unbanning of, 26, 89, 91, 112
South African Defense Force (SADF), 40,
59
black revolt and, 74, 80, 84, 88
breakdown of, 71
conscription and, 72–73
De Klerk and, 90–91, 93
main functions of, 69
total strategy and, 55–62, 69–73
South African Law Commission, 9, 112,
124–28, 130–33
South African Police (SAP), 8, 31, 37–38,
40, 42, 59, 94, 105
black revolt and, 73–78, 80, 82–84,
86–87
De Klerk and, 89–93
detention and, 7, 22–24, 35
growth, 62
homeland police compared with, 67
international criticism of, 89–90
lack of accountability of, 62–66
lack of discipline of, 63
SADF and, 69–70
total strategy and, 55, 59–64
violence of, 25
Southern African Catholic Bishops'
Conference, 25, 85
South-West Africa, 71–72
South West Africa People's Organization
(SWAPO), 121–22
total strategy and, 55, 61
Soweto, unsolved crime rate in, 63–64
Soweto uprising, 25, 38, 48, 56, 62
Special Branch, 61
Spoelstra, T. T., 108
Staatspresident v. United Democratic Front,
52
Star (newspaper), 41–42

State, nature of the, 116–20
State Security Council (SSC), 58–59
"Subversive statement," definition of, 46
Suppression of Communism Act (1950),
21
Supreme Court, Bophuthatswana, 68
Supreme Court, South Africa, 26–27,
41–42, 49–50, 96–100
Appellate Division of, 14, 17, 22, 27–
28, 30, 35–36, 51–53, 96–97, 100,
110
black revolt and, 74, 77
Supreme Court, U.S., 21, 129, 132
Suzman, Helen, 109
Swart, C. R., 33
Swaziland, 29–30
Swilling, Mark, 79

Tambo, Oliver, 99
TBVC states, 11, 16–17, 67, 95, 101. *See
also* Bophuthatswana; Ciskei;
Transkei; Venda
judges in, 98
Territorial segregation, 10, 13–16, 31
denationalization and, 11–12, 16–17
land division and population removals
and, 13–16
movement and, 17
residential zoning and, 17–18
Terrorism, 24
definition of, 22, 37
security laws and, 37
Terrorism Act (1967), 22, 24, 37
Toms, Ivan, 72
Torture, 24, 36, 42, 63, 66, 109
Total strategy, 55–94
black revolt and. *See* black revolt
demise of the securocrats and, 89–93
external dimensions of, 55–56, 61, 70–
72
origins of, 56–59
tactics of, 77–89
tactics used for, 55
Townships
housing shortage in, 17
security forces and, 59–62, 70
Transkei, 11–12, 16–17, 95, 117, 119–20
police in, 67–69
Transvaal, 4–5, 24, 29, 71, 83, 84, 88,
102, 113, 117–18
white backlash in, 20
Trespass Act, 17
Trojan Horse incident, 76–77
Tsenoli v. the State President, 51
Tshikalanga, David, 85–86
Twenty-First Battalion, 71

Unions, black, 19
Unitary state vs. federation, 118–20
United Democratic Front (UDF), 30, 41,
    45, 99, 124
  formation of, 24
  unbanning of, 13, 26
  vigilantes and, 82–84
United Nations (UN), 21, 93, 112
  Security Council of, 21, 114
United Party, 28
United States, 15
  courts, 129, 132
  courts in, 27, 30
  economic policy and, 132
  education in, 21
  freedom of speech in, 129
  South Africa policy of, 25
Universal Declaration of Human Rights
    (1948), 123, 130
Unlawful Organizations Act, 34

Vaal Triangle, 24–25, 73
Van den Bergh, Gen. Hendrik, 57
Van der Merwe, Gen. J., 92
Van Niekerk, Barend, 63, 107
Van Zyl Slabbert, Frederik, 115
Venda, 11–12, 16–17, 67–68, 69, 95,
    117, 119–20
Verwoerd, Hendrik F., 11–12, 124
Veto, minority, 121
Vigilantes, 80–84, 88–89
Viljoen, Gerrit, 90
Violence, 114. See also specific topics
  assassinations and, 84–89
  daily death rate and, 75, 78
  in homelands, 12
  1983 Constitution and, 25
  in 1984, 9
  in Vaal Triangle, 24–25
  vigilantes and, 80–84, 88–89
Vorster, B. J., 22, 57–58, 124
Vote pooling, 121
Voters' roll, separate, 121
Voting rights
  of blacks (Africans), 5, 11
  of Coloureds, 5, 8–9, 24, 28
  of Indians, 9, 24
Vrye Weekblad (newspaper) 85, 87

War Measures Act (1940), 33
Webster, David, 79, 85, 86
Welgemoed, Jan, 108
Westminster model, 118, 120
Westminster parliamentary form, 56
White Liberation Movement of South
    Africa (Blanke Bevrydingsbeweging
    van Suid Afrika), 45

White Paper on Defense and Armaments
    Supply, 1982 (Dept. of Defense), 70
Whites, 71. See also Afrikaners
  definition of, 9–10
  education of, 20–21
  in justice system, 98
  1983 Constitution and, 5–10
  residential zoning and, 17–18
  sentencing of, 107–9
  in SAP, 61
Witwatersrand, 117
"Winning hearts and minds" campaign,
    80, 88
Working Paper on Group and Human Rights
    (South African Law Commission),
    125

Zimbabwe, 93
Zoning, residential, 17–18

Authors

John Dugard is the former director of the Center for Applied Legal Studies and a professor of law at the University of the Witwatersrand. A graduate of the Universities of Stellenbosch (B.A., LL.B.) and Cambridge (LL.B., LL.D.), he has written widely on international law and human rights.

Nicholas Haysom is an associate professor of law at the Center for Applied Legal Studies at the University of the Witwatersrand. He is a graduate of the University of Cape Town and holds the B.A. (Hons) and LL.B. degrees. He is a practicing attorney specializing in human rights law and has made a special study of the police and police methods in South Africa.

Gilbert Marcus holds B.A. and LL.B. degrees from the University of the Witwatersrand and an LL.M. degree from the University of Cambridge. He is an advocate of the Supreme Court of South Africa and was formerly an associate professor at the Center for Applied Legal Studies at the University of the Witwatersrand, where his work focused primarily on freedom of expression and state security.

Editor

John de St. Jorre, a journalist and author, has been visiting and writing about South Africa since the mid-1960s. His book *South Africa: A House Divided* was published by the Carnegie Endowment in New York in 1977, and he was a senior writer for the study commission that produced *South Africa: Time Running Out* in 1981. Born in London and educated at Oxford University, he joined the British Foreign Service and spent three years in different posts in Africa. After resigning, he became the (London) *Observer*'s Africa correspondent, based first in Zambia and later in Kenya. He covered the Nigeria-Biafra conflict, and his book on that subject, *The Brothers' War: Biafra and Nigeria*, was published in Britain and the United States. He was subsequently the *Observer*'s Paris, Middle East, and New York correspondent. His other books include *The Patriot Game* (a novel), *The Insider's Guide to Spain*, *The Guards*, and *The Marines*.

South Africa UPDATE Series